A HISTORY OF
Daggett County

A HISTORY OF *Daggett County*

A Modern Frontier

Michael W. Johnson
with Robert E. Parson
and Daniel A. Stebbins

1998
Utah State Historical Society
Daggett County Commission

ISBN 0-913738-18-2
Library of Congress Catalog Card Number 97-62121
Map by Automated Geographic Reference Center—State of Utah
Printed in the United States of America

Utah State Historical Society
300 Rio Grande
Salt Lake City, Utah 84101-1182

For my parents
Peter and Sandy Johnson

Contents

Preface

There are many ways to approach the writing of local history. In the Mountain West, grassroots local history books have become common. More often than not, they are a compilation of family histories, biographical sketches, and pioneer reminiscences. They do a fine job of telling the personal stories of a locale, but they generally fail to relate those stories to any kind of broader perspective. In this volume, I have tried to put the personal stories into a bigger picture. The history of a place is the story of its people, but it is also the story of distant wars, global economic changes, and large social movements. It is one thing to know that grandpa bought his first tractor during World War II; it is another to understand that wartime labor shortages and high farm profits prompted his decision. By providing historical context, we intend to provide more meaning.

As the research unfolded, we began to assemble significant events, movements, and people from the county's past into a more coherent story. A conscious effort was made to leave out redundant matter or material that might distract from the flow of the narrative. Characters appear as they make a significant contribution, and then they disappear from the narrative. Others are included because they left articulate descriptions of common experiences. Through them we gain insights into the lives of the everyday people who left few if any written records.

One of this project's obstacles was trying to make sense of a confusing historical record that occasionally jumbles fact, lore, and fabrication. The authors have tried to be judicious in the use of sources and have relied on primary accounts and scholarly books as much as possible. Even so, where the primary sources are few and at times questionable, no historian can guarantee perfect historical accuracy. Where there was no reasonable evidence to the contrary, stories that have been retold in a consistent manner over many years and that are generally accepted by the local community have been presented as genuine. If future scholars find conclusive data that changes this view of the county's past, we applaud them.

Organizing this complex story also proved to be a challenge. History writing is typically structured either chronologically or topically. In this case, no single method was judged entirely adequate. Some issues in the county's past lent themselves nicely to a simple chronological narrative; others required different treatment. Abandoning a comprehensive structure allowed each chapter to be handled in a way that seemed to suit it best. While the subject matter is arranged somewhat chronologically, each chapter has a thematic basis and was written to stand alone. The end product is a collection of essays dealing with the important themes, eras, and issues in the county's past.

Two chapters have distinctive approaches and merit further discussion. Transportation has been an important factor in every period of the county's history, and this topic seemed to lend itself to a retrospective approach. After extensive research, Daniel A. Stebbins decided to base the chapter on the unpublished memoir of Linwood rancher Keith Smith. Smith's reminiscences offer a fascinating perspective on area travel from 1901 through 1964. They present wide-ranging information on the development of various routes and forms of transportation. Keith Smith literally saw the pace of regional travel go from six to sixty miles per hour. Though his memoir talks of change, it also speaks to the continuing story of rigorous travel in a harsh mountain environment. The complex interaction between the geography of the West and the mobility of its people is deeply ingrained in the region's culture. Nowhere is this more true than in the rugged Uinta Mountains country, and nowhere is this story chronicled better than in Keith Smith's memoir.

The chapter on crime and violence in old Browns Park also requires some explanation. It builds on the groundbreaking work of historian Richard Maxwell Brown (who had no connection to the aforementioned valley, or "park," as many valleys were called in earlier times). Most books dealing with Browns Park outlawry consider the place some kind of social aberration. After reading Richard M. Brown's *No Duty to Retreat* and his essay "Violence" in the *Oxford History of the American West,* it became clear that many western places had similar climates of violence. Brown attributes this phenomenon to conflicting attitudes toward the law, justice, property, and honor. This chapter in our book merely extends his reasoning to the era of violent behavior in Browns Park. More than just a laundry list of notorious acts, the chapter tries to explain the cycle of violence as a consequence of deeply held social values. (Note: In keeping with current naming practices of government and mapmaking entities, the apostrophe has been dropped in the possessive forms of Brown's Park, Henry's Fork, etc. throughout this book, except in historical quotations and citations, although most such places are historically better-known with the apostrophe.)

Throughout all of the chapters, the reader will note the somewhat unconventional use of long block quotations. Standard practice is to paraphrase long quotations and insert short tidbits to emphasize a certain point. To the chagrin of the editors, we have chosen to let the people that made history speak as much as possible for themselves. By doing this, we hoped to give a better sense of the times and of who these people were. Their remarks are sometimes politically or grammatically incorrect, but they speak volumes about the virtues and vices of their day.

A final word of explanation about the book's epilogue. I have always felt that history should be didactic. To end the narrative, I wanted to make an eloquent statement about the dignity of the rural community. I wanted to write about people on the land facing change—how family, community, spiritual values, and tradition provide the grace to endure. While looking for inspiration, I happened across a true story that embodied the points I wanted to make. This story can be analyzed as a desperate tale of struggle against the juggernaut of global change, or it can be enjoyed as a simple faith-promoting story. The choice is up to the reader, who may draw his or her own conclusions. That's one of the great things about history.

Many people helped with the research and production of this work. First and foremost, I would like to thank the good people of Daggett County. Not only were they extremely generous about sharing their reminiscences, family histories, and photographs, they were marvelously interesting to write about. RaNae Wilde and the Daggett County Centennial Committee offered guidance and assistance throughout the project. Superintendent Gerold Erickson and librarian WaNeta Lamb of the Daggett School District provided copies of numerous manuscript items in their extensive local history collection. Lynne Ingram of the U.S. Forest Service and Pauleen Baker of the Flaming Gorge Natural History Association provided access to the files of the old Daggett County Historical Society. Forest Service archaeologist Byron Loosle provided material on prehistoric occupation and the history of the Ashley National Forest. Leta Wahlquist and Virginia Bennion Buchanan generously allowed the use of some rare family history and local history materials.

Many repositories also provided assistance to the authors. Special thanks go out to the helpful staff members at Utah State University's Merrill Library Special Collections, Brigham Young University's Harold B. Lee Library Special Collections, the Utah State Historical Society Library, and the Uintah County Library in Vernal. Additional assistance was given by several Wyoming institutions. The Sweetwater County Museum, the University of Wyoming Coe Library, and the Western Wyoming Community College library proved invaluable to the project.

Craig Fuller and Kent Powell of the Utah Division of State History have provided helpful oversight from beginning to end. Craig especially has offered research leads, guidance, and careful editing along the way. I thank them and historian F. Ross Peterson for their professional assistance and moral support.

Finally, I must express sincere thanks to co-authors Daniel A. Stebbins and Robert Parson. Both are talented historians and long-time friends who made extremely valuable contributions to the book. Bob researched and wrote the chapter on Flaming Gorge and provided much of the material in the final chapter. Dan researched and wrote the chapter on transportation. Our association was not only professionally rewarding, it was a lot of fun.

General Introduction

When Utah was granted statehood on 4 January 1896, twenty-seven counties comprised the nation's new forty-fifth state. Subsequently two counties, Duchesne in 1914 and Daggett in 1917, were created. These twenty-nine counties have been the stage on which much of the history of Utah has been played.

Recognizing the importance of Utah's counties, the Utah State Legislature established in 1991 a Centennial History Project to write and publish county histories as part of Utah's statehood centennial commemoration. The Division of State History was given the assignment to administer the project. The county commissioners, or their designees, were responsible for selecting the author or authors for their individual histories, and funds were provided by the state legislature to cover most research and writing costs as well as to provide each public school and library with a copy of each history. Writers worked under general guidelines provided by the Division of State History and in cooperation with county history committees. The counties also established a Utah Centennial County History Council to help develop policies for distribution of state-appropriated funds and plans for publication.

Each volume in the series reflects the scholarship and interpretation of the individual author. The general guidelines provided by the Utah State Legislature included coverage of five broad themes encompassing the economic, religious, educational, social, and political history of the county. Authors were encouraged to cover a vast period of time stretching from geologic and prehistoric times to the present. Since Utah's statehood centennial celebration falls just four years before the arrival of the twenty-first century, authors were encouraged to give particular attention to the history of their respective counties during the twentieth century.

Still, each history is at best a brief synopsis of what has transpired within the political boundaries of each county. No history can do justice to every theme or event or individual that is part of an area's past. Readers are asked to consider these volumes as an introduction to the history of the county, for it is expected that other researchers and writers will extend beyond the limits of time, space, and detail imposed on this volume to add to the wealth of knowledge about the county and its people. In understanding the history of our counties, we come to understand better the history of our state, our nation, our world, and ourselves.

In addition to the authors, local history committee members, and county commissioners, who deserve praise for their outstanding efforts and important contributions, special recognition is given to Joseph Francis, chairman of the Morgan County Historical Society, for his role in conceiving the idea of the centennial county history project and for his energetic efforts in working with the Utah State Legislature and State of Utah officials to make the project a reality. Mr. Francis is proof that one person does make a difference.

ALLAN KENT POWELL
CRAIG FULLER
GENERAL EDITORS

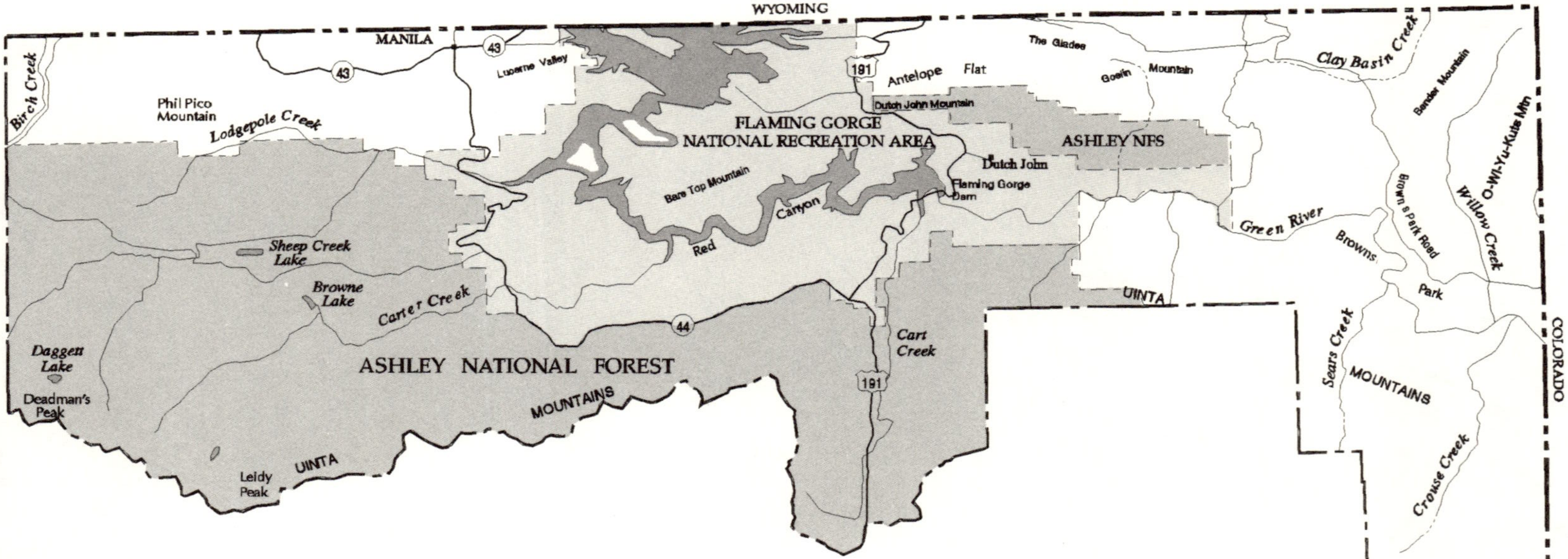

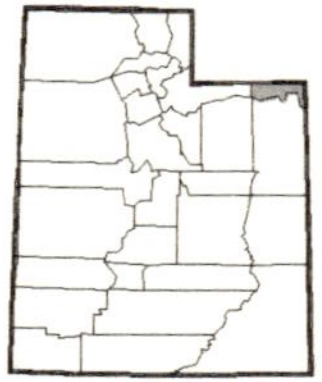

INDEX MAP

DAGGETT COUNTY

CHAPTER 1

NATURAL HISTORY AND EARLY INHABITANTS

The Uinta Mountains, some 150 to 160 miles long and 30 to 50 miles wide, run east and west, keen, snow-slashed peaks steeping in the sunlight, unique in their trend among the Rockies.

—ANN ZWINGER

It is a land of spectacular redrock cliffs, snowcapped mountains, tall pines, and whitewater rapids. Daggett County may be small in population, but it has landscape on a grand scale. This rugged countryside, a boon to modern recreationists, has generally made life difficult for the area's human inhabitants. Moreso than many places, climate and terrain have done much to shape this area's history.

Daggett County is a narrow strip of land along the northern slope of Utah's Uinta Mountains. Bounded basically by the crest of the Uintas on the south, the Wyoming state line on the north, the Colorado state line on the east, and Summit County on the west, it is Utah's twenty-ninth and youngest county. The east-west-trending Uinta Mountains and the Green River are the county's preeminent geographic features. The Green River generally flows from north to south, but where it strikes the Uintas it makes an abrupt turn to the east through Horseshoe and Red canyons. It curves southward again where it leaves Browns Park, a valley shared by Utah and Colorado.

Many creeks flow down to the Green River, and their drainages have been magnets for human activity. The valley of Henrys Fork, the Lucerne Valley, and Browns Park have historically been the important local areas of human settlement. Unfortunately, modern political boundaries were set without much thought to local geography. The rural communities along the north slope of the Uinta Mountains are interrelated and closely tied to the Green River-Rock Springs area of Wyoming, but they have been divided politically among three states. The Henrys Fork Valley is split between Utah and Wyoming, and the Utah-Colorado state line divides Browns Park. This land where Utah, Wyoming, and Colorado meet is sometimes called the "Three Corners," and it would not be unheard of for a resident of the area to live in Utah, work in Wyoming, and run livestock in Colorado.

The region is part of the Rocky Mountain Physiographic Province, bounded on the west by the eastern Great Basin Province and somewhat farther on the south by the northern portion of the Colorado Plateau Province. The climate is that of northern mountains, with short cool summers and long winters featuring abundant snowfall. Elevation ranges within the county move from 12,028-foot Leidy Peak to a low of about 5,365 feet where the Green River exits the county.

Life zones in the county begin with the Transition (from 5,500 feet to 8,000 feet in elevation), which features mountain brush plants including sagebrush and scrub oak as well as pinyon and juniper and ponderosa pine. The next zone is the Canadian (8,000 to 10,000 feet), where lodgepole pine, Douglas fir, and quaking aspen are dominant plants. The Hudsonian zone ranges from about 10,000 feet to timberline at about 11,000 feet; its largest plants are spruces and firs. Grasses and small plants are found in the Arctic-Alpine zone above timberline.[1] Animals in the county are typical of those zones in the West and represent a wide variety of many types and species, particularly insects, birds, and mammals, although some reptiles and even amphibians can be found in the county. Large mammals include mountain lion, bobcat, black bear, elk, mule deer, badger, skunk, raccoon, and other species common to the Rocky Mountain region.

Meadows at the Summit of the Uinta Mountains in southern Daggett County. (Utah State Historical Society)

Dominating the landscape and history of the county are the Uinta Mountains, the only major east-west mountain range in North America. The Uinta Mountains are of rather recent origin, however; much of the exposed rock in the Uintas is of great antiquity—some being Precambrian metamorphic rock well over one billion years old. Some of this rock has been broken and uplifted—faulted and folded in geologic terms—in the relatively recent past, after having been buried by increasing layers of sedimentation for hundreds of millions of years.

The Uinta Range actually began its formation as a trough—a depression in the earth periodically washed and submerged by ancient shallow seas. Over many millennia, the trough sank and filled with several layers of sediment. The Uinta uplift began some 80 million years ago during the mountain-building event called the Laramide (Rocky Mountain) Orogeny. Ancient layers of rock pushed up and through more recent strata, and the Uintas began to take shape as they are known today—an anticlinal fold about 160 miles long and thirty miles wide. The mountains contain twenty-six major formations, most of which are sedimentary rocks dating from the Precambrian to the Cenozoic periods. Though they contain almost no known commercially viable mineral deposits, they reveal a fossil record spanning 500 million years.[2]

The mountain range actually consists of two elliptical domelike segments that merge near the present town of Manila. The western dome, or High Uintas, grew to have a well-defined ridgeline with a number of peaks approaching 13,000 feet in elevation. Their barren snowcapped peaks are a marked contrast to the eastern portion of the range. The eastern Uintas, the eastern dome, which lies within Daggett County, are much lower and drier, and their ridgeline is less distinct. Deadman's Peak, at 12,280 feet, is the highest point on the eastern section. The crest of this dome, between two inward-dipping faults, eventually collapsed, leaving an irregular complex of ridge lines that has been a vexation to modern surveyors.

During the Ice Ages, the summits, ridge lines, and canyons of the Uintas were scoured by glaciers, which produced the wide valleys in the mountains. The most dramatic glaciation occurred in the High Uintas, but glacial activity also took place along the eastern portion of the range. Significant glaciated areas include Burnt Fork, the several forks of Sheep Creek, Beaver Creek, and Carter Creek. According to one geological study, the Burnt Fork glacier was about eleven miles in length.[3]

Complementing the geologic epic of the Uinta Mountains is the story of the Green River, a legendary river of the fur trade and the Mountain West. At their greatest height, the Uintas separated what are now the upper and lower basins of the Green River. The upper (northern) basin drained eastward toward the Platte River, while the lower (southern) basin, as today, drained southward. When the area of Wyoming known as the Great Divide Basin started to rise during the Laramide Orogeny, it dammed off the northern basin's outlet and created a lake. The subsequent collapse of the eastern Uinta summit provided this lake a new route to the sea, and upper-basin water carved a channel through Flaming Gorge, Red Canyon, Browns Park, Lodore Canyon, and Split Mountain Canyon to join the lower Green River in the Uinta Basin. In the process, the north slope tributaries—Birch Creek, Birch Spring Draw, Sheep Creek, Carter Creek, Spring

Browns Hole. (Utah State Historical Society)

Creek, Cart Creek, Jackson Creek, Red Creek, Crouse Creek, Willow Creek, and others—were altered to flow southward.[4]

The intense geologic forces that built the Uintas and influenced the carving path of the Green River also produced other impressive features of the terrain. Extensive faults parallel the mountains on both the north and the south. Action along these faults created the dramatic Palisades in lower Sheep Creek Canyon as well as the Flaming Gorge cliffs. Anticlinal movements also formed the Glades, which are parallel hogback ridges at the east end of the county, and erosion scoured out the Green River's magnificent Red Canyon.

While beautiful to behold, this tortured landscape has impeded human movement. The broken canyon country and often snow-packed mountains form a natural barrier that is traditionally impassable during much of the year. Yet, within this difficult country there are sheltered drainages, valleys, and basins that are far more hospitable to people and livestock than are the surrounding windswept badlands. Henrys Fork, Browns Park, and other smaller valleys in the county have microclimates that have made them inviting to humans for thousands of years.

Indeed, throughout the area there is extensive evidence of longstanding human occupation. Stone chips, projectile points, firepits, middens, and petroglyphs suggest that the Green River corridor has been both a thoroughfare and an area of habitation for ancient peoples. Remains of Clovis, Folsom, and Plano cultures have been found in southwestern Wyoming and northeastern Utah, testimony to as much as 11,000 years (or more) of human activity in the region. These Paleo-Indian people are thought to have engaged in a hunting-and-gathering subsistence lifestyle that relied heavily on the taking of large game animals.

The Paleo-Indians were followed by a cultural stage archaeologists identify as the Archaic people, who flourished from about 8000 B.C. to the beginning of the Christian era. Early and Middle Archaic peoples sometimes constructed pithouses, indicating that they had a sedentary lifestyle at least at certain times of the year. Their subsistence pattern was more generalized than that of the earlier Paleo-Indians; they relied on the hunting of all manner of game as well as the collecting and cooking of various plant species. Their tools and clothing were more advanced than those of the Paleo-Indians, and they are known to have used the atlatl (spear thrower) for hunting large game. Snares and traps were fashioned to capture small animals. Excavations from Late Archaic sites have yielded bones of bison, antelope, deer, and rabbit.[5]

Around the beginning of the Christian era, the Archaic period ended with the appearance of what archaeologists call the Fremont culture. The Fremont Indians were an agricultural people with a semisedentary lifestyle. They built dry-masonry structures and made ceramics. Moreso than their predecessors, they relied on flora gathered from wetlands, marshes, and streams for food and clothing. The Uinta variant of this culture seems to have flourished between about 450 and 1,000 A.D. The Uinta Fremont farmed at sites along the Green River, storing their corn in nearby granaries constructed under overhangs and other protected areas along the canyon walls. This group relied more on hunting than the Fremont of southern Utah. They used the bow and arrow to hunt large animals, and excavations at the Summit Springs hunting camp reveal numerous bones of bighorn sheep.[6]

Looking back toward Browns Hole from Lodore Canyon of the Green River. (Utah State Historical Society)

Most Fremont Indians were located in the eastern Great Basin and the Colorado Plateau country. The scattered remains they left in Daggett County suggest that few of them lived north of the Uinta Mountains. Those that did were primarily at lower elevations with the vast majority of identified Fremont Indian sites located along the Green River and its tributaries. At a Fremont site several miles south of Manila, the Indians built dry-wall masonry structures to store their seasonal harvests. Several petroglyph and pictograph panels were found at this site. Here and at other sites, remains of ceramics were found. Clay pots were used to carry and store all kinds of seeds, especially pinyon nuts. Metates (slabs used for grinding seeds) and various kinds of tools made of bone or stone have also been found at Fremont sites in the county.[7]

The Fremont peoples were highly accomplished as builders, tool and implement makers, and as craftsmen and artists. They were able to adapt to harsh environments, and they lived in the region for well over one thousand years. Their rather mysterious disappearance occurred about the same time as that of the Anasazi to the south.

There is currently no consensus of opinion regarding the demise of the Fremont peoples. Archaeologists and ethnohistorians speculate that they were driven out by prolonged drought or that they were destroyed or assimilated by other invading Indian peoples. Whatever the case, it is unfortunate that we do not know more about the Fremont. They raised food, built shelters, and fashioned clothing, tools, and weapons. They hunted game in the mountains, and their petroglyphs and pictographs suggest that they contemplated the mysteries of the universe. The Fremont Indians made a living in and called home a country that Europeans would later describe as a hostile wilderness.

By A.D. 1350, the Fremont culture in most of Utah had been replaced by Numic speakers, the ancestors of the modern Shoshoni and Ute indians. This country was a vast improvement over their original homeland of southern Nevada, California, and northwestern Mexico. These were among the most primitive tribes on the continent. Sparse resources had forced them to hunt and gather in small family groups, and social organization was only minimally developed.They were often on the brink of starvation, and only at certain

Flaming Gorge Reservoir, looking southwest from the Visitor's Overlook north of the dam. (Allan Kent Powell)

times and places when the food supply permitted were they able to gather in large groups.

It is easily understood why, given the opportunity, these people migrated to a more hospitable territory. As in earlier times, the Uinta Mountains presented a formidable natural barrier. The mountains traditionally marked the frontier between the two Indian nations that occupied the region into the historic period. To the south lived the mountain Utes; to the north were the Eastern Shoshoni.

The Shoshoni, sometimes referred to as the Snake Indians, were active traders long before the coming of Europeans. They traded with the rich tribes along the Columbia River, with the Utes to the south, and, through their Crow neighbors, they obtained goods from the Missouri River villages of the Mandan-Hidatsa. They were an enterprising people and an important link in the protohistoric North American trade network.[8]

Shoshoni culture adapted to and flourished in this new homeland. Skins of large game animals were tailored into clothing, replacing the rabbitskin robes that had been worn in the Great Basin

The Henrys Fork near Linwood before the area was covered by Flaming Gorge Reservoir. (Courtesy Pauleen Baker)

winters. The diet also diversified. Besides large game, the Eastern Shoshoni are known to have eaten roasted pine nuts and juniper berries, a bread made from sunflower seeds, powdered serviceberries, and various wild vegetables and tubers. The greater food resources allowed larger concentrations of people and a more sophisticated social structure. Gender roles became more specific, as men spent more time hunting and women specialized in gathering foods and cultivating the domestic arts.[9]

Henrys Fork and Browns Park became favorite wintering grounds for the members of the tribe. On his Green River expedition of 1825, William H. Ashley camped in Browns Park. He wrote of the site as:

> a spot of ground where several thousand Indians had wintered during the last season. . . . Many of their lodges remained as perfect as when occupied. They were made of poles two or three inches in diameter, set up in circular form, and covered with cedar bark.[10]

Like the Eastern Shoshoni, the Ute Indians also advanced both materially and socially in the new land. Ironically, it was the intru-

Looking west up Sheep Creek Canyon from Highway 44 south of Manila. (Allan Kent Powell)

sion of European civilization that brought these Indian cultures to their apex. As the Ute and Shoshoni nations moved into Utah, the empire of New Spain, bringing horses and trade goods, advanced

Daggett County Petroglyph. (Utah State Historical Society)

north from Mexico into the American Southwest. The result was an intense period of cultural dynamism and intertribal conflict. This activity reached the Flaming Gorge area with the introduction of European manufactures about 1550, and it ended with the beginnings of permanent white settlement in the early 1840s.[11]

Of all the things that the Europeans introduced to the Indians of the West, the horse proved to be the most revolutionary. The mountain Utes are believed to have acquired horses around 1650, and the Shoshoni acquired the animals perhaps fifty years later. Mounted bands of these people quickly took on traits associated with the Plains culture—particularly increased hunting and raiding activities due to their much greater mobility. Buffalo assumed great importance as a source of food and raw material, and both tribes engaged in buffalo hunts east and west of the Rocky Mountains. Hide-covered teepees began to replace the traditional brush-covered wickiups, the size of bands increased, and more authority inured to head chiefs. Reminiscent of the Cheyenne and Sioux, the Kohogues, or Green River Snakes, developed two warrior societies. The Yellow Noses were a warrior group, while the Logs organized camp and formed a rear guard on the march. To the horror of traditional rivals, the mounted

Ute and Shoshoni bands were also able to raid far into the homeland of their enemies.[12]

Trapper Warren Angus Ferris penned this description of a large Shoshoni camp that he observed in 1830:

> Their village consisted of about one hundred and fifty lodges, and probably contained above four hundred fighting men. The lodges were placed close to each other, and taken together had much the appearance of a military camp. . . . We were obliged to carry clubs to beat off the numerous dogs, that were constantly annoying us by barking, and trying to bite our legs. Crowds of . . . children followed us from lodge to lodge, at each of which were seen . . . industrious women, employed in dressing skins, cutting meat into thin strips for drying, gathering fuel, cooking, or otherwise engaged in domestic labour. At every lodge, was a rack or frame, constructed of poles tied together, forming a platform, covered over with half-dried meat, which was curing over a slow fire.[13]

Fortunately for the Ute and Shoshoni, Spanish expansion sputtered on the borders of the Apache country. Catholic fathers Francisco Atanasio Domínguez and Silvestre Velez de Escalante explored the Uinta Basin and much of the Ute domain during their famed expedition of 1776, but no serious attempts at settlement followed. For the Shoshoni, contact with whites would not occur until their encounter with the Lewis and Clark expedition.

At the close of the eighteenth century, the land that would become Daggett County was generally considered Shoshoni country. Both the Shoshoni and the Utes were flourishing. White men's horses, blankets, and ironware had brought a new material prosperity and increased leisure time. There was a flowering of the arts and spiritual pursuits.

But while New Spain's conquests had stalled in the Southwest, Britain and the young American republic continued to probe the unexplored regions of the continent. Their explorers, trappers, traders, and missionaries were traveling the inland waterways and pushing toward the Rocky Mountains. They brought more of the goods that the Indians wanted, but they also brought trouble and heartache in the form of smallpox, venereal disease, whiskey, and firearms. It was only a matter of time before white men would enter the upper basin of the Green River, and this would not bode well for the native peoples of the Uinta Mountains.

ENDNOTES

1. *Atlas of Utah* (Provo: Brigham Young University Press, 1981), 17, 31.

2. G.E. Untermann and B.R. Untermann, *Field Guide to the Geology of the Uinta Mountains* (Salt Lake City: Utah Geological and Mineral Survey, 1961), 1; Stokes, *Geology of Utah* 145–46.

3. Howard R. Ritzma, *Geological Atlas of Utah: Daggett County* (Salt Lake City: Utah Geological and Mineralogical Survey, 1959), 47.

4. Dick Dunham and Vivian Dunham. *Flaming Gorge Country* (Denver: Eastwood Printing, 1978), 8–9; Stokes, *Geology of Utah,* 146.

5. "Two Cultural Resource Studies for the Questar Pipeline Company Near Flaming Gorge Reservoir," report prepared for Bureau of Land Management, Rock Springs District, 1992, 13–30.

6. Byron Loosle, Lora Broadbent, Lynne Ingram, "The Other Side of Life: Hunting with the Fremont"(unpublished paper presented at the 1st Rocky mountain Anthropological Conference in collection of Byron Loosle, 1993)

7. Kent C. Day and David S. Dibble, *Archaeological Survey of the Flaming Gorge Reservoir Area Wyoming-Utah, University of Utah Anthropological Papers No. 65 (Upper Colorado Series No. 9* (1963), 1–14, 39–77.

8. Raymond W. Wood and Margot Liberty, eds., *Anthropology on the Great Plains* (Lincoln: University of Nebraska Press, 1980), 101–3.

9. Virginia Trenholm and Maurine Carley, *The Shoshonis: Sentinels of the Rockies* (Norman: University of Oklahoma Press, 1969), 27.

10. Harrison Clifford Dale, ed. *The Ashley-Smith Explorations and the Discovery of a Central Route to the Pacific* (Glendale, CA: Arthur H. Clarke, 1941), 87.

11. "Two Cultural Resource Studies," 32.

12. Trenholm,*The Shoshonis,* 30.

13. Warren Angus Ferris, *Life in the Rocky Mountains* (Denver: Old West Publishing Co., 1940), 49.

Chapter 2

The Fur Trade Era

> Beyond the horizon, for the Spanish and all others, there were many provinces where as Raleigh said "the graves have not been opened for golde, the mines not broken with sledges, nor their Images puld downe out of their temples."
>
> —Bernard DeVoto

Lust for wealth was the driving force behind most early European incursions into the New World. Spain grew fat on the looted wealth of Central and South America, but native civilizations to the north of Mexico's Aztec empire were not nearly as wealthy. The elusive Seven Cities of Gold, to Spanish explorer and military leader Francisco Coronado's dismay, proved to be nothing more than Pueblo villages. Coronado and others spent years searching for treasure, and, though myths of gold and silver treasure persisted, the European powers that expanded into North America turned their attention to the extraction of less-glamorous commodities.

The quest for furs would become the driving force behind European expansion into North America—the force that eventually would lead to the settlement of the Mountain West and the establishment of Daggett County, Utah. English, Dutch, French, American, and Spanish fur companies worked along the inland waterways toward the unknown interior of the continent. They generally relied on Indians to do most of the work. Tribal peoples did the trapping and preparation of the pelts, which were then traded for European manufactured goods. As an area became trapped out, the traders worked onward into the heartland, and with them went the imperial claims of their respective monarchs.

For the Indian tribes, white traders were new players in an already existing game of territorial alliances and rivalries. European goods and weapons, especially firearms, were greatly prized, and the tribes that acquired these items gained great advantages. Whites were powerful allies, and Indian nations often aligned themselves with a fur company and its national sovereign. Wars, revolutions, and treaties changed the players with the passage of time, but the nature of this geopolitical chess game remained remarkably the same.

At the beginning of the nineteenth century, most of North America was dominated by European powers. England had taken control of Canada; Spain controlled California, the Southwest, and Louisiana. America was expanding toward the Mississippi Valley and had laid claim, along with Britain, to the Columbia River drainage in the Pacific Northwest. Meanwhile, British, French, and Spanish interests were vying for the trade of the upper Missouri Valley, and American merchantmen had begun trading for sea otter pelts with the Indians of the Pacific Northwest coast. This situation was soon to be shattered.

To his pleasant surprise, President Thomas Jefferson's attempt to purchase New Orleans from France resulted in the acquisition of all the Louisiana territory—France having regained control of the territory from Spain. The Louisiana Purchase of 1803, coupled with the existing claim to Oregon, suddenly made the United States a continental empire. It now included an immense area of 828,000 square miles in the heart of the continent—all of France's claims in North America. Lying south of the 42nd parallel and west of the Louisiana Purchase, most of the Green River drainage remained Spanish territory; but Spain (and later Mexico) was never able to exert much control over the area. This ensured that the rich Green River beaver

Ashley National Forest above Palisade Park near Summit Springs Ranger Station. Photo taken 1 March 1939 by B.W. Schubert. (Utah State Historical Society)

country would become a no man's land open to trespass from trappers and traders from Canada and the United States.

On their return trip down the Missouri River in 1806, Captains Meriwether Lewis and William Clark and their exploratory company encountered several parties of fur trappers heading upriver. The American fur business was burgeoning, particularly the trapping of beaver for their pelts to supply the fashion demand for beaver top hats, and it was St. Louis merchants like Manuel Lisa, Pierre Chouteau, and Andrew Henry who were in the forefront. These men and a few others came together in 1808 to form the Missouri Fur Company, and their brigades went up the Missouri River the following year.

After wintering at Fort Raymond, near the juncture of the Bighorn and Yellowstone rivers, the Missouri Fur Company men moved westward to the Three Forks region of Montana. This was fine beaver country, and the catches proved excellent. The Blackfeet Indians, however, who were allied with the British Hudson's Bay Company, attacked the Americans on several occasions. The conditions proved so hazardous that Pierre Menard's brigade retreated to Fort Raymond, and Andrew Henry's group moved south to the branch of the Snake River now known as Henrys Fork.[1] Here they built a fort and began trapping. The next year, 1811, John Hoback, Edward Robinson, and Jacob Reznor of Henry's brigade are said to have worked the headwaters of the Bear River and were likely the first white men on the northern slope of the Uinta Mountains. These three encountered returning fur trappers of John Jacob Astor's fur company under Robert Stuart the following year, and their advice guided the Astorians home over the now-famous South Pass.[2]

The War of 1812 and the hostility of the powerful Blackfeet Indians disrupted American efforts in the Far West. The British North West Company dislodged the American Fur Company from Oregon, and British trappers made the Snake River and the upper Green River their domain. Donald MacKenzie led several North West Company expeditions through the Green River country from 1817 through 1821, discovering Bear Lake in 1819.

It was not until the middle 1820s that Americans returned to the Green River. General William H. Ashley formed a partnership with Andrew Henry in 1822 for the purpose of trapping the upper Missouri River drainage. Ashley would eventually reap a fortune from the fur trade, but his first two years were not auspicious. In

Jim Bridger. (Utah State Historical Society)

1822, one of the partnership's two keelboats, laden with $10,000 in trade goods, was wrecked near Fort Osage. The following year brought severe harassment from both the Blackfeet and the Arikara Indians. In the wake of these disappointments, Henry and Ashley revised their plans. They decided to move their operations away from the Missouri River to the safer central Rockies. Furthermore, they planned to eliminate the expense of maintaining trading posts by adopting a system of annual rendezvous.

The rendezvous was a long-established trading practice among the Shoshoni and other Native American tribes. At given times of the year, tribes would meet at prearranged locations to celebrate and trade. Ashley and Henry adapted this practice to their own purposes. They determined to pack supplies from the east into the heart of the mountain country. At a given time and place, Indians and trappers would meet the caravan, and pelts then could be exchanged for the next year's supplies. This was a daring departure from accepted practice, and it would make Ashley a very wealthy man.

During 1824, brigades led by Andrew Henry and Jedediah Smith trapped the Black Hills, the Wind River Mountains, the Bighorn Mountains, Cache Valley, the Weber River, and the Bear River. They found the upper Green River country extremely rich in beaver, and this news was passed to Ashley when pelts were transported to St Louis in the fall. Ashley immediately moved to resupply his outfits and set out with a pack train in November.

Ashley's train reached the Green River, which the Shoshoni called the Seeds-ke-dee Agie (Prairie Hen River), in April 1825. He then divided his men into four small groups. While the other groups went trapping in various directions, Ashley's men built bullboats for an exploring trip downriver. The crude vessels were probably about sixteen feet long, seven feet in the beam, and made of buffalo hides stretched over a light willow frame. Before separating, the groups had agreed to rendezvous in July a short distance downriver at a point to be chosen and marked by Ashley.

The General found his meeting place a few days later: "Here also a creek sixty feet wide discharges itself on the west side. This spot I selected as a place of general rendezvous, which I designated by marks in accordance with the instructions given to my men."[3] The small creek became known as Henrys Fork of the Green River, named after Ashley's partner. The spot was marked so the others might recognize it, and the small group continued their journey. Ashley's hope was that the Green River might provide a navigable waterway over which he could transport his goods and pelts. Instead, canyon walls closed in and the current quickened.

Upon entering Red Canyon, the expedition had its first serious encounter with rapids. The channel was entirely blocked by boulders that had tumbled from the surrounding cliffs, creating a dropoff about a dozen feet in height. The boats were laboriously unloaded and lowered by rope over the obstructions. During the process, the General climbed an overlooking cliff and painted "Ashley 1825" in black letters. The place would later become known as Ashley Falls.[4]

Whitewater continued the next day, with men and baggage getting a severe soaking. Ashley noted a substantial Indian trail along the north side of the river. Finally, on 7 May, the country opened up, the waters calmed, and the beleaguered argonauts entered Browns Park. Ashley wrote:

> . . . we encamped on a spot of ground where several thousand Indians had wintered during the last season. . . . Many of their lodges remained as perfect as when occupied. They were made of poles two or three inches in diameter, set up in circular form, and covered with cedar bark.[5]

Browns Park provided a welcome but short respite. Downriver, passing through the massive Gates of Lodore, a spirit of foreboding swept through the party. Sometimes unloading the boats and lining them down, sometimes shooting the rapids, Ashley's men worked through Lodore, Echo Park, and Whirlpool Canyon. In Split Mountain Canyon, Ashley's boat swamped in a rapid. Fortunately for the General, who could not swim, two of the men leaped into the water with ropes and pulled the boat ashore.

This incident was fancifully recalled much later by James Beckwourth. In his memoirs, Beckwourth told how he plunged into the current and effected Ashley's rescue. It made a fine tale, but Beckwourth was with James Clyman's group at the time of the event and was nowhere near Split Mountain Canyon. Like many mountain men, Beckwourth was not one to let the facts get in the way of a good story.[6]

Ashley's party continued downriver toward the valley that now bears his name. The men cached supplies near the mouth of the Uinta River, figuring they would return and make an overland exploration of the Uinta Basin. Another fifty miles, however, convinced Ashley that further exploration of the treacherous river was pointless, and the boats were abandoned. The expedition met a party of

Utes and acquired horses. Not long after, it joined with a group of Taos trappers led by Etienne Provost. Ashley's return to the rendezvous took him up the Uinta and Duchesne rivers and through the upper portion of Strawberry Valley. There the group crossed over to Heber Valley, turned northeastward to the Kamas Valley, and headed eastward.

Ashley had cached his goods near the confluence of Henrys Fork and the Green River, and he had sent word that this was to be the rendezvous ground. Mountain men and Indians assembled there, near the site where the town of Linwood eventually grew, waiting for the General. However, Ashley traveled down Henrys Fork on his return from the High Uintas and must have noted the lush grasslands in the area of Burnt Fork and Birch Creek. After retrieving his goods, he chose to move the rendezvous upstream about twenty miles to this site, depriving the future Daggett County to a claim as the site of the first rendezvous.[7]

In the meadows of the Henrys Fork Valley, near the mouth of the Burnt Fork, the parties were arranged in two camps just a few miles north of the present Daggett County line. The group consisted of twenty-five men under Ashley, twenty-nine Hudson's Bay Company deserters, Etienne Provost's band of thirteen, Jedediah Smith's group of seven, twenty-five to thirty men captained by John H. Weber, perhaps some free trappers (not in the employ of any fur company), and numerous Indians.[8]

James Beckwourth recalled that:

> When all had come in, he opened his goods, and there was a general jubilee among all at the rendezvous. We constituted quite a little town, numbering at least eight hundred souls, of whom one half were women and children. There were some among us who had not seen any groceries such as coffee, sugar, etc. for several months. The whiskey went off freely as water, even at the exorbitant price he sold it for. All kinds of sports were indulged in with a heartiness that would astonish more civilized societies.[9]

Though the mountaineers probably took several days to gather, the formal rendezvous took place in one day, 1 July. Ashley's records indicated the price of the goods traded:

coffee	[$]1.50 per pound
sugar	1.50 per pound
tobacco	3.00 per pound
powder	2.00 per pound
fish hooks	1.50 per dozen
flints	1.00 per dozen
scissors	2.00 each
knives	2.00 each
blue cloth	5.00 per yard
scarlet	6.00 per yard
lead	1.00 per pound
blankets	9.00 each (3 point North West Company blanket)
buttons	1.50 per dozen[10]

The next day, Ashley and fifty men departed for St Louis with the beaver packs they had acquired at the rendezvous. He made only one more trip to the mountains, but the rendezvous system that he established on the banks of Henrys Fork flourished for another fifteen years. Subsequent rendezvous were held throughout the mountains of the northern region, with the upper Green River being the favored location. Ashley sold his interest in the company to Jedediah Smith, William Sublette, and David Jackson at the rendezvous of 1826, and he left the business a wealthy man. To him and the stalwart members of his expedition must go the credit for being the first white Americans to float the canyons of the upper Green River and to explore the eastern Uinta Mountains.

Over the next several years, many fur trappers and traders frequented Browns Park, the Green River, and the eastern Uintas. Among those who passed through were Ceran St. Vrain, Kit Carson, Uncle Jack Robinson, and Warren Angus Ferris. It has been suggested that Baptiste Brown, a trapper of French descent, settled in Browns Park with his Indian wife in the late 1820s and that the valley was named for him. However, this story is probably false. Baptiste Brown was a character in Colonel Henry Inman's book *The Santa Fe Trail,* and there is compelling evidence that his character was based on the life of Jean Baptiste Chalifoux, a Taos trapper and known historical figure. Though Chalifoux is known to have traveled the lower Green

Uncle Jack Robinson. (Utah State Historical Society)

River, there is no evidence to suggest that in real life he ever used the name Brown.[11]

The story of Baptiste Brown may be apocryphal, but it was common in fur trade days to name a valley after someone associated with it. Examples such as Jackson's Hole, Pierre's Hole, and Ogden's Hole abound. Brown's Hole, later called Brown's Park by explorer John Wesley Powell, was probably named for a trapper or trader who wintered there. The area's namesake may have been "Bibleback" Brown, an old trapper remembered by area settlers, or it may have been some shadowy figure who has disappeared from the historical record. Others assert that the valley was named for its dried brown appearance. Whatever the case, people started to refer to the valley as Browns Hole in the late 1830s, and by then it had become a favorite place for mountain men to spend the winter.[12]

Indeed, the sheltered valleys of the Uinta Mountains region became popular winter campsites during the fur trade era. Henrys Fork, Little Hole, and Browns Hole provided somewhat temperate microclimates where people and livestock could survive the cruel winter months. Indians and trappers at times wintered together, living in brush lodges or teepees and feeding their horses cottonwood bark when snow was too deep for grazing.

The later 1830s brought many changes to the Mountain West. Beaver populations declined, and the market value of beaver pelts, or plews, dropped. In order to cut costs, fur companies began to establish permanent trading posts throughout the Mountain West. Antoine Robidoux reportedly built Fort Uintah (sometimes called Fort Robidoux) on the banks of the Green River in the middle 1830s, and Jim Baker opened a post near the mouth of Henrys Fork in 1839.[13]

One of the most notable trading posts in the region was in Browns Hole. At the juncture of several trails, and being one of the most popular winter camp areas in all the West, the Hole seemed a prime business location. With that in mind, Prewitt Sinclair, William Craig, and Phil Thompson constructed Fort Davy Crockett on the banks of the Green River in 1837. The partners chose the name in tribute to the famous frontiersman recently killed in Texas at the siege of the Alamo. Though its exact location is a matter of controversy, the fort most likely was situated on the eastern shore of the river a short distance upstream from the mouth of Vermillion Creek (in present-day Colorado). It was described as a few log buildings with dirt floors and roofs arranged to form a square enclosure.[14]

Kit Carson became a frequent visitor at Fort Davy Crockett.

James Baker. (Utah State Historical Society)

During its first winter of operation, Carson was the post's hunter, supplying the tables of the twenty or so residents with freshly killed game. By 1839, Carson and his colleagues had done their job too well. Game was scarce, provisions had run low, and the fort's staff and patrons were relegated to dining on roast dog. One summer visitor commented that the place had become known among the trappers as Fort de Misere (Fort Misery).[15]

There was also competition from other traders. Traveler Thomas Jefferson Farnham arrived at the post in August noting:

> Here also were the lodges of Mr. Robinson (Uncle Jack), a trader, who usually stations himself here to traffic with the Indians and white trappers. His skin lodge was his warehouse; and buffalo robes were spread upon the ground and counter, on which he displayed his butcher knives, hatchets, powder, lead, fish hooks, and whiskey. In exchange for these articles he receives beaver skins from trappers, money from travellers, and horses from Indians. . . . And indeed, when all the "independent trappers" are driven by approaching winter into this delightful retreat, and the whole Snake village, two or three thousand strong, impelled by the same necessity, pitch their lodges around the Fort, and the dances and merry-making of a long winter are commenced, there is no want of customers . . . [16]

Farnham, who was with an ill-starred emigrant party heading to Oregon, found Fort Davy Crockett a delightful oasis. Other visitors were not of the same opinion. Dr. Frederick A. Wislizenus, a German adventurer, commented:

> The fort itself is the worst thing of the kind we have seen on our journey. It is a low one-story building, constructed of wood and clay, with three connecting wings, and no enclosure. Instead of cows the fort had only some goats. In short, the whole establishment appeared somewhat poverty stricken, . . . the people at the fort seemed to be worse off than we were.[17]

Better times returned with cooler weather. Phil Thompson and William Craig returned from the Arkansas River country with fresh provisions, and a sizable winter camp began to develop. Several dozen trappers and the inhabitants of a large Shoshoni village spent the winter of 1839–40 in the proximity of the fort. Kit Carson returned to the hole, Joseph Walker arrived, and Joe Meek showed up to do some trading. That winter, Meek lead a party on horseback far down the ice-covered Green River to explore the canyon country, and hostile Indians stole about one hundred of the trappers' ponies.[18]

Despite the good times in Browns Hole, the beaver trade had fallen into a slump from which it never recovered. European fashion discarded the beaver hat in favor of hats made of silk. 1840 saw the collapse of the Rocky Mountain Fur Company and the last major rendezvous. However, people in the Mountain West still needed to make a living, and horse stealing became a popular alternative for both Indians and former trappers. Large bands were formed to steal horses from as far away as California; but Phil Thompson, one of the partners in Fort Davy Crockett, made the mistake of stealing horses too close to home.

In an effort to replenish the trappers' herd, early in 1840 Thompson helped lead an expedition that rode to Fort Hall to steal horses from the Hudson's Bay Company. After nabbing fourteen British horses, the group pilfered some thirty more from an unsuspecting group of friendly Shoshoni. Fort Davy Crockett was in Shoshoni territory, the Shoshoni were important customers, and Thompson's complicity in this act drove a wedge between the fort's partners.

When the aggrieved Shoshoni arrived at Fort Davy Crockett demanding restitution, partner William Craig and most of the assembled trappers denounced the theft, and a recovery party was organized under the command of Joseph Walker. The group headed south and finally located the stolen animals near the mouth of the Uinta River on an island in the Green River. Although the horses were recaptured, Thompson and the other thieves slipped away.[19]

Thompson's bad judgement caused a rift that broke up the Sinclair, Craig, and Thompson partnership. This incident, competition from other traders, and the general demise of the Rocky Mountain fur trade soon brought about the abandonment of Fort Davy Crockett. A detailed account of an 1842 visit to Browns Hole makes no mention of Fort Davy Crockett, and a report from 1844 by John Charles Frémont states that the fort was in ruins.[20]

Despite the untimely end of Fort Davy Crockett and hard times in the fur trade, Browns Hole remained a favorite haunt of Indians and the few remaining trappers. William Hamilton wrote that in August 1842 he and some others

Mr. and Mrs. John Jarvie. (Sweetwater County Museum)

> with Washakie and his Shoshones, moved to Brown's Hole on Green River. . . . A few Utes and Navajos came up on their annual visit with the Shoshones to trade and race horses . . . three tribes were parading on horseback. Indians and horses were decorated with paint and trappings of finery, according to the taste of the owner. Each man was trying to outdo the other in horsemanship, stopping ponies when in full career, halting at a mark, at a jump—the one who succeeded in stopping the nearest to the mark winning the trophy. . . .
>
> We remained at Brown's Hole until the first of September, making several excursions to the Uintah Mountains, a beautiful and romantic country and then a trappers' paradise for small game.[21]

Hamilton, in the company of Old Bill Williams, moved out of the hole around 1 September, traveling and trapping the Uinta Mountains. The group returned to Browns Hole, late in November for a trappers' rendezvous. Though the grand old-time rendezvous was a thing of the past, a vestige of the tradition hung on at Browns Hole into the late 1840s. Indians and trappers met with traders from the "States" to exchange furs for needed provisions. Hamilton remembered:

Philip Mass. (Daggett County)

> The days were given to horse racing, foot racing, shooting matches; and in the evening were heard the music of voice and drum and the sound of dancing. There was also an abundance of reading matter for those inclined in that direction.[22]

The colorful Rocky Mountain rendezvous, which began in the Daggett country, ended in the Daggett country. As a trapping area, a location for rendezvous, and a winter campsite, the three-corners region became one of the most significant places in the history of the North American fur trade. The names of the people who passed through read like a who's who of the mountain men. Jim Bridger, Thomas Fitzpatrick, Kit Carson, Bill Williams, Jim Baker, Uncle Jack

Robinson, William H. Ashley, Joseph Reddeford Walker, and Joe Meek all traversed the eastern Uintas and wet their moccasins in the Green River.

Their place in the nation's story is secure. These frontiersmen established an American presence in the Far West. For good or ill, they forged the first relationships between the United States and the Indian tribes of the Rocky Mountains. Their knowledge of western geography was indispensable to the explorers and emigrants who followed them, and their mere presence helped put the American stamp on a large portion of the continent. Furthermore, the mountain man's legendary fearlessness, rugged individualism, and colorful lifestyle has given him an unparalleled status in the pantheon of American folklore.

The fur trade era was just the beginning of Euro-American expansion in the Far West, but it marked the cultural apogee of the region's native people. With large numbers of horses, firearms, and ironware, western Indian tribes enjoyed a material prosperity unrivaled in their existence. Disease and warfare did reduce native populations, but this served to concentrate the increased wealth among fewer individuals. Spiritual and cultural life flourished, band size grew larger, and governance became more complex. Associating with the whites was not without benefits.

The fur trappers were small in number and did not permanently occupy the land. They moved with the seasons and the supply of beaver. Their ways, however, were about to change. As the fur trade came to a close, the juggernaut of Euro-American settlement turned its attention to Oregon and California. Emigrants were coming, and for the Indians and mountain men alike, life would never be the same.

ENDNOTES

1. In keeping with current naming practices of government and mapmaking entities, the apostrophe has been dropped in the original possessive forms of Brown's Park, Henry's Fork, etc. throughout this book, except in historical quotations.

2. Dick Dunham and Vivian Dunham, *Flaming Gorge Country*, 31.

3. Harrison Clifford Dale, *The Ashley-Smith Explorations and the*

Discovery of a Central Route to the Pacific 1822–1829, (Glendale, CA: Arthur H. Clark, 1941), 140.

4. Ibid.

5. Ibid., 142.

6. James P. Beckwourth, *The Life and Times of James P. Beckwourth as told to Thomas D. Bonner* (Lincoln: University of Nebraska Press, 1972), 90; Roy Webb, *If We Had a Boat* (Salt Lake City: University of Utah Press, 1986), 25–26.

7. Fred R. Gowans, *Rocky Mountain Rendezvous: A History of the Fur Trade Rendezvous 1825–1840* (Layton, UT: Peregrine Smith, 1985), 17.

8. Ibid., 19.

9. Beckwourth, *Life and Times,* 75.

10. Gowans, *Rocky Mountain Rendezvous,* 19.

11. Janet LeCompte, "Jean-Baptiste Chalifoux," in *The Mountain Men and the Fur Trade of the Far West,* vol.vii, Leroy R. Hafen, ed., (Glendale, CA: Arthur H. Clark, 1955), 57–60.

12. Dunham and Dunham, *Flaming Gorge Country,* 48–49; J.S. Hoy, "The J.S. Hoy Manuscript," James G. Hodgson, ed., 1952, unpublished manuscript in author's collection, 90.

13. Dunham and Dunham, *Flaming Gorge Country,* 64. See also Scott J. Eldredge and Fred R. Gowans, "The Fur Trade in Utah," in Powell, ed., *Utah History Encyclopedia,* 208–13.

14. Thomas Jefferson Farnham, *Travels in the Great Western Prairies, The Anhuac and Rocky Mountains, and in the Oregon Territory,* (n.p., n.d.), 59, Merrill Library, Utah State University. See also Dunham and Dunham, *Flaming Gorge Country,* 68–71.

15. Frederick A. Wislizenus, *A Journey to the Rocky Mountains* (St Louis: Missouri Historical Society, 1912), 129; Kit Carson, *Kit Carson's Own Story of His Life,* Blanche Grant, ed. (Santa Fe, NM: Kit Carson Memorial Foundation, 1956), 42.

16. Farnham, *Travels in the Great Western Prairies,* 59.

17. Wislizenus, *A Journey to the Rocky Mountains,* 129.

18. Carson, *Kit Carson's Own Story,* 48; Frances Fuller Victor, *The River of the West* (Oakland, CA: Brooks-Sterling, 1974), 260.

19. Victor, *River of the West,* 259–60; Leroy R. Hafen, "Prewitt Sinclair," in *The Mountain Men and the Fur Trade of the Far West,* vol. 4, Leroy R. Hafen, ed.(Glendale, CA: Arthur H. Clark, 1955), 308.

20. William T. Hamilton, *My Sixty Years on the Plains: Trapping, Trading, and Indian Fighting* (Norman: University of Oklahoma Press,

1960) 71–72; Donald Jackson and Mary Lee Spence, *The Expeditions of John C. Fremont,* vol. 1 (Urbana: University of Illinois Press, 1970), 707–8.

21. Hamilton, *My Sixty Years on the Plains,* 70.

22. Ibid., 72.

CHAPTER 3

MORMONS, MOUNTAINEERS, AND UTAH'S FORGOTTEN COUNTY

> I visited immediately—this section of the country—found a company of Mormons under the charter Legislature of Utah, had assembled on Green River, and commenced construction of a bridge; finding much opposition on the part of the Indians, they determined to abandon for the present, and all returned to Salt Lake City—should the Mormons persist in determination, a war will be the consequence.
>
> —J.H. HOLEMAN

In 1831, four Indians from Oregon arrived in St. Louis. It is likely they were nothing more than curious tourists, but a Methodist journal reported that they had come seeking Christian salvation. Three years later, Reverend Jason Lee was on his way to the Oregon country to establish a mission in the Willamette Valley. Other missionaries, including Marcus and Narcissa Whitman, soon followed, and the glowing reports they sent back to the "States" did much to stimulate interest in the West.

In the grips of an economic depression in the late 1830s, thousands of Americans searching for hope were eager to hear tales of a new Eden, and numerous Oregon emigration societies sprang into existence. In 1840 Joel Walker's family, accompanying a party of missionaries, followed the trail to Oregon; the following year the Bartleson-Bidwell company completed a difficult overland journey to California. These people inaugurated a westward migration that would assume epic proportions; by 1860 a quarter of a million emigrants had traveled westward on the Oregon, California, and Mormon trails.[1]

These trails followed the route of the old fur-trade caravans up the Platte River, the Sweetwater River, and over South Pass; they then diverged in the Green River Valley. For the mountain men, whose chief livelihood had died with the beaver trade, the trails provided new opportunities to make a living. Thousands of westbound emigrants needed food, ammunition, draft animals, guides, and blacksmithing services. They also needed ferry services to cross the Green River during periods of high water. For many of the mountaineers and their families, this was the beginning of a new and prosperous way of life.

Among those who made the change was the legendary Jim Bridger, known to his fellows as "Old Gabe." Bridger saw the possibilities of trading with the emigrants and Indians, and, in partnership with Henry Fraeb, he built the first of the three trading posts that bore his name. The first Fort Bridger was built in 1841 near the Green River between the mouths of the Big Sandy and Blacks Fork rivers. Fraeb was killed by Indians before the fort was completed, and the site was abandoned not long thereafter. Early in the summer of 1842, Bridger started constructing a new post on a bluff overlooking the Blacks Fork. He then traveled to St. Louis to procure goods, and it is likely that while there he arranged his partnership with Louis Vasquez, another Ashley veteran and an experienced trader.[2]

The second Fort Bridger was also short-lived. Work began on a new site near the river bottom, and the third and final Fort Bridger was occupied in August 1843. This bottomland along the Blacks Fork, with its lush grass and shade trees, was an oasis along an otherwise desolate stretch of the emigrant trail. It was an excellent location for weary travelers to rest themselves and their stock and to obtain necessary supplies and repairs. John McBride described the site in 1846:

> It is only a camp where some fifty trappers were living in lodges. A single cabin of logs where the roof composed of willow brush covered with earth composed the fort. There was a large village of Indians of the Snake Tribe encamped here and a brisk traffic in dressed deer skins, buffalo robes, and logs went on during our stay with them which was half a day and the following night.[3]

Bridger and Vasquez were not the only mountaineers to take advantage of the new opportunities. Many began trading in livestock; among them was Uncle Jack Robinson, who is said to have started in the business in 1843. After months on the trail, many of the emigrants' draft animals were badly broken down when they reached the Green River. Stockmen like Robinson often traded one sound animal for two that were broken down. A long rest on good pasturage generally restored the oxen, horses, or mules to health, and then they were once again marketable. Smart trading and natural reproduction combined to increase herd sizes quickly. This could be a lucrative business.[4]

Like most of the mountaineers, Uncle Jack Robinson had taken many Indian wives during his tenure in the wilderness. He lived in a skin lodge during the summer, trading his cattle during the annual emigration period. Winters were generally spent along with other area stockmen herding on the Smiths Fork or Henrys Fork rivers. He was a regular visitor at Fort Bridger for some forty years, and he was remembered as a gentleman and an extraordinary storyteller. Sometime during this phase of his life, he constructed a cabin near the mouth of Henrys Fork, possibly the oldest structure in Utah built by whites.

Other frontiersmen went into the lucrative ferry business. There were eventually five ferry sites on the Green River that operated during times of high water. Fees could range between three dollars and six dollars a vehicle. Jim Baker, who in 1839 had operated a trading post on Henrys Fork, was one of the ferry operators.[5]

In 1847 a different group of emigrants came through the Green River Valley. They were not headed for Oregon or California but intended to colonize the valley of the Great Salt Lake. This was the first company of Mormon pioneers, members of the Church of Jesus Christ of Latter-day Saints (LDS, or Mormon). Under the leadership of Brigham Young, they were fleeing religious intolerance and intended to build the "Kingdom of God on Earth" in the Rocky Mountains. Near the Little Sandy River, they encountered Jim Bridger. He entered their camp and spoke at length of the geography to the west and what they might encounter along their way. In the words of historian Bernard DeVoto, "The pilgrims of eternity were children come a little way into the kingdom of Old Gabe. As a monarch he instructed them."[6]

Brigham Young, the Mormons' "Lion of the Lord" met Jim Bridger, the monarch of the mountains. Both men were strong, independent, and highly competent; both were leaders and builders. On this day they parted on good terms, but eventually their ambitions and their kingdoms would collide.

For the United States, the late 1840s were a time of great change. West of the continental divide and south of the 42nd parallel, the land officially belonged to Mexico. In reality, much of this territory was a no man's land. Like its predecessor Spain, Mexico had never been able to exercise any real authority in the region. The Green River Valley was effectively still Indian country, and the mountaineers, by virtue of intermarriage and attained respect, had become part of that social milieu. Land ownership derived from the ability to sieze and hold ground. Justice was a matter of folk tradition. There was no established law.

This situation was soon to change. The murder of Mormon church founder Joseph Smith and increasing persecution in Illinois propelled the members of the LDS church toward the West. The Mormons were a pre-millenial sect that believed their sacred charge was to build a utopian society to be ruled by Jesus Christ after the Second Coming. Attempts to create the kingdom in Missouri and Illinois had failed in part because of intolerance and persecution, and Brigham Young and the church's Quorum of Twelve Apostles opted to try once more in the Rocky Mountains. They felt that beyond the boundaries of civilization they might realize their dreams without harassment. The Latter-day Saints' plan was to build a spiritual and temporal empire in the West.

In the midst of this movement, the United States went to war with Mexico in 1846. The conflict ostensibly began as a boundary dispute over the location of the Texas border, but the underlying cause was the United States' continental ambitions. It was the nation's first great military adventure on foreign soil, and it was successful. The Treaty of Guadalupe Hidalgo ending the war in 1848 ceded California, New Mexico, and the Mountain West to the United States. Both the Mormon Zion and Fort Bridger came under American authority.

Almost coincidental with America's taking of the Far West was the discovery of gold in California. Victory in the Mexican War had wrested this land for the United States, but it was the California Gold Rush that motivated the American people to occupy and hold it. In 1848, on the eve of the gold rush, a total of some 19,000 people had emigrated to the West. In 1849 alone, 27,000 traveled the trails to Oregon and California, and in 1852 the number was 70,000. A trickle of emigration had turned into a flood.[7]

Two groups of Forty-niners spurned the accepted trails and detoured through the Uinta Mountains country. One was a sizable party of Cherokee Indians. They traveled up the Front Range and the Cache la Poudre River, across the Laramie plains, and down Bitter Creek toward Fort Bridger. Arriving at the fort late in the season, the company opted to spend the winter in Browns Hole. After resting themselves and their stock, they continued their journey in the spring. Their route became known as the Cherokee Trail and would later become the route of the Overland Stage.[8]

William Manly was with another group that started late in the season in 1849. Manly had worked his way west as a driver with a wagon train from Missouri. On reaching the Green River, the train was informed by soldiers that it was too late to cross the Sierra Nevada that year; the party would have to spend the winter in Salt Lake City among the Mormons. For Missourians, this was anathema. The bloody conflict in which they had driven the Mormons from their state was a very recent memory. They not only distrusted the

Looking southeast into Browns Park from the top of Jesse Ewing Canyon. Photo by William Purdy. (Utah State Historical Society)

Mormons, they feared retribution. Remembering a group of Mormons he had met earlier on the trail, Manly commented:

> They were dressed in buckskin and moccasins with long spurs jingling at their heels, the rowells fully four inches long, and each one carried a gun, a pistol, and a big knife. They were rough-looking fellows with long matted hair, long beards, old slouch hats, and a generally backwoods get-up in every way. . . . I had heard much about the Mormons, both at Nauvoo and Salt Lake. . . . I am sure I would not like to meet them if I had a desirable mule that they wanted, or any money, or a good looking wife.[9]

Not wanting to chance a winter in Salt Lake City, Manly and some of the other drivers determined to try to float the Green River to the Pacific Coast. They dug an abandoned ferryboat out of the sand, found a couple of paddles, and bought supplies. Manly was elected captain, and the group set out in high spirits:

> It looked as if we were taking the most sensible way to get to the Pacific, and we almost wondered that everyone was so blind not to

> see it as we did. . . . We commenced to move down the river with ease and comfort, feeling much happier than we would had we been going toward Salt Lake with the prospect of wintering there.[10]

When they entered the canyon country, their mood changed. The old ferryboat was quite unmaneuverable in the rapids. Somehow they got past Ashley Falls, but the next day the awkward vessel was dashed to pieces against a boulder. Fortunately, the boat had been unloaded before running this rapid, and the party's gear, including some axes, was intact. Discouraged but still determined, they set to work felling pine trees and fashioned dugout canoes. Lashing the canoes together for stability, the emigrants moved on.

In Browns Hole the expedition halted to replenish its larder. They managed to shoot a deer, two elk, and several ducks. After eating their fill and drying the meat that was left, the beleaguered argonauts returned to the river and headed toward the Gates of Lodore. Like the mountain men of 1825, Manly's party somehow was able to reach the still waters of the Uintah Valley, where they encountered a band of Utes. Chief Wakara persuaded Manly and most of his men that continuing downriver was sheer folly. Following a brief respite with the then peaceful Utes, the men traded for horses and rode toward Salt Lake City. However, two dissenters, McMahon and Field, returned to the dugouts and headed downstream. Desolation Canyon soon convinced them that Wakara had been correct, and they too abandoned the river and traveled to Salt Lake City.

Both the Mormons and mountaineers prospered as tens of thousands of gold rushers crowded the trails of the Mountain West. For Brigham Young's followers, the emigrant trade generated hard cash at a time when it was desperately needed. It helped solidify the Mormon colony in Salt Lake City, and it financed the movement of many fellow believers to the new Zion.

Their improved condition allowed the Mormon hierarchy to proceed with plans for a western empire. In March 1849 they organized the "State of Deseret," a self-proclaimed government whose huge jurisdiction covered parts of eight present-day western states. Bridger Precinct was organized the following year, and the Deseret census indicated that twenty-two males and twenty-four females resided along the Green River, or at Bridger Precinct. At least on paper, the domain of the mountaineers had been brought under the control of the Latter-day Saints' civil government.[11]

The United States never recognized the State of Deseret; instead, it created the Territory of Utah on 9 September 1850. Much smaller than Deseret, Utah still encompassed a sizable area, including all of what is now Nevada and Utah and large portions of Wyoming and Colorado. Brigham Young was appointed territorial governor and superintendent of Indian affairs.

Even at this early date, relationships between the Mormons and mountaineers had become strained. Brigham Young seemed to trust Louis Vasquez, but he felt that Jim Bridger was his enemy. In 1849 he commented:

> I believe that Old Bridger is death on us, and if he knew 400,000 Indians were coming against us, and any man were to let us know, he would cut his throat. . . . I believe Bridger is watching every movement of the Mormons, and reporting to Thomas Benton at Washington.[12]

Bridger had reason to be hostile. Salt Lake City had become the trading center of the region, and Bridger's business suffered from the competition. Emigrants were bypassing his fort to make cheaper purchases in the Mormon capital. Furthermore, it was becoming clear that the Mormons planned to expand their political and economic control over the Green River area.

This was done by the Utah Territorial Legislature in 1852 through the creation of Green River County. One of the first counties created in the territory, it was an immense jurisdiction, bounded on the north and east by the territorial lines, on the west by Weber and Davis counties, and on the south by an extension of the southern boundary of Davis County. Taxes were levied against the mountaineers and license fees were exacted for their businesses.[13]

Even more odious to the mountaineers were Mormon attempts to take control of the lucrative Green River ferry business. In 1852 the legislature granted ferry rights on the Green River to Thomas More; unlicensed operators were to be subject to a $1,000 fine. A company of Mormons was sent to colonize the area and build a bridge, but it

Browns Park, looking southwest toward the confluence of Vermillion Creek and the Green River. Photo by William Purdy. (Utah State Historical Society)

met so much Indian opposition that the project was abandoned. The Shoshoni were understandably angered by the rapid growth of Mormon settlement, and their mountaineer allies easily exploited this discontent.

Undaunted, the Mormons made another attempt to take the Green River ferries the following year. Daniel H. Wells received exclusive ferry rights from the legislature in 1853. He assigned these rights to the company of Hawley, Thompson, and McDonald, but it was soon found that having rights and exercising them were two different things. The company was forcibly excluded from all but one of their sites by the area's mountain men, who understandably claimed prior possession.[14]

Incensed by armed resistance to their civil government, and with a firm conviction that Jim Bridger was inciting Indian insurrection, the Mormon leadership decided it was time to "Mormonize" Green River County. In August, Salt Lake County Sheriff James Ferguson organized a posse of 150 riders to take the ferry sites and to arrest Jim Bridger. "Old Gabe" must have been alerted, because he was nowhere to be found when the posse arrived at the fort. Believing that Bridger had been selling powder, lead, and liquor to the Indians, possemen confiscated these commodities. The ammunition was sent to Salt Lake City while, according to Bill Hickman, the posse destroyed the "good stock of whiskey and rum in small doses."[15]

After taking Fort Bridger, a detachment moved on the mountaineers at the ferry sites. In a pitched battle, two or three mountaineers were killed and the rest were driven off. The posse confiscated much of their property, including liquor and several hundred head of livestock. Though a few of the lawmen stayed on until October, the elusive Bridger was not apprehended and the mountaineers reoccupied most of the ferry sites.[16]

This was not the end of the matter. The way for the Mormons to effectively control this country was to occupy it, and a mission to the Green River was organized under the leadership of Apostle Orson Hyde. At the LDS general conference in October 1853, Hyde called thirty-nine people to permanently settle the region. John Nebeker led the first company to Fort Bridger, and Hyde set about organizing a second company to follow.

Nebeker's group did not receive a warm reception. Still smarting from the attacks of Ferguson's posse, the mountaineers and Indians around Fort Bridger were in no mood to welcome Mormon settlers. Thoroughly intimidated, the colonists moved on to Smiths Fork while their leaders searched for another suitable townsite. Fort Supply was soon established about two miles above the confluence of Willow Creek and Smiths Fork, some twelve miles from Fort Bridger. With the arrival of a second company under Isaac Bullock late in November, Fort Supply became a well-armed community of ninety-two people. Completion of a blockhouse brought further security. Orson Hyde and Hosea Stout visited the place the following spring, and Stout wrote:

> It is the most forbidding and godforsaken place I have ever seen for an attempt to be made for a settlement and judging from the altitude I have no hesitancy in predicting that it will yet prove a total failure but the brethren here have done a great deal of labor. . . . Elder Hyde seems to have an invincible repugnance to Fort Supply.[17]

With a permanent Mormon presence finally established there, Brigham Young appointed officials for the administration of Green River County. W.I. Appleby became probate judge, Robert Alexander was made clerk of the probate court, and William Hickman fulfilled multiple roles as sheriff, prosecutor, assessor, and tax collector. Hickman, who established a trading post at Pacific Springs and a ferry on the Green River, was a good choice as lawman and tax collector. A tough and resolute frontiersman, and rumored to be one of the church's "avenging angels," Bill Hickman was a man who could command the respect of mountaineers and Indians.[18]

Hickman wisely pursued a policy of accommodation, trying to undo the ill feelings generated by the Mormon invasion of the previous year. He gained the trust of Uncle Jack Robinson, in Bridger's absence the most influential of the mountaineers, and he befriended Elisha Ryan, the dissident ferryman who had led mountain men and Indians against the Mormon posse. In a letter to Brigham Young, Hickman stated that Ryan

> talks much to the Indians in favor of the Mormons. . . . Jack Robinson tell[s] him to mind me and he will get along well. The Mountaineers all feel well. They say there has never been as good feelings here as now exists—there are many of them that are the greatest of scamps but they are as good to us as they can be. . . . We have affected these feelings by telling them there is good feeling toward them, and none will be robbed. That some Mormons talk and act foolishly but not to mind it—this we had to do to get the good feeling of the Indians, for they were so linked together we could not separate them.[19]

By the spring of 1855, relationships between Green River County's opposing factions had improved enough that Jim Bridger felt he could safely return to his fort. After escaping Sheriff Ferguson's

Ranch along the Green River in Browns Park. (Utah State Historical Society)

posse in 1853, Bridger had traveled to Washington, D.C., where he aired his grievances against the Mormons to federal officials. In July 1855 he was back at Fort Bridger.

Bill Hickman, acting as agent for the LDS church, proposed to Bridger that he sell his trading post to the Mormons. Bridger was in no hurry. His fellow mountaineers had urged him to hold on, so he set a price he believed the church would find unacceptable. On 2 August, Lewis Robison, representing the Mormons, traveled from Fort Supply to meet with the venerable mountain man. To Bridger's surprise, Robison finally acceded to the $8,000 purchase price; $4,000 was to be paid immediately and the balance was to be paid in fifteen months. Bridger accepted the terms and his attorney drew up the contract. H.F. Morell acted on behalf of the absent Louis Vasquez.[20]

The Mormons now owned Fort Bridger, had another colony at Fort Supply, and had occupied some of the Green River ferry sites. Fair dealing had accomplished what highhanded force in 1853 had not. Mormons, mountain men, and Indians settled into an uneasy peace. Forts Supply and Bridger became important stations for reprovisioning Mormon handcart companies and wagon trains. Meanwhile, Robison and his workers kept busy improving the post, putting up hay, tending livestock, and trading with emigrants and Indians.

As Hosea Stout had predicted, however, life at the Green River outposts proved difficult. Farming was problematic, and much of the food had to be freighted in from the Salt Lake Valley. Killing frosts and hordes of grasshoppers ravaged fields and gardens. Horseflies, gnats, and mosquitos in the summer plagued man and beast alike. Such problems were borne somewhat more easily at Fort Supply, which had a semblance of social activity, but Fort Bridger was a dull place where wives and children made it a point to be away as much as possible.[21]

Jim Bridger was not the only one to make protests to the federal government over affairs in Utah. W.M.F. McGraw, superintendent of the South Pass Wagon Road, wrote to President Zachary Taylor in October 1856:

> No vestige of law and order left. . . . An ecclesiastical organization, as despotic, dangerous and damnable, as has ever been known to exist in the country . . . whose laws, or rather conspiracies, are framed in dark corners, promulgated from the stand of Tabernacle or Church, executed at midnight, or upon the highways, by an organized band of braves and assassins whose masters compel an outraged community to tolerate.[22]

Relations between the Mormon-dominated territorial government and federal officials were deteriorating, and controversies surrounding the appointment of federal judge W.W. Drummond only increased the alienation. Drummond outraged the Latter-day Saints by leaving his wife in the East and coming to Utah in the company of a Baltimore prostitute. The judge made no secret that he detested the Mormons, and the Mormons tended to ignore the writs of his court. This prompted Drummond to complain to the president that Utah was in a state of rebellion.

These and other complaints, many of questionable validity, prompted President James Buchanan to act. Feeling compelled to uphold the authority of the United States government, he appointed Alfred A. Cumming to replace Brigham Young as territorial governor. To make sure that Cumming was properly installed and that federal officials were obeyed, a massive army escort was to accompany him to Utah.

Jarvie Store in Browns Park. (Daggett County)

General William S. Harney was placed in command of the military expedition, which was composed of three infantry regiments, a regiment of dragoons, and two artillery batteries. These regiments started their march on 18 July 1857 from various locations and were to rendezvous west of South Pass. Harney, however, was embroiled in the highly contentious Kansas political situation and could not remove himself. With troops already en route, Colonel Albert Sydney Johnston was chosen as the new commander.

Word of the approaching army reached Salt Lake City on 24 July. Remembering their treatment in Missouri and Illinois, Brigham Young and the church hierarchy surmised that a new wave of persecution had begun and that they were to be robbed, killed, and turned out of their homes. Young issued a proclamation that the army would not be allowed within the territory. On 4 August 1857 Young wrote to Lewis Robison at Fort Bridger: "We do not intend to be taken this time . . . they will not be permitted to come into this Territory to plunder, rob and murder as seems to be their wishes and designs."[23]

In early September, Brigham Young assured Robison that the occupants of the fort would be safe through the winter; however,

Colonel E.B. Alexander's 10th U.S. Infantry had arrived at Hams Fork by the end of the month. Just twenty-five miles from Fort Bridger, the soldiers established Camp Winfield, where they waited to be joined by the other units.

Recognizing the danger, the Mormons adopted a scorched earth policy. They vowed to leave nothing in their country that might aid or sustain the U.S. troops. On 29 September Mormon militiamen heading eastward to confront the army met some fifty families fleeing with their livestock from Fort Supply and Fort Bridger. Both places were set afire on the night of 2 October. Militiaman Jesse W. Crosby was present at the destruction of Fort Supply:

> The company which I belonged left Salt Lake City September 25, 1857. We took out our wagons, horses, etc., and at twelve o'clock set fire to the buildings at once, consisting of one hundred or more good hewd log houses, one sawmill, one gristmill and one thrashing machine, and after going out of the fort we set fire to the stockade work, straw and grain stacks, etc. After looking a few minutes at the bonfire we had made, thence on by the light thereof. I will mention that owners of property in several places begged the privilege of setting fire to their own, which they freely did, thus destroying at once what they had labored for years to build and that without a word. We then went our way a few miles and stopped to set fire to the City Supply, a new place just commenced; there were ten or fifteen buildings perhaps, and warmed ourselves by the flames. Thus was laid waste in a few hours all the labor of settlement for three or four years, with some five or six hundred acres of land fenced or improved.
>
> Our work of destruction was now finished and we moved silently onward and reached Bridger after daylight and found it in ashes, it having been fired the night before.[24]

While the various U.S. Army units assembled on Hams Fork, the Mormon militia, known as the Nauvoo Legion, kept up a constant harassment. The commands of Lot Smith, Robert Burton, and Porter Rockwell captured and burned three federal supply trains and drove off several hundred of the army's cattle. In early October Colonel Johnston had not yet arrived to take charge, and Colonel Alexander determined to push on toward Salt Lake City. His plan was to avoid ambush in Echo Canyon by taking a circuitous route along the Bear River. Snowstorms and impassable conditions halted progress just thirty-five miles from Camp Winfield, however, and Colonel Johnston sent word to abandon the march and return to Hams Fork.

Johnston took command in early November. Realizing that Hams Fork was no place to spend the winter, Johnston pushed his already depleted army toward the relative shelter of Bridger Valley. In the shadow of the burned-out fort the troops established Camp Scott, the expedition's winter quarters. Men and livestock had both suffered greatly. Thousands of cattle had been lost to cold, starvation, and Mormon harassment.

About 2,500 soldiers, teamsters, and federal officials spent the winter of 1857–58 at Camp Scott. Tents and huts spread for miles along the banks of the Blacks Fork River. Despite a few expected incidences of drinking, desertion, and insubordination, the command was kept in an acceptable state of military discipline and preparedness. Regular drills were maintained, and several tents were put together to form a makeshift theater. For several months Camp Scott was one of the largest communities in the West.[25]

Forage in the neighborhood of the camp was quickly depleted, and the remaining livestock were sent to winter on Henrys Fork. A detachment of troops under Colonel Philip St. George Cooke accompanied the herds. Another command under Captain Randolph Marcy of forty soldiers, twenty-six civilian mountain men, and some sixty-six mules was dispatched to Fort Massachusetts in New Mexico to secure replacements for lost horses and mules. Marcy's group made a difficult winter crossing of the Uinta Mountains on Indian trails. After almost perishing in the San Juan Mountains of southwestern Colorado, they finally made it to the fort. They returned on a longer but well established route east of the Rockies with some sixty horses and 1,000 mules.[26]

Many of the region's old mountaineers readily assisted the federal army. Rough treatment at the hands of the Mormons was still fresh in their memories. Jim Baker, who had become one of the Green River ferrymen, had many reasons to scout for Johnston's Army. Several mountain men guided Marcy on his arduous mission to New Mexico, and others sold cattle that helped the hungry soldiers survive the winter.

Near the end of the long winter, negotiations opened between the Mormons and Governor Cumming. The heated words of the fall were replaced by more pragmatic rhetoric. A compromise was reached that allowed the new territorial officials to take office and the army to enter the Salt Lake Valley. Johnston's Army marched through Salt Lake City on 26 June 1858. The men kept their ranks; looting and vandalism were not permitted. Federal authority was reestablished in Utah, and the army moved south to build a post west of Utah Lake. This post, named Camp Floyd, was far enough away from Salt Lake City so that the soldiers would not be a daily menace to the Mormon capital, but it was still close enough to exert some oversight on the affairs of government.

The legacy of the bloodless "Utah War" in the Green River country was a permanent shift in the balance of power. The federal government took control of Fort Bridger, creating an army post and a sizable military reservation. Elements of the 10th U.S. Infantry were stationed there until they were withdrawn for duty in the Civil War. Civilians associated with Johnston's force stayed on to settle the region, and Governor Cumming refused to allow the legislature the granting of exclusive ferry rights on the Green River. Green River County remained a part of Utah Territory and Mormons remained active there, but the LDS church was no longer the dominant force in the area. The large military reservation effectively precluded the establishment of other settlements in the vicinity.

One of the newcomers, Phil Mass, had been a civilian scout with the federal troops. Like the mountaineers before him, Mass took a Shoshoni wife and became a prominent stockman on Henrys Fork. To him goes the credit for naming Phil Pico Mountain, while Phil Mass Mountain, a flat-topped prominence just north of the present Wyoming border, was named for him. However, the most influential of the new non-Mormon settlers was William A. Carter.[27]

Carter was a Virginian and a friend of General Harney. Harney had used his influence to get Carter appointed as a sutler to the army's Utah expedition. Sutlers were officially appointed by the federal government and attached to military organizations as traders

Bridge across the Green River. (Courtesy Pauleen Baker)

and merchants. Large sums could be made purveying merchandise to soldiers, and such appointments were highly prized. With the end of the Utah troubles, Carter became sutler at Fort Bridger.

A man of culture who carried himself as a southern gentleman, William A. Carter soon became Green River County's most prominent citizen. His wife, Mary, was certainly the area's most celebrated woman, entertaining guests in a grand manner. In addition to his work as sutler, Carter also became a merchant, rancher, postmaster, justice of the peace, and probate judge. He was a gracious host to military men and travelers, and his house was known for its Steinway piano and impressive library. One army officer commented:

> We found him to be a high toned and intelligent and hospitable Virginia gentleman. Universally popular with all who associated with him. And deservedly so. His store contains a larger assortment of goods and wares than any other establishment West of the Mississippi River. . . . This large trade is by no means confined to those at the post but principally with the miners and immigrants. . . . I have seldom met a more hospitable gentleman than Judge Carter and there is always a place at his table for a visitor at the

post or a passing friend. The pleasure of entertaining a guest is the only remuneration he will receive for his liberality.[28]

When the Civil War prompted the withdrawal of Fort Bridger's garrison, Judge Carter organized the local mountaineers into a militia for the defense of the fort. He also used his influence with Chief Washakie to defend the post from hostile Indians. This force remained active until California volunteer troops under Colonel Patrick Connor occupied Fort Bridger in 1862. During the Civil War, soldiers at Fort Bridger guarded the emigrant trails, the new transcontinental telegraph line, and the mail route, and they kept a watchful eye on the Mormons. In 1865, Nevada volunteer soldiers under post commander Noyes Baldwin constructed a military road from the fort to Browns Hole.[29]

Carter continued to prosper after the Civil War. He had several daughters who were sent to eastern schools, and the judge and his wife continued to entertain in grand style. The Carter's southern hospitality as well as their liquor cellar became known throughout the West. James T. Rusling visited Fort Bridger in 1866 and later wrote that the judge was

a striking character in many ways, already had several tracts under cultivation, by way of experiment, and the next year he expected to try more. His grass was magnificent; his oats, barley, and potatoes, very fair; but his wheat and Indian corn wanted more sunshine.[30]

Judge Carter's fortunes may have been on the rise, but this was not the case for Green River County's Shoshoni inhabitants. White people did not take all the land, but they had the habit of taking the very best. Euro-American settlements and military posts usurped the rich riparian areas that had done much to support Indian life. White hunting near the settlements and along the emigrant trails decimated game populations. In the late 1850s, Utah Superintendent of Indian Affairs Jacob Forney reported:

There is no tribe of Indians in the territory with whom I have any acquaintances that have been so much discommoded by the introduction of white population as the Shoshones. For the past few years they have been compelled to live in the mountains as the

> game has been driven off the lowlands where the snow frequently falls to such depths as to be a disadvantage to man and beast. Not withstanding all the disadvantages under which they labor from the introduction of the white populace I cannot learn that they have ever molested our citizens but on the contrary have always been friendly.[31]

Some credit for these good relations must go to the Mormons, who generally believed it was better to feed the Indians than to fight them, and to the mountain men who had dealt fairly with them and married into their tribe. Most of the credit, however, must go to the pragmatic Shoshoni themselves. Washakie's band of Eastern Shoshoni faced threats from the Blackfeet to the north and the Sioux, Cheyenne, Crow, and Arapaho Indians to the east. The tribe's southern neighbors, the Utes, had also become enemies. Even though the whites were taking their lands, they were still a powerful ally against the Shoshonis' enemies. When other bands of Shoshoni harassed the Mormon settlements or raided along the mail route, Washakie's band generally maintained peace with the whites.

In 1858 Superintendent Forney aided both the Shoshoni and Ute people by negotiating the end of their longstanding enmity. Forney helped to resolve the tribes' grievances and got both parties to agree on a boundary between their respective homelands.[32]

Peaceful relations between the United States and the Eastern Shoshoni were codified in a treaty signed at Fort Bridger in 1863. The treaty set the boundaries of Eastern Shoshone territory and required that white settlements, river ferries, telegraph lines, stage lines, and military posts go unmolested. The government agreed to pay the tribe a $10,000 annual annuity for twenty years to compensate them for lost lands and game, and $6,000 worth of food and clothing were distributed when the treaty was concluded. The agreement was signed by Washakie and other chiefs and was witnessed by Indian commissioners James Doty and Luther Mann. The venerable mountain man Jack Robinson acted as interpreter.[33]

The Eastern Shoshoni continued at peace even as trails and settlements closed in around them. In what has now become known as the Treaty of Fort Bridger, a government delegation under General William T. Sherman met again with Washakie and other chiefs in

1868. Whites and Indians agreed that the Eastern Shoshoni would move to a reservation in the Wind River Valley in Wyoming where white men would not be allowed to trespass. A military post, later named Fort Washakie, was built near the site to protect the Shoshoni from hostile Indian neighbors. The 1868 Fort Bridger Indian treaty effectively removed all remaining Eastern Shoshoni Indians from southeastern Wyoming and northeastern Utah. On the reservation, Washakie maintained peaceful relations with the whites. During the Sioux campaign of 1876, he and his Shoshonis fought with distinction under General George Crook at the Battle of the Rosebud.

Time had run out for the free-roaming ways of the Eastern Shoshoni, and so also went the fortunes of Utah's Green River County. Disgust with the Mormon practice of polygamy and bitter memories of the Utah War motivated Congress to whittle away at Utah Territory. Green River County was reduced in 1861 when Colorado Territory was established, and enlargement of Nebraska Territory the following year brought a further reduction. The creation of Wasatch County in Utah also moved back Green River County's southern boundary.

Following the Civil War, the Union Pacific Railroad advanced its survey line along the Platte Valley and the Overland Trail, and thousands of construction workers and merchants swept along the route. The arrival of the rails in the fledgling town of Cheyenne, late in 1867, spawned a movement to create a new territory. Judge Carter, who would become even wealthier as a railroad tie contractor, lobbied to include Fort Bridger in the new jurisdiction. A longtime foe of the Mormons, Carter used his influence to have the southern boundary of Wyoming established at the forty-first parallel, not the forty-second, which was the northern boundary of Utah. When the Territory of Wyoming was created in 1868, it was made rectangular, and Utah lost its northeast corner. Nothing was left of Green River County but a narrow strip of land on the northern slope of the Uinta Mountains. This strip of land was added to Summit County in 1872, and Utah's contentious Green River County became only a memory.[34]

ENDNOTES

1. John D. Unruh, *The Plains Across* (Urbana: University of Illinois Press, 1979), 119–20.

2. Fred R. Gowans, *Fort Bridger: Island in the Wilderness* (Provo: Brigham Young University Press, 1975), 10–12.

3. Ibid., 12–13.

4. Dick Dunham and Vivian Dunham, *Flaming Gorge Country*, 98.

5. Ibid., 101.

6. Bernard DeVoto, *The Year of Decision: 1846* (Boston: Little, Brown and Company, 1943), 447.

7. Unruh, *The Plains Across*, 119–20.

8. Gowans, *Fort Bridger*, 35; Dunham and Dunham, *Flaming Gorge Country*, 75.

9. Roy Webb, *If We had a Boat* (Salt Lake City: University of Utah Press, 1986), 35.

10. Ibid., 37.

11. Gowans, *Fort Bridger*, 37.

12. Ibid., 41.

13. "Green River, Sweetwater County Once Part of Territory of Utah," *Green River* (Wyoming) *Star*, 23 July 1937; Gowans, *Fort Bridger*, 44–47.

14. Gowans, *Fort Bridger*, 49.

15. Hope Hilton, *"Wild Bill" Hickman and the Mormon Frontier* (Salt Lake City: Signature Books, 1988), 40; Gowans, *Fort Bridger*, 52.

16. Hilton, *"Wild Bill" Hickman*, 42.

17. Gowans, *Fort Bridger*, 60.

18. Hilton, *"Wild Bill" Hickman*, 43.

19. Ibid., 46.

20. Gowans, *Fort Bridger*, 66.

21. Ibid., 95.

22. Hilton, *"Wild Bill" Hickman*, 56.

23. Gowans, *Fort Bridger*, 95.

24. Ibid., 101.

25. Ibid., 108.

26. Ibid., 109.

27. Dunham and Dunham, *Flaming Gorge Country*, 81.

28. Gowans, *Fort Bridger*, 146.

29. C.G. Coutant, *History of Wyoming and the Far West* (New York: Argonaut Press, 1966), 2:666.

30. Gowans, *Fort Bridger,* 147.

31. Ibid., 132.

32. Ibid., 132.

33. Ibid., 134–35.

34. Dunham and Dunham, *Flaming Gorge Country,* 97–98.

CHAPTER 4

INTO THE FAR WEST

> Ashley, Fremont, the Manly party of Forty-niners, Henry Adams, Clarence King and his helpers Hague and Emmons, Powell himself—a curiously diverse history would casually brush that little-known [Uinta] range. From the mountain man's uncomplicated and ferocious dynamism to Adams' dynamo and second law of thermo-dynamics, ideas significant to the continent's knowledge and use of itself passed here.
>
> —WALLACE STEGNER

In the years following the Civil War, America turned westward. The advancing iron of the Union Pacific Railroad signalled the nation's intent to explore and occupy the frontier. It was the age of steam and of science, and these would be the potent tools with which the United States would accomplish its mission. Into the Far West went great explorers and scientists. They were more than mapmakers; they included geologists, paleontologists, naturalists, and ethnologists. In the late 1860s and the 1870s, some of the finest minds in the country were set to the task of surveying and studying the western domain, and many of them traversed the Uinta Mountains and the canyons of the Green River.

A few had come before them. Guided by Jim Baker, Joseph Reddeford Walker, Auguste Archambeault, and "Broken Hand" Thomas Fitzpatrick, John C. Frémont returned through Browns Hole on his epic journey of 1843–44. The party found the Green River badly swollen by spring runoff and went into camp across from the ruins of Fort Davy Crockett. Here they repaired a boat Frémont had purchased at Fort Uintah and ferried themselves across the channel. With the river at their backs, Frémont's men ascended the Vermillion Creek drainage and continued eastward to the parks of the Rockies.[1]

Later, Captain Howard Stansbury's expedition to the Great Salt Lake skirted the country on its return trip in 1850. Shunning the familiar route over South Pass, Stansbury engaged Jim Bridger to lead his party east over the Cherokee Trail.[2]

In spite of these explorations, and those of Ashley and the mountain men earlier, the scientific community had only vague knowledge of the geography and resources of the Mountain West. Thus were born the great surveys of the post–Civil War period. They included the United States Geological Survey of the Territories under Ferdinand Vandiveer Hayden, the United States Geological Survey of the Fortieth Parallel directed by Clarence King, John Wesley Powell's Geographical and Geological Survey of the Rocky Mountains, and the Geographical Surveys West of the 100th Meridian commanded by Lieutenant George Wheeler. Bitter rivalries sometimes flared between the competing surveys over funding, power, and intellectual prestige, and their work often overlapped.

The most famous of the scientist-explorers was one-armed Civil War veteran Major John Wesley Powell. Though enrolled for brief periods at the Illinois Institute, Illinois College at Jacksonville, and Oberlin College, this magnificently able scholar and administrator was largely self-taught. Following his army service, Major Powell became a professor at Illinois Wesleyan College, but he yearned for greater challenges. With an eye toward funding an expedition to the West, Powell helped found a state natural history museum. The Illinois legislature funded the institution, Powell was named curator, and he was given $500 for a collecting trip to the Rocky Mountains.

Major John Wesley Powell in about 1872. (Smithsonian Institution)

This began a chain of events that would take him overland across the Rockies, on two float trips down the unexplored canyons of the Green and Colorado rivers, and establish his reputation as one of the preeminent scientists of his day.[3]

Powell quickly moved to secure further backing from various universities and railroads. Through his acquaintance with General Ulysses S. Grant, he was given authority to draw rations at cost from military posts, and the Smithsonian Institution was persuaded to supply scientific instruments for his expedition. Consisting of a few college students, teachers, amateur naturalists, relatives, the Major, and his wife, Emma, the Rocky Mountain Scientific Exploring Expedition set out for the mountains in 1868. There they fell in with Oramel G. Howland and Jack Sumner, both experienced outdoorsmen, and they learned the ways of the back country. It was likely Sumner who first suggested the exploration of the Colorado River, but the ambitious Powell was ready and willing to accept the challenge.[4]

In the fall, Sumner and Howland found a few other mountaineers who wanted to throw in with the company, and the augmented expedition moved west over the old Berthoud Trail to the country of the White River Utes. Here in late October they built winter cabins and put up hay for their livestock; but not all were up to the rigors of wintering over. On 2 November, Powell, Oramel Howland, and the less-adventurous souls set out for Green River, Wyoming, and the Union Pacific Railroad. People and mules suffered terribly from thirst until they reached Little Bitter Creek several days later. Remaining in Browns Hole for a day or two, the company continued on its way, and by mid-November it had reached the railroad station at Green River. After depositing the tenderfeet on a train east on 15 November, Powell and Howland returned to White River by way of the eastern Uintas and Browns Hole.[5]

The winter was not spent idly. When weather permitted, Powell roamed extensively along the valley of the White River and through the surrounding country. He gazed over vast expanses of rugged terrain, learning the nature of the wildlands his upcoming river expedition would traverse. He also spent many hours among the White River Utes. The bands of Antero and Douglas were wintering in the vicinity, and the Major indulged his incipient ethnological interests. He learned the rudiments of the Ute language, customs, and beliefs, and he traded extensively for the traditional artifacts that defined Ute culture.

These studies were rudely interrupted in March when the swollen White River overflowed its banks and flooded the cabins. It seemed like a good time to move on, and the now hardened explorers headed toward the Green River. The party split at the Yampa River. Emma Powell, the Major, Seneca Howland, and Billy Hawkins headed for the Union Pacific tracks in Green River town. The Powells needed to go east to secure more funding and have boats constructed. On the way out, they cached rations and instruments at the mouth of Henrys Fork. These would be retrieved when they returned by boat.[6]

The others, Jack Sumner, O.G. Howland, and Bill Dunn, took a more leisurely trip over to the Little Snake River and down Vermillion Creek to Browns Hole. Spring waterfowl migration was in full swing, and the frontiersmen lingered in the area for two weeks indulging themselves on roast duck. Duck finally became tiresome, and the three continued their relaxed pace to Fort Bridger and the town of Green River. It was here that they rendezvoused with Seneca Howland, Hawkins, and Walter Powell (the Major's brother) and, in the words of the Major's biographer, "camped below the Green River bridge, spending their days and nights trying to drink up all the whiskey in town, but finding that Jake Fields could make it faster than they could drink it."[7]

On 11 May 1869, the day after the transcontinental railroad was completed at Promontory, Utah, Major Powell returned with the boats. Inexperienced as boatmen, the crew spent the next two weeks training on the river and learning flag signals for communication. They mastered use of the sextant and barometer, and O.G. Howland learned how to chart the river. The roster, in addition to the Major, eventually included nine men. From the previous year were Sumner, both the Howlands, Bill Hawkins, Bill Dunn, and Powell's brother Walter. In addition, there was George Bradley, a soldier from Fort Bridger who would do anything to get out of the army, a young frontiersmen named Andy Hall, and Frank Goodman, an English traveler and sportsman.[8]

At noontime on 24 May, with the residents of Green River, Wyoming, looking on, the party's four boats slipped into the current and disappeared downriver. In the lead boat, the *Emma Dean*, rode Major Powell, Sumner, and Dunn. Then came Walter Powell and George Bradley in the *Kitty Clyde's Sister*, Andy Hall and Bill Hawkins in the *Maid of the Canyon*, and Frank Goodman and the Howland brothers in the *No Name*. They would not be heard from again until weeks later when they reached the Uinta Valley.[9]

The first few days were easy going. Although the Green River ran swiftly, there were no rapids or canyons. The inexperienced navigators learned the feel of their heavily laden boats, and loads were redistributed so that the vessels were more equally maneuverable. On the third day out they reached the Henrys Fork. Powell wrote:

> We land a short distance above the junction, where a cache of instruments was made several months ago in a cave at the foot of the cliff, a distance back from the river. Here they were safe from the elements and wild beasts, but not from man. Some anxiety is felt, as we have learned that a party of Indians have been camped near the place for several weeks. Our fears are soon allayed, for we find the cache undisturbed. Our chronometer wheels have not been taken for hair ornaments, our barometer tubes for beads, or the sextant thrown into the river as "bad medicine," as had been predicted. Taking up our cache, we pass down to the foot of the Uinta Mountains and in a cold storm go into camp.
>
> The river is running to the south; the mountains have an easterly and westerly trend directly athwart its course, yet it glides on in a quiet way as if it thought a mountain range no formidable obstruction. It enters the range by a flaring, brilliant red gorge, that may be seen from the north a score of miles away. The great mass of the mountain ridge through which the gorge is cut is composed of bright vermillion rocks; but they are surmounted by broad bands of mottled buff and gray, and these bands come down with a gentle curve to the water's edge on the nearer slope of the mountain.
>
> This is the head of the first of the canyons we are about to explore—an introductory one to a series made by the river through this range. We call it Flaming Gorge. The cliffs, or walls, we find on measurement to be about 1,200 feet high.[10]

Before venturing onward, the expedition paused for three days. It rained on the 27th, and they repaired a barometer; the next two days were occupied in exploring the country. Powell and his companions climbed to various high points to view the surrounding geography, and they must also have visited among the small local community of stockmen. He recorded that:

> For many years this valley has been the home of mountaineers, who were originally hunters and trappers, living with the Indians. Most of them have one or more Indian wives. They no longer roam with the nomadic tribes in pursuit of buckskin or beaver, but have accumulated herds of cattle and horses, and consider themselves quite well to do. Some of them have built cabins; others still live in lodges. John Baker is one of the most famous of these men, and from our point of view we can see his lodge, three or four miles up the river.[11]

In spite of the mountaineers' warnings that the canyons of the Green River could not be run, the Powell expedition returned to the river on 30 May. They easily handled their first rapid, exhilarated by the speed and whitewater. Proceeding through Red Canyon, more rapids were encountered, and the Major felt he was speeding along at almost the pace of a locomotive.

The *Emma Dean* was the lighter scout boat and took the lead. When the Major heard the approaching roar of rough water, he carefully scanned the river for the best passage. At the worst rapids, the boats were unloaded and let down by ropes. Lines were attached to both bow and stern, and the bow line was made fast to some object below the rapid. Straining against the stern line, five or six men carefully lowered the boat into the tempest. When they could no longer hold it back, the stern line was released and the craft bounded over the fall. The downstream men on the bow line hauled the boat in. All the cargo had to be lugged along the rocky shore and reloaded below. This was a laborious process that the men detested. They often felt the Major was overcautious and would gladly have taken their chances shooting the whitewater much of the time.[12]

On 2 June they came to the falls that had bedeviled William H. Ashley's bullboat party in 1825. Powell's boats were unloaded and the

Emma Dean was lined down before camp was made for the evening. The other boats were let down the next morning. As the men trudged along the bank to reload their gear, they noticed Ashley's inscription on a rock above the trail. Ashley's narrative would not be published until 1918, and Powell was unaware of his voyage. He thought the inscribed date was 1835 or 1855 and surmised that Ashley had been part of a prospecting expedition mentioned to him by John Baker.

> The story runs that the boat was swamped, and some of the party drowned in one of the canyons below. The word "Ashley" is a warning to us, and we resolve to use great caution. Ashley Falls is the name we give to the cataract.[13]

They continued a short distance beyond the falls before making camp. The following day they dried their rations, clothing, and equipment on the rocks and went exploring, and on 4 June they arrived in Browns Hole in the early afternoon. Setting up camp under a large cottonwood, the men spent the rest of the day killing a number of wild ducks and catching fish.[14]

Browns Hole offered a wonderful respite from the claustrophobic canyons and roaring whitewater. The now-seasoned rivermen climbed and gazed over the countryside and leisurely floated down the valley. They rose in the morning to a chorus of bird songs, but the halcyon moment was not to last. Peering down the valley to where the river disappeared into a rocky defile, the Major penned a letter to the *Chicago Tribune:*

> . . . I am sitting on the same rock where I sat last spring, with Mrs. Powell, looking down into this canon. When I came down at noon, the sun shone in splendor on its vermillion walls . . . the sun is going down, and the shadows are settling. . . . Now 'tis a portal to a region of gloom.
>
> And that is the gate way through which we enter our voyage of exploration tomorrow—and what shall we find?[15]

What they found were towering cliffs looming over a narrow canyon that seemed like one continuous cataract. In one exhilarating rapid Andy Hall exclaimed, "Oh how the waters come down from Lodore," a line he had memorized in his school days. Lodore became the name of the canyon, and the rocky defile at its entrance was

The first camp of the Second Powell Expedition, May 4, 1871. Shown from left to right are: Almon Harris Thompson, Andrew Hattan, S. V. Jones, John Steward, W.C. Powell, Frank C.A. Richardson, Frederick Dellenbaugh, F. M. Bishop. Three other members of the expedition, , John Hillers, Major Powell, and the photographer E. O. Beaman are not shown. (Courtesy U.S. Geological Survey and Utah State Historical Society)

dubbed the "Gates of Lodore." This irritated Jack Sumner, who wrote in his journal that it was un-American to pull names for a new continent from such "musty trash."[16]

Lodore was a terror. On the afternoon of 9 June, Powell pulled the *Emma Dean* to shore to avoid a rough spot, signalling with the flag for the other boats to do likewise. Two of them did reach shore, but the *No Name,* swamped with water, did not respond to the oars. It went racing down the falls with Frank Goodman and the Howlands, eventually breaking in two against a large rock. The men were rescued, but the boat was a total loss. The stern was found some fifty yards downriver the next day, and Sumner and Hall volunteered to retrieve what they could from the watertight cabin. They saved the barometers, some thermometers, and, to their delight, a keg of whiskey surreptitiously smuggled aboard by Oramel Howland. Even so, some 2,000 pounds of provisions were lost, including the entire

The Green River looking south through the Gates to Lodore. Photographed by E. O. Beaman, 1871. (Courtesy U.S. Geological Survey and Utah State Historical Society)

outfits of the three crewmen and O.G. Howland's map. Powell named the place Disaster Falls.[17]

Lodore was bad luck. While lining the *Maid of the Canyon* through a rapid, the boat got away from its handlers and dashed downriver. Fortunately, it was found a short way below in a quiet eddy with only slight damage. Shortly thereafter, Hawkins's cooking fire got away and set the whole camp ablaze. Men's hair and beards were singed saving the boats, and some of the mess equipment was lost in the fracas. Downriver, Echo Park provided a much-needed rest and time was taken to repair the boats.[18]

Whirlpool and Split Mountain Canyons were passed in relative ease, and the expedition drifted into the valley of the Uintah River on 26 June. Some of the men, including Frank Goodman, hiked up to the Ute Agency to get mail and provisions. Goodman decided that he had had enough. When Powell's men headed back into the current on 6 July, Goodman was not among them. Interestingly enough, he stayed on in the Green River country the rest of his life. Goodman kept sheep in Browns Park until cattlemen ran him out in 1897, and his body is buried in Vernal.[19]

The nine remaining men now entered unknown territory.

Neither Ashley or Manley had gone much beyond the mouth of the Uintah River. Powell and his men forged on through Desolation, Labyrinth, and Stillwater canyons to the junction of the Green and the Colorado. They then continued through Cataract, Glen, and Marble canyons. By the time they entered the Grand Canyon, rations were low, the boats were battered, and the men were skinny and half-naked. They pushed on, fighting hunger and discouragement until, on 27 August, they encountered a torturous rapid that could not be lined or portaged and appeared impossible to run.

At this place, which Powell named Separation Rapid, the Howland brothers and William Dunn decided to quit the river and climb out. The leaky *Emma Dean* was abandoned. Somehow the remaining men worked their two boats through the tumult. They then fired their guns, hoping Dunn and the Howlands would rejoin them; but it was to no avail. After conquering one more difficult rapid later in the day, the cliffs began to recede and the water slowed down. On 30 August they left the canyons behind them, their journey completed. Ironically, the three who had feared the rapids and had decided to climb out were killed on the plateau above by Indians.[20]

The year after John Wesley Powell first explored the Green River, Ferdinand V. Hayden's United States Geological Survey of the Territories made an overland exploration of the Uinta Mountains country. Like Powell, Hayden was largely self-taught. His concern was identifying the geology and natural resources of the country he traversed. The celebrated western photographer William Henry Jackson recorded the journey on glass-plate negatives as the explorers visited Henrys Fork, the Green River, Browns Hole, the Uintas, and Bridger Pass.[21]

Also in 1870, noted paleontologist Othniel C. Marsh of Yale University led an expedition to the West. Most of the funding came from Marsh himself, and the members were volunteer Yale students and recent graduates. The plan was to make a number of side trips along the route of the railway; the country south of Fort Bridger was of special interest.[22]

George Bird Grinnell, who later became a well-known writer and naturalist, accompanied Marsh's expedition. At Fort Bridger he met

Uncle Jack Robinson. He recalled, "Uncle Jack . . . was a kindly, friendly man and very ready to talk with the youngsters who questioned him. It is a great pity that some of them did not know enough to ask the old man for a multitude of details about his experiences, and to set them down."[23]

Grinnell's horse was small and only partially broken, and he determined to replace it before the expedition set out. As the only horses available were with the mountaineers on Henrys Fork, Grinnell mounted his recalcitrant pony and made for their camp. His account of the visit provides a marvelous description of the Daggett country's early residents:

> It was almost sundown when I reached Henry's Fork, and following a well-worn trail, approached a little camp of three buffalo skin lodges standing close together along the stream. As I rode into the camp, Ike Edwards came in from the other direction, and we met and I explained my errand. He took me into his lodge and gave me food, and a little later I met the other men. John Baker and Phil Mass each had a Shoshoni wife and . . . a large flock of children of various sizes. . . . Ike Edwards told me to turn my horse out into the general horse herd which was feeding nearby, and gave me robes and blankets for my bed; then by the small lodge fire, which was needed for light only and not for warmth, we talked far into the night.[24]

The next morning, the men checked beaver traps along the river before breakfast. Grinnell and Edwards went together and found two of the animals. These were tied onto the horses, Edwards carefully reset the traps, and they returned for their morning meal. The young naturalist watched the mountaineers deftly skin their catch and then rode to the horse herd, where he traded his mount to Phil Mass for a seasoned hunting horse. Grinnell thought this life idyllic:

> All about in the stream bottom, on the hills, and among the mountains there was game—birds, deer, antelope, and at a distance, elk. The stream furnished trout in numbers, and a certain amount of fur. The men each had a few cows which ranged about in the river bottom and were driven in morning and evening to be milked. It was really a place where every prospect seemed to please . . . the camp was rather a permanent one so that the bed . . . and fireplaces

> were built up to be comfortable and useful. There was plenty of food, plenty of covering, and plenty of shelter.[25]

The mountaineers still dressed in buckskin. Their coats, shirts, trousers, and moccasins were decorated with fringe, beads, and stained porcupine quills. The cuffs and collars of some of their coats were trimmed in beaver fur. Edwards was tall and lean—an excellent hunter and equestrian. John Baker, the celebrated Jim Baker's brother, had come west in the late 1830s and had lost a leg; this, however, did not interfere with his ability to ride and survive in the wilderness. Phil Mass was massive in build, with great strength and remarkable agility for a big man, yet he was quiet and reserved. Grinnell wrote:

> These men lived in just the fashion of the old-time trappers of early western days. They possessed that independence which all men seek. Theirs was everything that man needs—food, clothing, shelter, and family. They were masters of their own lives. When they felt like it, they pulled down their lodges, packed their possessions on their animals, and moved away to another place which pleased them. In winter, they camped in sheltered places or moved into comfortable log houses. The pursuit of food, the attention to their traps, and the care of livestock lent to their lives an interest which never failed . . . while I was with them I could not imagine, nor can I imagine now, a more attractive—a happier—life than theirs.[26]

Now well-mounted, Grinnell returned to Fort Bridger to join the expedition. With army wagons and an escort of soldiers, Marsh's fossil diggers set out for the Green River. It was tough going for the heavily laden wagons along the Henrys Fork bottoms, and a large quantity of grain was cached to lighten the load. Even so, the wagons continued to break down, and it was decided to leave them behind. A scout was sent back to Fort Bridger to obtain packs and ropes, and these were brought down to the mouth of the stream a few days later.[27] Grinnell remembered their camp:

> Near the base of one of the buttes our camp is pitched. Three or four tents, their white canvas showing bright against the green willows, stand a short distance from the water. Four government wagons are drawn up not far off, and the baggage of the outfit lies

> on the ground beside them. The horses and mules, dispersed over the plain, are cropping the luxuriant herbage, tended by their watchful herders, who occasionally drive in those that stray too far, and prevent the more restless from wandering away from camp.
>
> Around the glowing fire a dozen men are stretched upon the ground. Bearded, bronzed, and clothed in buckskin, you might take them all at first glance for a party of trappers; but their speech betrays their occupation, and shows you that they are members of some scientific expedition.
>
> The evening meal over, they have lighted their pipes, and are discussing in animated voice and gesture the various prizes obtained during the day. Some exult in a new fossil; others examine some rare bird; others still are looking over their tools, while two, who are cleaning their rifles, converse about to-morrow's hunt.[28]

The arrival of the pack outfit allowed the party to move on to Browns Hole. The place already had a bad reputation, and they feared an encounter with dangerous outlaws. None materialized, and the Yale men moved on toward the rich fossil beds of the Uinta Basin.

The return trip took Marsh's crew across the pine-covered Uinta Mountains on a military trail that ran from Fort Bridger to the Ute Agency. Still searching for fossils, hunting, and fishing for trout, they crossed an 11,000-foot pass and with difficulty made their way back to the wagons. These were found unharmed, but the horse thieves they had avoided in Browns Hole were camped at their grain cache. Cool heads prevailed on both sides, and violence was avoided. The Marsh expedition returned to Fort Bridger quite pleased with the large stock of fossils it had unearthed.[29]

So rich was the Green River country in fossils that paleontological expeditions in the area soon became quite common. In 1872, three parties were at work in the region searching for prehistoric remains. Marsh returned, then came Edward Cope of the Hayden Survey, and finally Joseph Leidy. There was great jealousy between these scientists—especially between Marsh and Cope. All three separately discovered bones of a prehistoric rhinoceros-like creature that summer, and each one tried to take credit for the discovery. Marsh and Cope exchanged vicious insults, each accusing the other of foul play and gross incompetence. Their bitter rivalry continued to rage for many years.

Dick Son, one of the younger mountaineers on Henrys Fork and John Baker's son-in-law, was a guide for Marsh that year. He was evidently so taken by the professor that he named one of his children William Othniel. Though Marsh did not return after 1873, Son, Jack Chew, and John Hersey continued to collect for him, shipping the fossils to Yale University at New Haven, Connecticut. Cope subsequently returned to the region several times.[30]

For John Wesley Powell, one trip down the Green and the Colorado rivers was not enough. Though his first expedition had made him a celebrity, it had been scientifically disappointing. Many of the notes and maps had been lost in the rapids, and broken barometers had made it impossible to judge altitudes in the latter part of the journey. Not long after he quit the river in 1869, Powell resolved to make a second voyage, and, on the basis of his new-found fame, he secured a federal appropriation toward that end.

Powell's brother-in-law, Almon H. Thompson, was chosen as topographer and second-in-command of the new expedition. Steven V. Jones, John F. Steward, and Francis Marion Bishop assisted him. E.O. Beaman was official photographer, and Powell's young cousin, Walter Clement Powell, would be Beaman's assistant. An artist, Frederick Dellenbaugh, accompanied the party, and Andy Hattan and Frank Richardson were picked to be general assistants. Jack Sumner was the only member of the first voyage who was invited to return. When impassable spring conditions delayed his arrival, a teamster from Salt Lake City was hired to replace him.[31]

This time there were three boats. On 22 May 1871, the *Emma Dean*, the *Nellie Powell*, and the *Canonita* drifted away from Green River, Wyoming. The group paused for a day in Flaming Gorge, and most of the men climbed out of the canyon to look around. Steward and the Major found a number of fossils, including a femur bone ten inches in diameter. Unfortunately, there was no way to transport the find. Dellenbaugh recalled:

> Flaming Gorge is an easy place to get in and out of, even with a horse, and doubtless in the old beaver-hunting days it was a favourite resort of trappers. I am inclined to think that the double turn of the swirling river is the place known at that time as the Green River Suck. Our camp under the cottonwoods was delight-

ful. We took advantage of the halt to write up notes, clean guns, mend clothes, do our washing, and all the other little things incident to a breathing spell on a voyage of this kind.[32]

In Horseshoe and Red canyons the men encountered their first rapids. On 2 June, the crew of the *Nellie Powell* misread the Major's signal and made for the wrong side of the river. Their boat upset against the rocks, and Richardson was trapped underneath the boat. Responding quickly, Professor Thompson reached down and pulled the lad to safety. Two days later, they came upon the grave of Theodore Hook and the wreckage of his boats. According to Dellenbaugh:

One rapid, where Theodore Hook, of Cheyenne, was drowned in 1869, while attempting to follow the first party, gave us no trouble. We sailed through it easily. Hook had declared that if Powell could descend the river he could too, and he headed a party to follow. The motive I believe was prospecting. I do not know how far they expected to go but this was as far as they got. Their abandoned boats, flat-bottomed and inadequate, still lay half buried in the sand on the left-hand bank, and not far off on a sandy knoll was the grave of the unfortunate leader marked by a pine board set up, with his name painted on it. Old sacks, ropes, oars, etc., emphasized the completeness of the disaster.[33]

The group made a difficult portage of Ashley Falls on 5 June and drifted into Browns Hole two days later. Here they met the Harrell brothers, a man named Bacon, and several Mexican drovers who were pasturing a large herd of Texas cattle. Much to the surprise of the boatmen, the Harrells were waiting for them with mail. Beaman also noted a group of silver prospectors, though his companions made no mention of it in their journals and diaries. A steer was butchered, and the cowboys and boatmen dined on fresh beef.[34]

Powell arranged with the Harrells to pack out notes, mail, and specimens to be sent east. Frank Richardson would be going out, too. Richardson seems not to have fit in with the group, and, according to Clem Powell, was dispatched at the Major's request. Clem Powell's journal recorded:

We rose at 4 1/2, had an early breakfast, it being the last meal that

Clarence King. A geologist and mining engineer who from 1867–1874 made a geological exploration along the 40th parallel approximately 100 miles wide that was the first systematic mapping of northern Utah including Daggett County. (Utah State Historical Society)

> Frank will eat with us. He left us about 6:00 on Horseback with Harrel[l] and a pack mule and away went "Little Breeches" over the hill and out of sight.[35]

The next few days were spent drifting lazily through Browns Hole, with occasional stops to explore or hunt. The boats were sometimes lashed together, with the men swimming alongside. Afternoon temperatures rose into the high 90s. The Major, sitting in his armchair atop the cabin of the *Emma Dean,* read aloud from Sir Walter Scott's *The Lady of the Lake.* During this respite, and for reasons known only to himself, Powell decided to rename the valley "Browns Park." It was hoped that Harrell would return to them with a new sack of mail, but on 17 June they received word that their letters had already been forwarded to the Ute Agency. Disappointed, they resumed their journey down the Canyon of Lodore.[36]

This second expedition did not command Powell's full attention. At the mouth of the Yampa River, his boat went ahead toward the Uintah Valley so that he could make an overland visit to his pregnant wife in Salt Lake City. At other times he left the expedition for various reasons. Almon Thompson was actually the man in charge a good portion of the time. The 1871 voyage was just as arduous as the first—the men suffered a variety of illnesses and malnutrition—but somehow it seemed more mundane. Writing of it, Wallace Stegner commented:

> . . . somehow it doesn't make a story. It hasn't the thrill or suspense, the fear, the fateful climax, the ending muted by tragedy; it doesn't come to us with either the terror or the triumph of the first. The second passage down the river was not an exploration, but a survey; what rendered it scientifically important rendered it dramatically second-hand.[37]

Scientifically, the second expedition was indeed quite significant. The travels of its members both overland and on the water provided a wealth of information on the geography and Indian cultures of the region. Accurate maps were drawn of a country that until that time was virtually unknown. It elevated Powell to the directorship of his own ongoing government survey. Eventually it propelled him to become head of both the United States Geological Survey and the Bureau of Ethnography.

At the same time that Powell's second expedition was shooting the rapids, members of Clarence King's United States Geological Survey of the Fortieth Parallel were traversing the Uinta Mountains. They had begun their survey of the area in 1869 and in 1871 were following up earlier work. King's ambitious charge was to explore the country along the route of the transcontinental railroad. His survey was especially interested in commercial mineral deposits. Trained at Yale University's prestigious Sheffield Scientific School, King was athletic, intelligent, and highly charismatic. The eminent nineteenth-century historian Henry Adams once described him as "the best and brightest of his generation, with talents immeasurably beyond that of his contemporaries."[38]

Adams joined the King survey for a time during the summer of 1871 at the invitation of his childhood friend S.F. Emmons. Emmons was the geologist in charge of the Uintas field crew, and Adams accompanied that group into the fall months. He delighted in riding and hunting in the pristine mountain country, testing himself against rugged nature. Adams also enjoyed the scholarly discourse at day's end. He commented that, "In Emmons's camp, far up in the Uintahs, these talks continued till the frosts became sharp in the mountains. . . . they delighted Adams, for they helped, among other things, to persuade him that history was more amusing than science."[39]

One of King's greatest adventures came that fall during his final survey of the Uintas. He sighted a grizzly bear and gave chase for miles across deep gullies and sage-covered hills. The bear eluded him but was found a few hours later holed up in a cave. Undaunted, the plucky King crawled into the cave with his single- shot rifle. All that he could make out in the darkness were the bear's glowing eyes. King fired and suddenly felt himself being dragged backward; it was one of his companions attempting a rescue. The animal did not emerge, and, after summoning courage, the hunters carefully crawled back into the cave. They found the bear dead—shot through the brain.[40]

Just a year later, the climactic event of King's career took place in the Green River country. In the spring of 1872, two grizzled prospectors deposited a sack of uncut diamonds in the Bank of California at San Francisco. So intrigued were William Ralston and his financial cronies that they tracked down the depositors, Philip Arnold and John Slack. The cautious prospectors would not disclose the site of the bonanza, but they volunteered to take a blindfolded representative to the site. Arnold and Slack took David Colton aboard a Union Pacific train. Eyes covered, Colton disembarked at an unknown station and traveled for four days through difficult terrain. When the blindfold was removed, he marveled at diamonds, rubies, and other precious stones.[41]

In New York, Charles Tiffany confirmed the authenticity of the stones. Ralston and his associates quickly formed the New York and San Francisco Mining and Commercial Company, and, with diamonds shining in their eyes, they bought out Arnold and Slack for about $600,000. A public stock offering for $12 million was put into motion. The California businessmen then hired Henry Janin, a highly respected mining engineer, and he issued a glowing report following his examination of the diamond field. Though Janin had almost no experience in the area of gemstones, he reported that he was absolutely convinced the find was genuine and quite rich.

News of the diamond discovery spread like wildfire, but the syndicate maintained secrecy. Prospecting parties searched throughout the West to no avail. The find was of special interest to Clarence King and his associates, who rightly surmised that the field must be somewhere within the bounds of their survey. They were puzzled, however, because they had spent years covering the region and had seen no evidence whatsoever of gemstones.

In October 1872 Emmons and an associate stumbled into Janin's prospecting crew on a train in Nevada. Though Janin was evasive, Emmons gleaned a certain amount of information about the location of the field. Shortly thereafter, A.D. Wilson reported that the prospecting party had gotten off the train between Green River and Rawlins, Wyoming. By comparing what they had learned and could surmise, King's assistants concluded that the diamonds could only be in one place. King agreed, and on 29 October he and his men left Fort Bridger for Browns Hole.

Their ultimate destination was a mountain just north of the hole now known as Diamond Peak, which was in the Colorado portion of the region. It was windy and bitterly cold, and their horses were at times covered with balls of ice. King's party crossed the frigid waters of the Green River on the fourth day out and went into camp on the peak. A short search revealed Henry Janin's water claim and posted mining notices. Before dark, each of them had found a diamond. They too were convinced that great wealth lay at their feet.[42]

Judge William A. Carter. (Utah State Historical Society)

Careful searching the following day, however, brought suspicions of a hoax. The geologists found the same ratio of twelve rubies to one diamond wherever they located stones. Also, some of the gems rested in highly unlikely positions. When they found no precious stones in surrounding streambeds or in a test hole, King knew he had uncovered a fraud.

Minutes after the scientists reached this conclusion, a stranger appeared. He was a diamond speculator, and he had been spying on the party through field glasses for days. When the speculator announced, "What a chance to sell short," King realized the gravity of the situation. King and Wilson set out before dawn the next morning and rode across forty-five miles of badlands. They arrived at Black Butte Station just in time to catch the train to San Francisco.

Back in California, King confronted Janin with his findings. They went together to present the evidence to the company's directors. Janin and King returned to the site for a final confirmation, but the facts remained. Full public disclosure of the hoax was made upon their return to California, and Ralston's syndicate repaid the stockholders. The perpetrators of the fraud got away clean. Slack disappeared; Arnold was murdered a few years later in Kentucky. None of their loot was ever recovered.

In 1872 Lieutenant George Wheeler's Geological Surveys West of the 100th Meridian did topographical work in the Uinta Mountains; and all four of the great government surveys had by then explored the surrounding country. Marsh, Leidy, and Cope had also scoured the region for fossils. Surely no other part of the American West was more thoroughly studied or visited by so many illustrious scholars.[43]

Their mark on the Uinta Mountains country is clear. They made the first accurate maps, and many places in the region were either named by them or named for them. Flaming Gorge, Emmons Peak, Leidy Peak, and Browns Park are just a few examples. The information they discovered and the theories they advanced stretched the boundaries of geology and natural history, and they hastened the development of the Mountain West.

But if they left their mark on the country, the country also left its mark on them. It was in Horseshoe and Red canyons that the boatmen of both Powell expeditions learned to handle rough water. George Bird Grinnell discovered the idyllic life of the mountain men on Henrys Fork, and Henry Adams furthered his education on the slopes of the Uinta Mountains. In the blackness of a cave, Clarence King tested his mettle against king grizzly. The mountains and canyons of the Uintas shaped the experience of some of America's great thinkers, and America was the better for it.

ENDNOTES

1. Donald Jackson and Mary Lee Spence, *The Expeditions of John C. Fremont,* vol. 1 (Urbana: University of Illinois Press, 1970), 707–8; Dick Dunham and Vivian Dunham and Dunham, *Flaming Gorge Country,* 68–69.

2. Howard Stansbury, *Exploring the Great Salt Lake* (Washington, D.C.: Smithsonian Institution Press, 1988), 229.

3. William H. Goetzmann, *Exploration and Empire: The Explorer and Scientist in the Winning of the American West* (New York: Alfred A. Knopf, 1966), 534.

4. Ibid., 536.

5. Wallace Stegner, *Beyond the Hundredth Meridian: John Wesley Powell and the Second Opening of the West* (New York: Houghton and Mifflin, 1954), 35–39.

6. Ibid., 39–41.

7. Ibid., 42.

8. Goetzmann, *Exploration and Empire,* 541–42.

9. Ibid., 543; Roy Webb, *If We Had a Boat: Green River Explorers, Adventurers, and Runners,* 54–55.

10. John Wesley Powell, *Exploration of the Colorado River and its Canyons* (New York: Dover Publications, 1961), 127–29.

11. Ibid., 131.

12. Stegner, *Beyond the Hundredth Meridian,* 60; Powell, *Exploration of the Colorado River,* 141–42.

13. Powell, *Exploration of the Colorado River,* 143.

14. Ibid., 144–48.

15. Stegner, *Beyond the Hundredth Meridian,* 62.

16. Ibid., 62–63.

17. Ibid., 62–65; Webb, *If We Had a Boat,* 58–62.

18. Stegner, *Beyond the Hundredth Meridian,* 67.

19. Webb, *If We Had a Boat,* 67.

20. Stegner, *Beyond the Hundredth Meridian,* 101–11.

21. Goetzmann, *Exploration and Empire,* 500.

22. Ibid., 426.

23. John F. Reiger, ed., *The Passing of the Great West: Selected Papers of George Bird Grinnell* (New York: Winchester Press, 1972), 43.

24. Ibid., 44.

25. Ibid.

26. Ibid., 45–46.

27. Dunham and Dunham, *Flaming Gorge Country,* 124.

28. Reiger, *Passing of the Great West,* 47–48.

29. Goetzmann, *Exploration and Empire,* 427.

30. Dunham and Dunham, *Flaming Gorge Country,* 125–27.

31. Webb, *If We Had a Boat,* 71.

32. Frederick S. Dellenbaugh, *A Canyon Voyage: The Narrative of the Second Powell Expedition* (Tucson: University of Arizona Press, 1991), 20.

33. Ibid., 25.

34. Webb, *If We Had a Boat,* 75; Charles Kelly, ed., "The Journal of Walter Clement Powell," *Utah Historical Quarterly* 16–17 (1948–1949):270.

35. Kelly, "Walter Clement Powell," 270–71.

36. Dellenbaugh, *A Canyon Voyage,* 31–32.

37. Stegner, *Beyond the Hundredth Meridian,* 137.

38. Henry Adams, *Henry Adams: Novels, Mont Saint Michel, The Education* (New York: Library of America, 1984), 1,100.

39. Ibid., 1,006.

40. Goetzmann, *Exploration and Empire,* 451–52.

41. Ibid., 452–57.

42. Emmons's notes are quite clear that the hoax was perpetrated on Diamond Peak just over the border in Colorado, not on Diamond Mountain in southeastern Daggett County.

43. Dunham and Dunham, *Flaming Gorge Country,* 127.

Chapter 5

Ranching Communities

> Next day I was through the Indian country into the Diamond Mountain cattle country. . . . It was like a little of cowboy Wyoming lapping down into Utah.
>
> —Matt Warner

Matt Warner was right. When the young Mormon boy from Levan drifted into the eastern Uinta Mountains in 1878, he encountered a way of life very different from that which he had known. This was not a land of small irrigated farms and compact villages; it was an open range cattle culture. People lived on isolated homesteads. There were no towns, no churches, and there was very little authority of any kind. An ambitious lad with a long rope and a running iron could do well.

Ever since the mountain men had taken to herding livestock in the early 1840s, the eastern Uintas had been cattle country. The old mountaineers had developed a sort of subsistence ranching lifestyle. Their cattle and horses provided meat, milk, leather, and transportation, and surplus animals were marketed to the U.S. Army or to emigrants. Herd sizes stayed small and manageable because livestock was only a part of

Oscar Swett Ranch. (Allan Kent Powell)

their overall economy. The mountaineers continued to hunt, trap, and trade, living in skin lodges and roaming with the seasons.

In the three decades following the end of the fur trade, the Henrys Fork area became a small subsistence ranching community. Jack Robinson, Phil Mass, John Baker, Ike Edwards, and others spent considerable time in the Henrys Fork Valley, and a few built cabins for wintering over.

Browns Park was much less settled during this period. A few prospectors, like Sam Bassett and Louie Simmons, moved in and out of the valley. There were attempts at cattle ranching, but nobody stayed. The place remained a grazing area for transient herds. Browns Park was on a cattle trail that crossed the central Rockies, linking Texas with the California Trail at Fort Bridger. A few herds of Texas cattle, bound for the gold-rush country of California, are believed to have wintered there. W.H. Snyder was one of the first to bring cattle through the area to California from Texas. W.A. Peril was another. Animals which cost about ten dollars in Texas could be sold for three times that in the gold mining camps.[1] Cattle belonging to the LDS church also may have grazed there in the 1850s. J.S. Hoy once

This two-room log house was built by Oscar Swett in 1919. (Allan Kent Powell)

described the climatic conditions that made the valley a desirable winter herdground:

> Snowfall is usually accompanied by high winds that blow the snow into drifts or tear it away, leaving most of the ground bare. The prevailing winds are from the West, affording a full sweep the entire length of the Hole. A thawing wind called a "chinook" occasionally visits the Hole during the winter, which usually melts all the snow away in the low country and up to say, 500 feet along the sides of the mountains. This peculiarity is what gave Brown's Hole the reputation as a favorite winter resort for . . . any one who likes to see bare ground occasionally during the winter time.[2]

About as close as Browns Park came to permanent settlers in those days were Warren P. and "Snapping Annie" Parsons. According to an entry in Sam Bassett's diary, "Snapping Annie" expertly drove her oxen "Turk" and "Lion" into the valley on 22 June 1854, and the Parsons started a place near Vermillion Creek. For reasons unknown, they too later moved on, leaving "Snapping Annie" a claim to fame as the first white woman inhabitant of the region.[3]

Ranch along Henrys Fork near Linwood. (Courtesy Pauleen Baker)

It was not until after the Civil War, when America seriously turned its attention to the development of the West, that ranching as we understand it came to the Uinta Mountains country. Most of the Shoshonis and Utes had by then been moved to reservations, and the newly completed transcontinental railroad put the northern range in contact with the nation's urban markets. Western stockmen were no longer limited to trading with emigrants or the military; the railroad could ship their cattle to Omaha, Chicago, or San Francisco.

Many of the animals that stocked the new ranges of the Mountain West were driven north from Texas. In the spring of 1871, Major John Wesley Powell's expedition happened on the Harrell brothers' herd of some 8,500 cattle there, and the following winter George Baggs grazed about 900 head in Browns Park en route to Evanston, Wyoming.[4]

The country began to fill up. Large cattle companies prospered east of the continental divide, and Judge William Carter's herds near Fort Bridger grew to considerable size. The eastern Uintas, however, remained the home of small operators—small on money but often large on ambition. To this day, there is a saying on Henrys Fork that

Eleanore Pruett Stewart on a hay cutting machine. (Sweetwater County Museum)

all the local ranches were started with Judge Carter's cattle. The same ethos prevailed in Browns Park, where pioneer stockmen increased their holdings at the expense of passing trail herds.

The West of the Indian and the mountain man was fading. Elijah "Lige" Driskell arrived in 1868 and became the first stockman in the region to break out of the old subsistence ranching pattern. Driskell originally came to the region with Colonel Patrick E. Connor as a California Volunteer soldier during the Civil War. He then stayed on in the Fort Bridger country. With his Shoshoni wife, Cora, and stepson George Finch, he started a ranch near the mouth of Henrys Fork. Driskell quickly built up large herds of horses and cattle and eventually established a horse ranch at Birch Springs in Dry Valley. Driskell's large herds, rapid expansion, and dependence on hired labor show a clear departure from earlier methods. Commercial ranching, integrated into regional and national markets, had come to the Uintas.[5]

Another Civil War veteran from Fort Bridger, a German immigrant named George "Dutchy" Stoll, brought his wife, Mary, four children, and forty cows to a new ranch on Burnt Fork the following year. They settled near the home of Phil and Irene Mass, living in a dugout during their first winter.[6]

Jimmy Ramsey, helping with haying. (Courtesy Pauleen Baker)

Growth on Henrys Fork accelerated in the 1870s. Shadrach "Shade" Large came into the area early in the decade and worked for John Baker. Large married a Shoshoni woman, Maggie Bazil, who was said to be a granddaughter of Sacajawea, famous for accompa-

A team of horses pulling a beaver slide hay stacker. (Courtesy Pauleen Baker)

nying the Lewis and Clark expedition. With his partner Charley Davis, he built a ranch near the territorial line. Davis moved on, but the Large family stayed. Shade's brother William later acquired Jack Robinson's old cabin. Ambroise Messier had a cabin and field south of the Large's homestead which was taken over by the Henry Perry family in 1879.[7]

The Herefords were other early settlers. Robert Hereford was married to Jack Robinson's daughter Lucinda, and his family drifted in and out of the Fort Bridger area. His son George, at age ten, decided not to accompany his parents to Montana and instead went to work for Lige Driskell. The elder Herefords returned to the area in a few years and went into the cattle business with Uncle Jack Robinson. Eventually, Robert and Lucinda Hereford took over an old cabin on Birch Creek and developed their own ranch. Young George Hereford married Sarah Perry in 1881 and took control of the Perry ranch. He continued to ride for Driskell while he built his own outfit. He became well known as a top hand and reportedly turned down an offer to ride with Buffalo Bill Cody's Wild West tour.[8]

In the 1880s, Zeb Edwards, Garibaldi Gamble, and George

Solomon became partners in Connor Basin. Edwards and Solomon both had a background in the timber business and Gamble was a schoolteacher. Edwards and Solomon are remembered to have run a sawmill on Phil Pico. Edwards eventually took up a ranch on Birch Creek. His brothers David and Isaac later established a ranch between Birch Creek and Burnt Fork which their sister Irma maintained.[9]

Other early residents of the Henrys Fork area included Benjamin and Florence Hill, whose daughter Catherine married Zebulon Edwards, Adam and Frank Stillwell, Joe and Maud Steinaker, James and Ellen Widdop, their son Tom Widdop, and Dick Son. By the 1890s this group also included Charles Wyman, Clark Logan, Bill Felshaw, Frank Easton, Si Eardley, Alec Hayden, Jimmy Hauser, Bill Harvey, and Dave Washam.[10]

As cabins proliferated along Henrys Fork and its tributary creeks, a sense of community developed among ranch families on both sides of the territorial line. Burnt Fork, Wyoming, where the creek of that name flowed into Henrys Fork, became the hub of this dispersed rural community. Despite their isolation, these people valued education and opened the first public school in the region. The "Henry's Fork Joint District with Uinta County, Utah" was formally organized on 10 September 1877. The Henrys Fork community also developed a rich social life. Parties and dances hosted at the various ranches became commonplace, and when the Oddfellows Lodge in Fort Bridger closed, the building and chapter were moved to Burnt Fork. Some lodge brothers rode as far as twenty-five miles to attend meetings. George Stoll was active in the lodge, and George Stoll, Jr., was the first postmaster.[11]

At the same time that the Henry's Fork Valley was growing up, another rural community was taking root in and around Browns Park. "Dutch" John Honselena, a horse trader from Germany, came into the area in the 1860s. He ran his string near Red Canyon, trading with the emigrants and railroad contractors. His range eventually became known simply as "Dutch John." Prospector Jesse Ewing also arrived about this time. He is believed to have been part of the ill-fated Hook expedition whose boats were wrecked in Red Canyon in 1869. Ewing stayed on in the area, building a cabin and an assay office near Bandbox Butte.[12]

Threshing in Browns Park. (Sweetwater County Museum)

Jimmie Reed, who had come to the region with his uncle Auguste Archambeault, was also an early resident of Browns Hole. Jimmie and his Shoshoni wife, Margaret, who as a child had survived the Bear River Massacre, herded horses and cattle there in the late 1860s. An unusually severe winter killed virtually all of Reed's stock, and a trading venture with the Utes also proved disastrous. The Reeds went back to living off the country and in 1876 built a cabin on what is now Crouse Creek.[13]

One of the more notorious early settlers of the area was Juan Jose Herrera, known by the nickname "Mexican Joe." With his brother Pablo and several countrymen, Herrera built a ranch on the Colorado side of the park near Vermillion Creek. Some writers have asserted that Jose Herrera had been in and out of the valley since the 1850s, but this is speculation. A contemporary remembered that Herrera had been a freighter during the South Pass gold rush and had come to Browns Park during the summer of 1870:

> Conditions here were better for making a home than in New Mexico—and to gather stray cattle. They made a beginning toward redeeming the wilderness. . . . He managed by hook and crook to

Threshing in Browns Park. (Sweetwater County Museum)

> keep a scant supply of provisions always on hand, enough to attract any of his wandering, homeless, moneyless countrymen stranded within a hundred miles around. He was a hard task master, making his followers work, work, work without pay. They commenced operations by building a dam in the Vermillion Creek to raise the water to irrigate his land, and clearing off sagebrush and rabbitbrush.[14]

In 1871 the Herreras were joined by their friend and attorney Asbury B. Conway, formerly of South Pass. In keeping with local custom, Conway had a habit of acquiring other people's cattle and horses. It is ironic that after his departure from Browns Park he had a successful career in the law and in 1897 became Chief Justice of the Wyoming Supreme Court.[15]

Later in the 1880s, Juan and Pablo Herrera returned for a time to San Miguel County, New Mexico, where Juan organized a group of Latino nightriders. Known as las Gorras Blancas (the White Caps), they fought against the persistent encroachment on the land by the Anglo community. Juan also served as a district organizer for the

Jared Williams working in the hay fields with a buck rake. (Courtesy Pauleen Baker)

Knights of Labor and at one time acted as a translator for the New Mexico territorial legislature. He eventually returned to Browns Park.[16]

The Herreras' rivals in the eastern end of the park were the Hoys. J.S. Hoy helped winter Crawford and Thompson's cattle there in 1872, and, though there were losses, he was sufficiently impressed by the valley that he moved in the next year. His brother Valentine soon followed, and other relatives arrived in succeeding years. The family had a certain amount of money and apparently planned to build a grazing empire. Hemmed in by neighboring outfits, the Hoys' dreams of a baronial ranch never quite materialized.[17]

Another early settler was Dr. John Parsons, son of Warren P. and Snapping Annie Parsons. He arrived in Browns Park around 1874 and built a cabin on the south side of the Green River at Sears Creek. Medicine was not his only occupation; the doctor had a forge and smelter north of the river, operated a ferry, and became the first postmaster of Browns Park. His son Warren lived nearby for a short period. Dr. John Parsons died of natural causes in 1879.[18]

A number of men and women moved into the valley in the late 1870s; they included Billy Tittsworth, whose cabin was across the

An early Daggett County rodeo. (Courtesy Pauleen Baker)

river from the house of Dr. Parsons, and Charlie Crouse, who, along with Aaron Overholt, started a horse ranch on upper Pot Creek. Crouse later bought Jimmie Reed's place. Other early settlers included James Warren; Griff and Jack Edwards; George, James, and Walter Scrivner; Tom Davenport; Tommy Dowdle; Jimmy Goodson; Frank Goodman (who had been on the first Powell expedition); Harry Hindle; Herbert and Elizabeth Bassett; and George Law. Another early settler, Charles Allen, was the first justice of the peace in Browns Park, but he later moved to Illinois because he didn't want his children growing up in such a rough and lawless area.[19]

Notable among the park's residents were two African-Americans. Isom Dart had a ranch on the Colorado side and had formerly been an outlaw known as Ned Huddleston. Albert "Speck" Williams (also known in some accounts as Welhouse), nicknamed for his speckled complexion, came into the valley with Tom Davenport. He worked for Davenport and other people in the area and ran John Jarvie's ferry for several years.[20]

John Jarvie's store and ferry, located on the Utah side of the territorial boundary, became the focal point for the Browns Park community. Newlyweds John and Nell Jarvie opened the store during the

A herd of horses on Henrys Fork River. (Courtesy Pauleen Baker)

summer of 1880. It was the only store for seventy miles and also served as the post office for six years. Josie Bassett Morris recalled, "He sold just about everything from Indian flour, through new saddles, boots, wagons, teepee poles for the Indians stacked outside. . . ." Whiskey was also a popular commodity. A school was started nearby in Warren Parsons' old cabin about 1882, with Mrs. Henry (Jennie) Jaynes as the first teacher. Her husband freighted for John Jarvie.[21]

By the 1880s, the settlers on Henrys Fork and in Browns Park had created rural communities. They could boast of schools, stores, and fraternal societies. At times they came together for dances and parties. There was remarkable diversity. Many on Henrys Fork were of mixed European, Hispanic, and Shoshoni heritage. Whites, Mexicans, and African-Americans lived and worked together in Browns Park, and a few Ute lodges were still scattered throughout the country. While there were differences among the settlers in wealth and prestige, they lived in a hard country where people of all kinds had to depend on each other.

The area's isolation meant that some things considered necessities elsewhere were for a long time luxuries in the Daggett region. Cooking stoves were rare in area homes until the 1880s—cooking was done in dutch ovens or over open fires. The homes themselves were built of rough logs until sawmills were established and roads

Getting ready to go on the cattle round-up. (Courtesy Pauleen Baker)

could provide wagons access to them. Judge Carter started two sawmills in the Fort Bridger area in the 1870s.[22] Domestic niceities were rare; store-bought goods were treasured since they were generally purchased at a premium locally or the object of hard travel if purchased elsewhere.

Garden produce was not very abundant and domestic animals were few, especially in the early years of homesteading; however, wild game was generally plentiful and quite varied. Little grain was attempted to be grown locally and flour was freighted in. The problem of getting water to farmland limited agriculture, and ranchers also disputed claims to water rights. A number of water squabbles are recorded. J.S. Powers filed on Davenport Springs, disputing the rights of Ben Kelly. Half of the water rights on Willow Creek were sold by Charley Crouse in 1887 to Jim Peterson, and the other half sold to Ed Rife. In 1888, however, Tom Davenport claimed rights to all the water. In 1887 Lum Tolliver filed for water on Sears Creek, but two years later John Jarvie claimed that the rights had long been his. It was becoming increasingly evident that a more ordered and better managed system was necessary, as water disputes could often turn violent.[23] By the mid-1880s many cattlemen had begun to fence ranges and begin irrigation projects.

Early residents longed for social outlets and were known to ride

Inoculating a calf. (Courtesy Pauleen Baker)

seventy miles to a dance or party. The ride could be worth it—such affairs in the rough-and-tumble frontier society often lasted all night and occasionally featured fights and even deaths. After schoolhouses were built, they became the centers for community events and entertainment. Those who had and could play musical instruments did so at the popular dances. Horse racing was another popular activity, and many folks would gather together to celebrate the Fourth of July.

Postal services were established at Browns Park in 1881 with John Jarvie as postmaster. However, this office was discontinued in 1887. A post office named Bridgeport was established at Charlie Crouse's house; his wife, Mary, was postmistress. In 1889 Herbert Bassett was named postmaster of a new Browns Park office named Lodore. Mail to this office came on the train to Rifle, Colorado, and was then brought by horseback to the Daggett area.

In 1889 a post office was established just across the territorial line in Burnt Fork, Wyoming, to help serve the Henrys Fork settlers. Mail was brought there from Fort Bridger by horseback. About 1893 John Berry established postal services at Shade Large's ranch; but Berry drowned in 1894 in the Henrys Fork River. Local service was then established at Dick Son's store, with Son as postmaster; however, for some reason, it was called Washam after David Washam, who lived next door. The Green River bridge cut forty miles off the route after it was completed in 1897.[24]

Life in the region was by no means rosy. By modern standards, these people lived in grinding poverty. Hours of work were long and the work was often dangerous. Isolation and drudgery were especially hard on the relatively few women. Health care was rudimentary or unavailable. Those who were physically strong and enjoyed the outdoor life adapted; the rest suffered or got out of the country.

There was also a growing threat from outsiders. The late 1870s and early 1880s brought a livestock boom to the northern range, and large cattle corporations spread across Wyoming and Colorado. The Middlesex Land and Cattle Company, a large firm headquartered in Boston, brought thousands of cows into southern Wyoming with designs to take over the Browns Park range. J.S. Hoy remembered that they threatened to "buy all the 'little fellows' out or drive them out of the country."[25]

Only two ranchers sold. The rest chose to resist. Jack and Griff Edwards liquidated their cattle and stocked the range just north of the park with sheep. Their plan was to strip the grass and create a barrier to Middlesex Company incursions. Competition from sheep, a bad winter in 1879–80, and rustling kept the company at bay. A

Sheep making their way along the frozen Green River. (Daggett County)

decline in cattle prices in 1884 dealt Middlesex another blow, and the legendary hard winter of 1886–87 finished it off. Only Clay Basin, named for a company official, remains as a legacy of the Middlesex Land and Cattle Company's ambition. Late in life, J.S. Hoy lamented his family's decision to turn down the $125,000 Middlesex had offered them: "Those two outfits were wise, the rest of us were foolish that we did not sell."[26]

The hard winter that destroyed the Middlesex herd devastated cattle populations all across the northern range. In the aftermath, increasing numbers of ranchers turned to sheepraising, and Browns Park ranchers were no exception. Frank Goodman and the Davenports went into the sheep business, and the Edwards's flock grew to about 60,000 animals. These sheepmen had the good sense to graze their animals mostly outside of the valley, and because of this they got along with their immediate neighbors. This kind of tolerance was at first commonplace; but, as the western sheep population expanded, cattlemen became increasingly hostile.[27]

By the middle 1890s, the situation on the northern plains had become explosive. Cattlemen's associations had come to believe that cattle and sheep could not co-exist on the same range, and the common practice was to establish "deadlines" to protect their traditional

Keith Smith's Sheep Camp. (Sweetwater County Museum)

grazing lands. Sheep outfits within the lines were driven out by threats or violence, and those sheepherders who strayed across the lines could end up dead. Henrys Fork cattlemen established one such protective boundary north of their valley. Originally it was just a line of old animal bones that ran east-west across Phil Mass Mountain and down to the Green River; the deadline was later marked by a plowed furrow and rock cairns. Trespassing sheep outfits might be attacked by gunmen in the dark of the night. The Henrys Fork deadline held until sheepman John Mackey bought out many of the small Henrys Fork ranchers in 1906.[28]

Over in Browns Park, the sheepherders got along with their close neighbors; but the members of the Snake River Stock Growers Association were determined to see them go. On 1 June 1896, Routt County (Colorado) cattlemen attacked one of Jack Edwards's flocks. Several sheep were clubbed to death, the rest were scattered, and two sheepherders were murdered. When Edwards went out to survey the damage, he was grabbed by a group of cowboys. They put a rope around his neck and discussed the removal of the remaining flocks. When Edwards refused, he was hoisted off his feet and left dangling for a while to reconsider. After being hoisted up a second time, the stubborn sheepman finally acquiesced. Edwards was released and eventually moved his flocks over the Wyoming border.[29]

This, however, was not the end of it. The Routt County cattlemen might be worried by Browns Park sheep, but Browns Park ranchers were concerned about encroachment from the east by Ora Haley's big Two Bar outfit. Haley, a New Englander, had come into the country following the Civil War and had acquired several large ranches in southern Wyoming and northwestern Colorado. His new manager at the Two Bar, Hi Bernard, visited Browns Park after Edwards's near lynching. His reason may have been to drum up enthusiasm for the anti-sheep campaign or to discuss the establishment of a general roundup. Whatever the case, instead of support he found antagonism over the Two Bar Ranch's expansion. The Browns Park response was the formation of the Brown's Park Cattle Association, headed by Matt Rash, and a demand to that the Two Bar stop its encroachment of Browns Park rangeland.

Rash and Bernard reached an uneasy compromise. A limestone ridge called the Divide became the demarcation line between the Browns Park and Two Bar ranges. Many from both sides patrolled the line to drive back strays. Browns Park cattlemen agreed to stop new flocks of sheep from coming onto their range, but they refused to move against neighboring sheepmen who were already established. This compromise did not please the Snake River Stock Growers. During the week of Christmas 1896, an army of Colorado cowboys descended on the park. The cowboys' overwhelming numbers made resistance unthinkable, and, in the face of massive intimidation, Griff Edwards and Frank Goodman agreed to move their sheep. The Davenports, who lived on the Utah side of the park, were not molested. Goodman left the area and sold his place to Matt Rash.[30]

The sheep were now gone from Routt County, but tensions did not abate. Like the big Wyoming producers, Ora Haley and the Snake River Stock Growers had become increasingly distraught with rustling by small ranchers. Conversely, the small Browns Park cattlemen felt besieged by the big-monied outfits around them. The new West, a West of law, authority, and big corporations, was closing in. For the traditional ranching communities of the eastern Uintas, it was a prescription for violence.

ENDNOTES

1. Dick Dunham and Vivian Dunham, *Flaming Gorge Country,* 83.

2. J.S. Hoy, "The J.S. Hoy Manuscript," James G. Hodgson, ed., 1952, unpublished manuscript copy in author's collection, 89; Diana Allen Kouris, *The Romantic and Notorious History of Brown's Park* (Greybull, WY: Wolverine Gallery, 1980), 12–13; Roy Webb, *If We Had a* Boat, 168.

3. William Lawrence Tennent, "The John Jarvie Ranch: A Case Study in Historic Site Development and Interpretation" (Master's thesis, Utah State University, 1980), 22; Dunham and Dunham, *Flaming Gorge Country,* 83–84.

4. Charles Kelly, ed., "The Journal of Walter Clement Powell," 270–71; Kouris, *Romantic and Notorious History,* 27.

5. Dunham and Dunham, *Flamimg Gorge Country,* 140.

6. Norma Gamble and Francie Anderson, eds., "George 'Dutchy' Stoll," in *Links to the Past* (Burnt Fork, WY: Gamble and Anderson, 1990), unpaginated.

7. Dunham and Dunham, *Flaming Gorge Country,* 141–45.

8. Ibid., 145–47.

9. Ibid., 95–96, 148–50; Gamble and Anderson, "Zebulon Edwards," in *Links to the Past.*

10. Dunham and Dunham, *Flaming Gorge Country,* 150–55.

11. Gamble and Anderson, "George 'Dutchy' Stoll."

12. Dunham and Dunham, *Flaming Gorge Country,* 93.

13. Hoy, "Hoy Manuscript," 110–16.

14. Ibid., 133.

15. Dunham and Dunham, *Flaming Gorge Country,* 89–90.

16. Tennent, "The John Jarvie Ranch," 32–33.

17. Ibid., 35.

18. Ibid., 35–36; Dunham and Dunham, *Flaming Gorge Country,* 170.

19. Dunham and Dunham, *Flaming Gorge Country,* 171–73; Hoy, "Hoy Manuscript," 103.

20. Dunham and Dunham, *Flaming Gorge Country,* 87, 184–86.

21. Tennent, "The John Jarvie Ranch," 51; Hoy, "Hoy Manuscript," 103.

22. Ibid., 202.

23. Ibid., 189.

24. Ibid., 211–12.

25. Hoy, "Hoy Manuscript," 216.

26. Ibid.; Dunham and Dunham, *Flaming Gorge Country,* 186–87.

27. Grace McClure, *The Bassett Women* (Athens, OH: Swallow Press/Ohio University Press, 1985), 76; Dunham and Dunham, *Flaming Gorge Country,* 299.

28. Dunham and Dunham, *Flaming Gorge Country,* 300–1.

29. McClure, *The Bassett Women,* 76.

30. Ibid., 77–78; Kouris, *Romantic and Notorious History,* 97.

Chapter 6

Violence and Values

> Out in the country there was an emphasis on highly traditional, not modern, values. Loyalty to family, individual self-reliance, and self-redress of wrongs were among the values most highly regarded. In reflection of a free-and-easy attitude toward rustling and outlaws throughout the rural West, there was little esteem for law and order as such.
>
> —Richard Maxwell Brown

In his book *No Duty to Retreat,* Richard Maxwell Brown offers vivid insights into the values and attitudes that led to the Earp-Clanton feud and the celebrated gunfight at the OK Corral. Brown's description is of Cochise County in early Arizona, but it could well have been of any number of places in the nineteenth-century West. Lincoln County, New Mexico; Johnson County, Wyoming; and Browns Park—these were just a few of the western battlegrounds where social conflicts turned into violent confrontations.

Utah largely avoided the social strife that characterized much of the developing West. Following the doctrines of their faith, members of the LDS church were inclined to reject violence and to accept authority. This was not the case in other western territories, where many rural settlers were highly independent and prone to violence. When such people came into conflict with large companies, wealthy businessmen, or civil governments, they sometimes resisted in criminal or violent ways. Indeed, it was the age of unbridled capitalism typified by the "Robber Barons," and people across the United States were outraged by the power and excess of the rich.[1]

It was also an age of banditry. Outlaws roamed the country, targeting banks, cattlemen, mines, and railroads. Some, like the legendary English Robin Hood, gave at least some of their loot to the poor. They relied on the vast rugged backcountry as well as on the goodwill of the rural population to provide them with safe havens. According to Richard M. Brown:

> Whether outlawed or not, those who resisted the dominant trend of society were often, in line with their traditional values, strongly prone to combat and violence. They were not offended by disorder, for in the accepted reality of their lives tumult was as likely as not to be the norm.[2]

The resisters' predilection to violence was closely tied to a cluster of attitudes now popularly known as the "Code of the West." This code is thought by many to have originated in Texas and spread along the nineteenth century cattle trails, and it established the rules of conduct that governed male relationships. "I'll die before I'll run," was the phrase that characterized the traditions of violent self-defense and self-redress of grievances. Historian Robert Utley commented that the code, "commanded practitioners to avenge all insult and wrong, real or imagined; never to retreat before an aggressor; and to respond with any degree of violence, even death."[3]

Utahns, in general, rejected violence as a means of conflict resolution, but the settlers of the three-corners region were of different stock. Most had drifted down from Wyoming and were not Latter-day Saints. They were highly independent small-time ranchers who still subscribed to traditional notions of family loyalty, Old Testament justice, and violent redress of grievances. Rustling, especially stock belonging to outsiders, was acceptable. It has been said that nobody ate their own beef, and, although cold-blooded murder was not tol-

Isom Dart. (Utah State Historical Society)

erated, many killings were justified by the "Code of the West." There was also sympathy for "Robin Hood" outlaws.

Tales of rustling, murder, and mayhem involving old Browns Park are legion, and it is now often impossible to separate fact from folklore. Some troubles were the result of simple crimes or local squabbles that turned violent; other tales speak of celebrated outlaws who considered the place home. Still more stories are reminiscent of the Wyoming range wars that pitted ambitious cattle barons against small ranchers. Most of the tales have one thing in common: they reveal a community of fiercely independent and sometimes violent people who put a high value on personal freedom. It was the kind of place that attracted such folk.

The Browns Park area was a good locale for those who desired to avoid the law. It was a long hard ride from the Uintah County seat in Vernal or any other place that had a sheriff. The area was also divided by three territorial jurisdictions, and for years there was little cooperation between law-enforcement agencies. When law officers did visit the region, it was easy to elude them by slipping away into another territory.

Most residents of Browns Park did not see themselves as outlaws, but their attitudes toward rustling and their proclivity for violence brought them in conflict with the new ways of a changing West. Rustling, the taking of unbranded cattle and horses, was almost universally practiced. Untended livestock roamed far and wide, and if one cowboy did not take an unbranded animal, the next one would. Hunting unbranded stock became the primary activity of some ranchers. One cowboy recalled that his outfit was "crowding the . . . brand as close to sucking calves and colts as they could get away with."[4]

In the late 1870s, young Matt Warner went to work for the Jim Warren ranch on Diamond Mountain. Warren encouraged his hands to take unbranded cattle and allowed them to keep some of the spoils. Matt Warner commented:

> I haven't been working more than a week when Warren begins to present me with cattle and horses and tells me I ought to be thinking of accumulating a herd of my own. I knew right away it was a bribe to keep my mouth shut and get me involved so deep in the rustling game that I would stick and become a good, dependable fighter for the Warren outfit. All the other cowboys on the Warren ranch had herds that they had got this-a-way and had their own

> brands. Every ranch outfit on the mountain but one was doing this.[5]

The traditional values embodied in the Code of the West also put many Browns Park residents at odds with the new order. Disputes that could not be resolved peacefully were often settled with a gun or a knife. It is true that courts and peace officers were distant and that citizens felt compelled to pursue their own justice; however, it is also true that personal redress, even to the point of violence, was ingrained in the local definition of manliness. All wrongs and insults, real or imagined, had to be avenged. To stand and fight was to prove one's manhood, and some young cowboys practiced with rifle and pistol to be ready.

Juan Herrera, the Hispanic rancher from the eastern part of the park, was a veteran of many fights and had a reputation as a dangerous man. A known cattle rustler and deadly with a knife, "Mexican Joe" was not generally considered an outlaw by community standards; however, J.S. Hoy, aspiring cattle baron, disagreed. After one of his steers came up missing, Hoy made the mistake of confronting Herrera at his camp. He reported:

> I was reckless enough to visit Joe's camp with a man as a witness, and asked permission to examine any beef hides lying around. This request was an insinuation that I thought they were stealing cattle. . . . They surrounded me chattering and jabbering in their own language, of which I understood but little, Joe saying, "You tink me steal, eh? Examine de hides! Look more! Here is anodder one," and like explanations. He fairly danced in his rage while his eyes scintillated steel and lightning. . . . Joe drew from his pocket a long-bladed knife sharpened to a razor edge, using it to point out brands for me to inspect. . . . Just at the most critical moment [A.B.] Conway's huge bulk appeared . . . if it had not been for Conway the enraged Mexicans would have killed me.[6]

Through Conway's intervention, Hoy was able to extricate himself from the confrontation; but Juan Herrera had become a bitter enemy. J.S. Hoy soon left the area in fear of his life.[7]

Charley Crouse was another resident who, though not an outlaw, was a hardened man and prone to violence. On one occasion, Crouse

Tom Horn. (Utah State Historical Society)

was driving his buckboard home and offered a ride to Albert Williams. Liquor flowed freely as Crouse, a southerner by birth, and Williams, an African-American, rode together. After a difficult crossing of the Green River, they stopped to turn out the horses and commenced a goodnatured rough-housing. According to Crouse's story, the sparring became serious. Williams had him pinned, and Crouse drew his pocket knife. Crouse stabbed the black man in the groin to extricate himself. The pair disengaged, but Williams grabbed a heavy stone to hurl at his opponent. Crouse delivered a second knife blow, and Williams went down badly wounded.

With the help of his wife, Crouse got the injured man to his house and ministered to his wounds. Williams was then moved to his own home on the Davenport place, where Crouse continued to look after him for several days. It was feared that Williams would die, but he eventually pulled through. No charges were filed. Crouse later remarked, "The nigger called me a liar and a son of a bitch. Now any one that calls me that ought to be killed."[8]

This incident was a powerful example of just how complex the values and attitudes of Browns Park's citizens could be. The leveling nature of the frontier helped Crouse to overlook his prejudices to the point that he could give Williams a ride, share his liquor with him, and indulge in a degree of camaraderie. Unfortunately, the whiskey and a tendency toward violence escalated playful sparring into serious combat. It is interesting to note, however, that Crouse immediately responded to assist his fallen adversary and continued to look after him. Violence, especially where liquor was involved, could come on in a moment and depart just as quickly. Prejudice was not forgotten, but at times it could be overlooked.

Charley Crouse also killed a man in a fight over a bad debt. A fellow named Travis had loaned him money, and when Travis pressed for repayment, an argument ensued that resulted in gunplay. According to Crouse, Travis fired first. The bullet missed its mark but killed Crouse's horse. Crouse used the dead animal for cover, returned fire, and delivered a fatal shot.[9]

Men like Crouse and Herrera became role models for the teenage buckaroos who worked for them. Some young cowboys yearned for the respect that went with a reputation, and they burned up box after box of ammunition practicing with their six-shooters. When Matt Warner learned that a Mexican named Polito had stolen his favorite mare, he yearned for a confrontation. He wrote: "It come all over me in a split second and give me a sorta thrill that here was the big chance I had looked forward to and expected during several years of gun practice, to meet my first test, and prove I was a good gunman."[10]

Warner searched unsuccessfully for weeks but could not locate the vaquero. Then, as luck would have it, Polito showed up on his own doorstep. Matt spied his adversary and spurred his horse in close, just itching for a fight. Polito denied any knowledge of the mare. Tempers flared, and Warner later wrote that

> underneath his loose, careless looks, I could sense a keg of dynamite ready to explode. . . . I watched his eyes and his face. I had learned that trick from the cowboys. . . . We shot practically together. Whether I saw that warning glint or death grin I never could remember after. . . . How in hell he missed me at that close range is more than I could ever understand. I think it was because he sacrificed everything to speed. I guess I hit him because I was more able to concentrate at the same time on speed and accuracy.[11]

Polito went down, and it was all Matt Warner could do to keep from emptying his revolver into the man. Fortunately, the vaquero told Warner where his horse could be found, and Matt's anger subsided. The doctor was called, and Polito amiably convalesced for several weeks at Warner's ranch.[12]

Despite this tolerance of rustling and violence, Browns Park residents did understand bounds of acceptable behavior. Theft of branded livestock and cold-blooded murder were serious offenses that were not condoned. A rancher who lost cattle or horses to thieves could justifiably track down and kill the perpetrators. A murderer might be subject to lynching. There was, however, a double standard. Crimes committed elsewhere could be overlooked as long as the offender got along in the local community.

Even before there was permanent settlement of the area, Browns Park had a reputation as an outlaw hideout. Tip Gault, the "Sagebrush King of Bitter Creek," led a gang of stock thieves that often used the park as a herdground. During the 1860s, Gault and his Hispanic lieutenant, Terresa, watched the emigrant trails for likely victims. Choice animals were run off at night. When the owners came looking, Gault befriended them and feigned a search for the missing stock. The stolen animals were never found, and Gault would offer to buy them from the travelers for pennies on the dollar, saying that he would endeavor to find them later. In this way he obtained legal title to his ill-gotten gains. The stolen cattle and horses were fattened in Browns Park and then resold to miners or travelers.

Daggett County Deer Hunters, left ro right: Derl Reed, Levi Reed Sr., Orvil Hoops, Bill Hoops, Lee Reed, Vaughn Christensen, Levi Reed Jr., Clifford Reed. (Daggett County)

Gault finally picked on the wrong man. As the story goes, his gang stole horses from a hard-nosed Wyoming rancher named Hawley. Hawley and his cowboys tracked the thieves and found them in the midst of burying a gang member. The outlaws were standing about the open grave when their pursuers opened fire. Terresa and Gault both fell with fatal wounds, and another man was shot while attempting to escape. Ned Huddlestone, a large African-American, dove into the open grave and played dead. He eventually slipped away and left the country. A top hand with a cheerful disposition, Huddlestone returned to homestead the area a few years later under the name of Isom Dart.[13]

The "Sagebrush King of Bitter Creek" had been sent to his final reward, but Browns Park continued as a haunt for cattle thieves. During the winter of 1875–76, young Henry Skaggs made the mistake of stealing his neighbors' livestock. Cattle were left untended in cold weather, and Skaggs easily acquired quite a large herd. He and a friend developed the "Window Sash" brand, a broad flat mark that covered up the largest brands on the range. When local ranchers noticed their cattle missing, obvious trails and other evidence pointed to Skaggs. He and his companion were spotted altering a brand, and local ranchers took justice into their own hands. Confronted by the vigilante cattlemen, the friend ran away, but Skaggs stood his ground and was killed.[14]

Charley Powers was another cattle thief who met a violent end; but facts surrounding his death are much less clear. Accounts agree that Powers was involved with a group of local stock thieves active mainly outside Browns Park. Billy Tittsworth claimed that he had found evidence of Powers' wrongdoing and had gone to confront him. When Powers attacked him with a knife, Tittsworth fired his revolver in self-defense. J.S. Hoy, however, asserted that Tittsworth was the ringleader of the gang and that the pair had argued over a split of the loot. When Powers threatened to expose the operation, Tittsworth rode him down and killed him in Little Hole. Billy Tittsworth was never charged in the affair, but his personal involvement tends to discredit his version of events.[15]

Cattle stealing was a dangerous profession that violated community standards, but encroachment on the range by large cattle companies made it a locally acceptable form of retribution. Big and small producers alike grazed their animals for free on the public domain. In communities like Henrys Fork and Browns Park, rangelands were acquired and maintained by local custom. Such customs, however, met with little respect from powerful latecomers. If a big outfit like the Middlesex Land and Cattle Company could not acquire a holding that it coveted, it often turned to intimidation, dirty tricks, and violence. Government was perceived to be on the side of the wealthy, so small ranchers turned to extralegal tactics of rustling and stealing in their fight against the corporate cattlemen. Range war had come to the three-corners country.

The war started slowly. During the years of the cattle boom in the late 1870s and early 1880s, profits were large and the huge livestock companies generally accepted a certain loss due to stealing and rustling. It was considered by them to be just another cost of doing business. Shrinking cattle prices, depletion of the range, and the great loss of cattle in the hard winter of 1886–87 reversed this attitude. In tough times any loss was unacceptable, and the conflict between big and small ranchers turned downright vicious.[16]

In the context of the range war, Matt Warner found the step from cattle rustler to cattle raider an easy one to make:

> These cattle kingdoms was so big they couldn't anywhere near be covered by men and watched. . . . In lots of places a man might ride a day or two and see nothing but unwatched, free-ranging cattle, and not a human being in sight. . . . Raiders then wasn't bothered by the idea they was doing wrong. They looked upon the cattle kings as range hogs having no legitimate right to their kingdoms and cattle they had grabbed, and they looked upon the cattle as legitimate spoils of war.[17]

In his original account of the Powers killing, J.S. Hoy asserted that Charley Crouse and Billy Tittsworth, close personal friends related by marriage, developed a ranch at Salt Wells Creek as a base for cattle stealing. This location would have put them in close proximity to the expanding Middlesex Land and Cattle operation. It is likely that the business of these partners was mostly legitimate but that they did consider encroaching Middlesex cattle spoils for the taking. Historian Grace McClure pointed out that, "As the land in the Park was homesteaded, continued attempts by outsiders to winter there caused serious overgrazing problems. . . . In retaliation, the ranchers were not too careful of an outsider's ownership rights."[18]

The demise of the Middlesex outfit in 1887 stemmed encroachment from the north, but the expansion of Ora Haley's Two Bar Ranch from Colorado signalled a new threat. It was common knowledge that Haley considered the Browns Park range underutilized and that he wanted a piece of it. In the 1890s, Two Bar stock became a favorite target for rustling and thievery. Noteworthy among Haley's adversaries were a trio of ranchers who erroneously have been referred to as the Bassett Gang. Elizabeth Bassett, whose husband, Herbert, was totally unsuited for ranch work, needed all the help she could get to build up her outfit. She allied herself with Madison "Matt" Rash and Isom Dart, and the three generally managed their herds together. Like many of their neighbors, they took unbranded

Hauling logs for the construction of a house in 1937. (Courtesy Pauleen Baker)

calves and stole an occasional steer from the Two Bar and from others they considered their adversaries.

Elizabeth Bassett died in 1892, but the cooperative arrangement continued. Rash became the de facto manager of the Bassett herd and was romantically involved with Elizabeth's daughter Ann. Isom Dart also remained close to the family. By the late 1890s, the resistance of the Rash-Dart-Bassett alliance had become a major concern of Colorado's Snake River cattle growers.[19]

While small cattlemen believed that the legal system was against them, big ranching companies considered the law ineffective. Time after time they had seen accused rustlers found innocent by juries made up of common citizens (who had no love for the big companies). The Snake River Stock Growers Association had cleared its range of sheep through means of murder and intimidation. When it turned its attention toward the rustling problem, it again chose direct action.

During the summer of 1900, several Browns Park ranchers found notes warning them to get out within thirty days or suffer dire consequences. Among the recipients were Tom Davenport, Longhorn Thompson, Matt Rash, and Isom Dart. Though nobody ran, the warnings were taken seriously.

On 10 July 1900, two cowboys found Matt Rash's decomposing body in a cabin on Cold Spring Mountain. It was lying on a bunk and was punctured by two bullets. A pool of dried blood stained the floor. According to a Colorado newspaper:

> A chair was at the table and the condition of the dishes showed that Rash must have been eating lunch at the time he was shot. While eating he was facing a window in the west side of the cabin: behind him was the open door on the east side. . . . Evidently Rash had been shot in the back and when he got up turned around only to be shot again through the right breast. He had fallen where the pool of blood was, then revived sufficiently to drag himself to his bed.[20]

Suspicion immediately fell on a cowhand named James Hicks. Hicks had drifted into the valley in the early spring, working for short periods at a number of local ranches. His sudden departure seemed to coincide with the appearance of the warnings. Hicks returned after the murder and began spreading a rumor that Isom Dart was the killer. Dart was respected and well-liked, and the assertions were given little credence.

Hicks disappeared once more. On 3 October Isom Dart was gunned down from ambush. He had been walking from his cabin to the corral when a shot rang out. The black rancher fell dead only twenty paces from his door. Not long after, an attempt was made on the life of Longhorn Thompson, and some ranchers who had received the mysterious warning notes decided to quit the country. Thompson moved to Craig, Colorado, and both Joe Davenport and Sam Bassett also left the area.[21]

These murders stunned the Browns Park community. It was apparent that, in the manner of the big Wyoming cattlemen, members of the Snake River Stock Growers had declared war on those they considered their enemies. That Matt Rash was the first to be targeted was no coincidence. He was the leader of the Brown's Park Cattlemen's Association, and his murder was a chilling message to the valley's other ranchers. The alleged assailant, James Hicks, was not seen again, and no charges were ever filed. Locals later came to believe that Hicks was, in fact, the notorious range detective and hired killer Tom Horn.

Decades afterward, a letter written by J. Wilson Carey to author John Rolfe Burroughs added credence to the small ranchers' suspicions. It revealed that representatives of five large ranches in the Snake River association had met to discuss the Browns Park rustling problem. Carey admitted to collecting $100 from each outfit for the purpose of hiring a range detective—money that was turned over to rancher Charles Ayers. Though he was never told the detective's name, Carey believed Ayers had hired Tom Horn. Late in his life, another cowboy recalled having seen Horn in the Two Bar bunkhouse just before the murder of Isom Dart.[22]

For the most part, the murders and intimidation achieved their desired effect. Rustling from the big Colorado herds declined, and the Brown's Park Cattlemen's Association fell into disarray. Regular patrols of the Divide, the boundary between the Two Bar and Brown's Park ranges, ended.

Ann Bassett, Matt Rash's sweetheart, proved to be an exception. Her resolve to keep fighting only intensified. Over several years, she carried out a one-woman vendetta against the Two Bar Ranch. There are numerous tales of her rustling Two Bar cattle or running them off to be lost in a distant canyon. Some believe she stampeded a large herd off a cliff into the Green River. At the insistence of Ora Haley, Ann Bassett was charged with cattle stealing in 1911 and brought to trial in Craig, Colorado. Newspapers nicknamed her the "Queen of the Cattle Rustlers." Her first trial resulted in a hung jury, and her acquittal in a second trial was a cause for major celebration. The *Denver Post* reported, "Businesses Close—Bands Blare—Town of Craig Goes Wild With Joy." The cattle barons might have won the range war, but they certainly had not won the hearts and minds of the people.[23]

While Browns Park ranchers fought the wealthy for control of the range, there were others who took the battle a step farther. Men like Butch Cassidy, Elza Lay, Harry Longabaugh (the Sundance Kid), and Matt Warner became bandits, robbing banks and trains and giving at least some of the money to the poor. In terms of background and values, they were not much different from the besieged ranch

Team of horses with a wagon. (Courtesy Pauleen Baker)

folk. Cassidy, Lay, and Warner had all cowboyed in Browns Park before becoming professional outlaws. Caught up in their own war with rich neighbors, it is no wonder that people in Browns Park found common cause with these outlaws and provided them a haven.

Sometimes called the "Wild Bunch," this loose aggregation of criminals plied their trade throughout the Mountain West from three remote bases: the Hole-in-the-Wall country of Wyoming, the Robbers Roost area of central Utah, and Browns Park. All were isolated and difficult for the law to penetrate. When things got too hot in one location, the outlaws just headed down the Outlaw Trail to another hideout.

Wherever they stayed, Butch Cassidy and his cohorts made it a point to get along. Cassidy had a genial manner that enabled him to make friends easily, and he tried to avoid violence. When he needed a meal or a horse, he always paid for it. More importantly, he and his group actively aided the poor. In part, this was a shrewd strategy that helped ensure aid and shelter from the community; but it also was motivated by a sense of altruism. Giving made the outlaws feel good and, in their minds, justified a life of crime. One gang member wrote:

> Like lots of cowboy outlaws in them days Butch and me liked to give lots of money to the poor, the needy, and the deserving. In this way we made sort of Robin Hoods of ourselves in our own eyes, gained a lot of popularity and protection from the public, and squared ourselves in our own estimation.[24]

Two incidents stand out as demonstrations of the outlaws' affection for the people of Browns Park. On one occasion, Matt Warner, Elza Lay, and two others held up a merchant who was freighting a load of merchandise from Rock Springs to Vernal. After taking what they could use, the robbers determined to donate the balance of the goods to their neighbors. Clothes and trinkets were given to storekeeper John Jarvie for distribution, and everyone was told to show off their new apparel at the next dance. When Friday night rolled around, some of the dancers sported rather outlandish ensembles.[25]

An even more fanciful event took place in the middle 1890s when the Bender Gang, Butch Cassidy, the Sundance Kid, and Elza Lay treated the residents of the valley to Thanksgiving dinner. No expense was spared. The menu included blue point cocktails, roast turkey with chestnut dressing, cranberries, Roquefort cheese, pumpkin pie, and many other delicacies. Held at the Davenport ranch, the affair attracted some thirty-five people. Isom Dart presided in the kitchen, and the outlaws donned white aprons to serve dinner. Ann Bassett recalled that Butch Cassidy got flustered pouring coffee and retreated from the dining room. "The boys went into a hud[d]le in the kitchen and instructed Butch in the formal art of filling cups at the table. This just shows how etiquette can put fear into a brave man's heart."[26]

When these Robin Hood bandits were not robbing banks or throwing parties, they often caroused in an old cabin on Charley Crouse's place. Drinking and poker were the favorite pastimes, and local residents could be trusted to send warning if law officers were nearby.[27]

By the dawn of the twentieth century, law officers were nearby a good share of the time. It became more and more difficult to elude the relentless pursuit of sheriffs and private detectives, and many of the Wild Bunch were apprehended and sentenced to prison. Hoping to avoid that fate, Butch Cassidy and the Sundance Kid left the country for Bolivia in 1902. Conventional wisdom holds that they were killed there in a shootout with law officers, but unsubstantiated reports persist that Cassidy returned to the United States and finished out his years in peaceful obscurity. Whatever the case, the long arm of the law had proved that it could now reach into the most remote corners of the West. The glory days of the Outlaw Trail were over.

In retrospect, the lawlessness of the Wild Bunch reflected the social and economic uncertainty that characterized much of America in the 1890s. Young men trying to find a life for themselves were caught in the worst economic depression of the nineteenth century. Agricultural prices dropped dramatically, and it was a time of bankruptcies and reorganizations of questionable legality for many banks and railroads. Mining in the West also declined, throwing thousands of men out of work. Frustrated by the lack of opportunity, it is little wonder that some people struck out at the monied institutions they blamed for their problems.

Not all of the illegal activity in old Browns Park was tied to social conflict. Several men met violent deaths under mysterious circumstances. Jesse Ewing and Cleophas Dowd were both reputed to have been killed in disputes over women. Mike Flynn was shot down from ambush, and John Jarvie was murdered in 1909 during a robbery of his store. One killing in particular, however, brought a terrible retribution and galvanized law-enforcement agencies of three states into a new spirit of cooperation.

In 1898 a teenage boy named Willie Strang was shot in the back by a cowhand named Pat Johnson. Strang, Johnson, and Jack Bennett had been hanging around the Hoy ranch, where the lad chose to play a prank on one of his new friends. Pat Johnson was not at all amused. Willie Strang turned and ran, and Johnson drew his revolver and fired, killing the boy.[28]

Fleeing to an old outlaw hideout at Powder Springs, Bennett and Johnson met up with Harry Tracy and David Lang. Joining company, the four decided to quit the territory. Bennett went for supplies and arranged to rendezvous with his companions on Douglas Mountain. In the meantime, outraged lawmen from Routt County, Colorado,

Costume Ball. (Courtesy Pauleen Baker)

Sweetwater County, Wyoming, and Uintah County, Utah, began the pursuit.

The Routt County posse was first on the scene. They struck the outlaws' trail and followed it toward Douglas Mountain. Unfortunately, Johnson, Lant, and Tracy had spied the approaching officers and were waiting in ambush. A shot rang out, and Valentine Hoy, the lead rider, went down dead. The outlaws were in a good defensive position, but the posse had them pinned down. As the siege went on, Bennett unwittingly returned and stumbled into the arms of his pursuers. Eventually, the lawmen broke off the engagement and spent the night in the warmth of the Bassett ranch.

The following day, the posse ran down the cold and hungry desperadoes and forced their surrender. Johnson was taken to Rock Springs, Wyoming, by a U.S. marshal, and Lant and Tracy were placed in the custody of the Routt County sheriff. Bennett, who had been left under a light guard, was taken by seven masked riders and lynched in the Bassetts' yard. A combination of deputies and vigilantes had served justice. In the aftermath, Lant and Tracy escaped from their Colorado jail cell, and Johnson was turned loose following an appeal. Even so, the law-enforcement agencies of the three-corners region had finally shown they could cooperate to apprehend criminals. Law and order were closing in on the last remnants and most remote places of the Wild West.[29]

In an age that respects the rule of law and renounces violence as a means of conflict resolution, it is difficult for many to understand the seemingly contradictory actions of people in old Browns Park. Those who abhorred cold-blooded murder thought nothing of drawing guns in an affair of honor. Someone who lynched a man for stealing cattle might feel justified in butchering a cow belonging to an antagonistic neighbor. Yet, within the traditions of folk justice understood by the people of the park, these actions were seen as understandable and consistent.

A long way from any kind of civil authority, Browns Park attracted people who were used to handling and settling their own disputes. Most had grown up in rural societies where the institutions of government had been weak. They were comfortable taking justice into their own hands, and violence was a tragic but accepted fact of life. To them, justice was a very personal matter. A wrong demanded satisfaction; the law was often seen as corrupt and ineffective, and retribution was a manly act.

In a sense, these folk still operated on the Old Testament principle of "an eye for an eye." They believed in settling a score. If someone rustled from you, it was all right to rustle from them. If someone was trying to muscle in on your range, you could get even by driving off their stock or butchering one of their steers. Stealing cattle or horses was like a declaration of war, and the aggrieved party could exact the ultimate penalty. In a small agrarian community where there was not much wealth and everyone understood the rules, it was a system that worked to some limited extent.

So it was in old Browns Park. The community handled its own problems until it was challenged by wealthy outsiders. Effective law enforcement had grown out of the need to protect property, and the wealthy were its strongest proponents. They believed in the rule of law—as long as it worked to their advantage. When the forces of wealth and order came into conflict with the traditional culture of Browns Park, it was a prescription for civil war.

At first, the isolation and rugged terrain of the three- corners area, coupled with lack of cooperation among the various jurisdictions, allowed Browns Park resisters to fight back with impunity. Rustling and thievery took a substantial toll on large operators who were trying to take over the range. Outlaw heroes like Butch Cassidy and the Wild Bunch found a safe haven in the community. This was not to last.

The late 1890s saw a new determination arise among the forces of wealth and order. Not only did law-enforcement agencies develop new strategies for cooperation, large stockraisers banded together to take direct action. They used murder, intimidation, and an army of cowboys to drive sheep from their range. Savoring that victory, association members hired a gunman from outside the area to murder their enemies. The desired effect was achieved. Robbing and rustling became less common, and Robin Hood bandits either left the country or ended up in prison. By 1910 the new West had triumphed.

The old Wild West, however, refused to die. As the years went by, it found new life in countless books, movies, and Wild West shows—and the outlaw days of Browns Park became grist for the mill. Local events were presented as simple morality plays: right versus wrong; good versus evil. This simplification, however, has obscured a more complex and interesting reality.

The people of old Browns Park had very traditional values and a proclivity for violence that put them into conflict with the encroaching mainstream society. They believed in personal redress of grievances and distrusted legal authority. They felt that protecting their range was a natural right of survival, and they accepted a degree of anarchy and violence as the price of unfettered independence. It is ironic that, in the end, the forces of order that opposed these people proved to be in many ways much more violent than they were.

ENDNOTES

1. Richard M. Brown, *No Duty to Retreat: Violence and Values in American History and Society* (New York: Oxford University Press, 1991), 43–44.

2. Ibid., 45.

3. Robert M. Utley, *Billy the Kid: A Short and Violent Life* (Lincoln: University of Nebraska Press, 1989), 4.

4. Matt Warner and Murray E. King, *The Last of the Bandit Riders* (New York: Bonanza Books, 1940), 37.

5. Ibid., 37–38.

6. J.S. Hoy, "The J.S. Hoy Manuscript," 173–74.

7. Ibid., 174–75.

8. Ibid., 212–13.

9. Ibid., 217.

10. Warner and King, *Last of the Bandit Riders,* 45.

11. Ibid., 47.

12. Ibid., 48.

13. Dick Dunham and Vivian Dunham, *Flaming Gorge Country,* 86–87.

14. Hoy, "J.S. Hoy Manuscript," 191–92.

15. Dunham and Dunham, *Flaming Gorge Country,* 254–55; Hoy, "J.S. Hoy Manuscript," 198–99.

16. Grace McClure, *The Bassett Women* (Athens, OH: Swallow Press/University of Ohio Press, 1985), 26; Michael W. Johnson and Bradford Cole, "Wyoming in the 19th Century: An Historical Report for the Wyoming Territorial Park," 171, paper in author's collection.

17. Warner and King, *Last of the Bandit Riders,* 63–64.

18. Hoy, "J.S. Hoy Manuscript," 198; McClure, *The Bassett Women,* 24.

19. McClure, *The Bassett Women,* 46.

20. Ibid., 80–81.

21. Ibid., 83, 86.

22. Ibid., 79, 85.

23. Ibid., 105.

24. Warner and King, *Last of the Bandit Riders,* 111–12.

25. Ibid., 54–58.

26. McClure, *The Bassett Women,* 58–60.

27. William L. Tennent, "The John Jarvie Ranch: A Case Study in Historic Site Development and Interpretation" (Master's thesis, Utah State University, 1980), 41–42.

28. Ibid., 77.

29. Diana Allen Kouris, *The Romantic and Notorious History of Brown's Park* (Greybull, WY: Wolverine Gallery, 1988), 91.

CHAPTER 7

BUILDING NEW TOWNS

> Where the . . . "Old Military Road" ascends the rugged north slope of the Uintah Mountains, the writer of this saw, in the fall of 1890, a low, flat valley surrounded by sunlit reefs, lying off some distance to the east. In contrast to the very broken, bleak and snow-covered country, this spot, where light and warmth appeared to dwell, seemed singularly attractive.
>
> —ADOLPH JESSEN

As the nineteenth century drew to a close, Utah was filling up with people. Most of the land that could be easily irrigated had been taken by 1880, and the high birth rate, coupled with the continual arrival of Mormon converts, brought increasing pressure to open up new farmland. The first response was to expand canal systems. More acreage was put under irrigation around existing Utah communities, and these lands were quickly taken. Demand for farmland, however, did not abate. New canal systems were built, requiring ever more money, effort, and technical expertise, and ever more marginal land was brought into production. Even so, the landless children and

Heber Bennion. (Courtesy Pauleen Baker)

grandchildren of the pioneers eagerly sought the security that farm ownership promised.

It was in this context that engineer Adolph Jessen contracted to complete the territorial survey of the rugged lands of the eastern Uinta Mountains. In the fall of 1890, Jessen noticed the agricultural possibilities of Dry Valley, the sheltered valley that was home to the Birch Springs Ranch. An assistant, Marius Larsen, later recalled:

> In making this survey, Mr. Jessen came in very close contact with every legal subdivision, its contour and soil, and I remember now, as I often heard him say, "what grain and lucerne this land would produce, if water could be brought into this valley."[1]

Jessen's preliminary investigation of the area determined that about 2,000 acres at the lower end of the valley could be brought under irrigation by diverting water from the Henrys Fork River. Armed with this information, Jessen approached several people with the purpose of forming a land-development company. They decided to change the name of Dry Valley to Lucerne Valley, lucerne being the common name for alfalfa at the time, and they incorporated the Lucerne Land and Water Company with a capital stock of $50,000. The company's plan was to acquire as much of the irrigable land as possible and then to resell it after the irrigation works were completed and values had risen. Other profits were to be made through the sale of water shares to homesteaders on the public land. On 24 May 1892 an article in the *Deseret News* announced:

> Articles of incorporation of the Lucerne Land and Water company were filed with the County Clerk today. The incorporators are: Adolph Jessen, James McGregor, Chas. C. Dey of Salt Lake, Benjamin E. Rich of Ogden, and Josiah Smith of Fort Bridger, Wyoming. . . . The general office will be in Salt Lake, but its business will extend over Utah and Wyoming. . . . The officers are Adolph Jessen president, B.E.Rich vice-president, and James McGregor secretary and treasurer.[2]

Other investors later got involved. Utah Surveyor General Ellsworth Daggett and mining magnate R.C. Chambers joined the enterprise. Together with Jessen, who continued to manage the company's affairs, they became the principal stockholders of the land-development project.[3]

During the summer, Jessen made further investigations of the countryside. He determined that upper Sheep Creek could be

Ellsworth Daggett. (Sweetwater County Museum)

diverted to water most of the Lucerne Valley as well as Antelope Flat, Phil Pico Bench, and South Valley. Designs on the Henrys Fork were

Crouse Bridge on the Green River in Browns Park. (Utah State Historical Society)

abandoned, and the Lucerne Land and Water Company worked to locate and appropriate all the waters of Sheep Creek according to law. In 1894 work commenced on the 14.5-mile Sheep Creek Canal. From a diversion on the west fork, the first 3.5 miles involved heavy rock work through Connor Basin Canyon. Tapping the flow of the north fork, the ditch then wound its way out of the canyon across gently rolling benchland to the head of Lucerne Valley. The main canal, rated at a capacity of fifty cubic feet per second, then divided into two twenty-cubic-feet-per-second laterals. One lateral flowed six miles along the northern slope of Lucerne Valley, while the other followed the southern slope for three miles. The Sheep Creek Canal irrigated several thousand acres, most of them in the western and central sections of the valley.

With the Sheep Creek Canal System well underway, the Lucerne Land and Water Company applied to the Uintah County Court and commissioners of Uintah County for its water right. The company was awarded all the waters of Sheep Creek for irrigation and other beneficent purposes. It acquired the Birch Springs Ranch for its headquarters, and widespread promotional efforts were begun.

The company also decided to employ an on-site manager to

Entering Linwood. (Sweetwater County Museum)

superintend its affairs. Frank Ellison of Grantsville was hired for the job, and he and his wife Eva arrived at the ranch late in 1895. Ellison did not last. Unable to get along with his superiors, he quit the following summer and was replaced by Edward Tolton. Tolton was a resident of Beaver who had come, in the company of Samuel and Joseph Warby, to learn more about settlement prospects in Lucerne Valley. Although the land was not as lush as the men from Beaver had hoped, they did see promise in the form of the already planted alfalfa fields and decided to stay. Tolton's employment as manager linked the project to the Beaver area, and several members of that west-central Utah community flocked to the valley, hoping to better their circumstances.

A number of people from Beaver immigrated to Lucerne Valley in 1896. The first to come were the families of George and Caroline Warby, Franklin and Maria Twitchell, and Daniel and Matilda Nelson. The Nelsons with their eight children were recent converts to Mormonism from Australia. Single men James, Steven, and Joseph Warby and Alvin Smith also accompanied the party. They left Beaver on 23 July and reached their destination on 16 August. The party consisted of twenty-four people, seven wagons, 150 cattle, sixty or

Eleen Williams, postmistress at Linwood, delivering mail to Timothy Potter. (Courtesy Pauleen Baker)

seventy horses, and two mules. They traveled by wagon via Provo, Heber City, Chalk Creek, Hilliard, Fort Bridger, and Henrys Fork.[4]

Ed Tolton's family arrived at the Birch Springs ranch in October, and the Sam Warby family, the James Reid family, and Axel Anderson settled in before winter. Years later, Warby's daughter wrote:

> We had two wagons and teams, some grain to plant, alfalfa seed, some household belongings, [and] a Dutch oven to cook in. . . . When we got to the top of the hill looking down into the valley, dad raised his hat and shouted aloud, "This is it." Mother, looking up, said, "I don't see anything to be that pleased with."[5]

Anderson, a Swede, was the only settler not from Beaver. Except for Tolton, they lived in crude huts, cabins, and a dugout—all clustered above the present site of Manila. The village was nicknamed "Sandtown," because blowing sand was a continual source of irritation. That first winter food came from wild game, an occasional old steer donated by Shadrach Large or George Hereford, and staples obtained on credit from Dick Son's nearby store.[6]

During 1897, most settlers began to prove up their homesteads and moved onto them. Water flowed through the canal system that rimmed the valley, but most of the land remained dry. People rebelled against the high cost of water proffered by the Lucerne Land and Water Company. The cost of a share, supposedly enough water to irrigate one acre, was five dollars. Those without cash could turn over half of their property for shares to water the remaining eighty acres. This arrangement seemed equitable, but things did not quite work out as expected. J. Kent Olson remembered:

> The homesteader had no money to buy water development, so the offer seemed natural and reasonable, and many such deals were consummated. Many disappointments followed, however, after discovering that the eighty shares on the ditch would irrigate but 15 acres.[7]

Shareholders felt swindled, and dissatisfaction with the irrigation company was widespread. Without adequate irrigation water there was little farming to do, and some of the men took jobs with canal contractors or hay crews. Fortunately, Sam Warby was able to dry farm a good crop of wheat and oats so that there was seed grain for the community the following spring. Willis and Annie Twitchell and Henry and Elizabeth Twitchell, all from Beaver, also arrived that year.

As Utahns became aware of the new Lucerne Valley settlement, would-be settlers came to investigate the area's potential. J.M. Pyper of Heber Valley visited the valley in the fall of 1897, and he reported to his local newspaper.

> J.M. Pyper and son of Midway returned home Saturday after an absence of eighteen days on a trip to Lucerne Valley in Uintah county. He says he found a nice little valley and a good climate, but he is not favorably impressed with it as a farming district. . . . Mr. Pyper says that there are but thirteen families settled in the valley altogether on a quarter section each. . . . The valley has been greatly

Manila Post Office in 1921. (Daggett County)

> exaggerated as a place in which to secure a home cheap, said our informant, and his advice to poor people is to remain away from there.[8]

Times were very difficult in the new settlement, but life was not all drudgery. The established families along the Henrys Fork put aside religious differences and welcomed the Mormons, some of whom were polygamists, into their midst. The Episcopal church had a mission at Burnt Fork, and some of them had reservations about the influx of Mormons, but soon virtually all in the area welcomed the newcomers. Latter-day Saints became regular visitors at the dances in Burnt Fork and reciprocated by holding dances in Lucerne Valley. When Dan Nelson's daughter Sarah Ann married Alvin Smith in the new settlement, both Mormons and non-Mormons celebrated together in hearty fashion. The first baby in the new settlement was a son born to George and Caroline Warby; sadly, the child was also the first to be buried in the town cemetery.[9]

In its third year, the Lucerne Valley community made considerable progress. The Lucerne Land and Water Company platted and developed a townsite it intended to name "Chambers" after company

Ladore School in Browns Park. (Daggett County)

Manila School built in 1912 and used as the county courthouse from 1922 to 1979. (Sweetwater County Museum)

investor R.C. Chambers. Jessen's men had bored a tunnel some sixty feet into a nearby hillside and developed a small but dependable spring of water. This was piped 1,600 feet to a tank at the center of the proposed town, which soon had a new name, Manila—named for a Spanish-American War naval victory. According to historian Dale Morgan:

> the name Chambers . . . had been decided on for the settlement, and Jessen had the plats all packed and ready for mailing to Washington, D.C., when news was received that Admiral Dewey had just won the battle of Manila Bay. To commemorate this victory, Jessen unpacked the plats and changed the name to Manila.[10]

Having been raised in the tradition of the Mormon farm village and accustomed to the social advantages of town life, many of the valley's new inhabitants purchased lots and moved in. Menfolk might spend considerable time away from home on their outlying farmsteads, but women and families generally lived in town—especially in winter when school was in session.

Manila's original houses were log cabins of only one or two

Manila School built in 1925. (Daggett County)

rooms. Four numbered streets ran east and west; three—named Jessen, Chambers, and Daggett—ran north and south. Each block was divided into ten lots. Barrels were mounted on drags and domestic water was hauled from the central tank. Livestock were driven to the tank for watering. The community felt that education was important, and Daniel Nelson crossed the mountains five times to lobby Uintah County officials to establish a school. The county appropriated a small amount for that purpose in 1898, and Benjamin Slagowski became the teacher at Lucerne Valley's first school.

Daniel Nelson also worked for the establishment of a local Latter-day Saint church organization. Sunday school meetings had begun in May 1898, but the community hoped for official church recognition. In August 1898 President John M. Baxter of the Woodruff LDS Stake traveled to Manila in the company of Apostle Abraham O. Woodruff and Joseph W. McMurrin of the church's First Quorum of Seventy to organize the local congregation. In his memoir, Baxter wrote of the trip down the Henrys Fork and the grinding poverty of the settlers:

> As the country was in its wild state, we would every few miles come to an Indian wigwam, or small village with a lot of Indian children and halfbreeds playing around the wickieup. . . . Leaving the river

> we turned into a low pass to the south. When we got near to it, a woman came to the door which was an opening with a blanket nailed up to serve as a door. The woman looked weather-tanned and ragged, showing evidence of a hard life. Brother McMurrin said, "Sister, you look to me like a Latter-day Saint Woman." She replied, "You bet I do, and you look to me like Latter-day Saint men, and I sure am glad to see you." She invited us into her humble home. It would be difficult to describe the destitute condition of that "home." She had two little children, one in her arms and one about two years old. Her husband was away at work on some of the ranches. There was not a fence, or any improvement on the place except the cabin, with a dirt roof, containing one room, no door, window or floor. The woman was cheerful, and told us they had lived there for two years, hoping to get water out on their land. Now they hoped they would be able to get it out next year.[11]

From there the travelers continued another three miles through heavy sand to the town of Manila. They found a small village of houses built closely together. Noticing the poverty of the people, the churchmen camped out in a yard rather than impose, and they gave away all the canned food they could spare. The next day, 7 August 1898, the three church officials held services in Manila's tiny log meetinghouse. It was about ten feet square, covered with a dirt roof, and had no door. Baxter remembered:

> We held meeting with the people in the little cabin, seated on slab seats, and had the satisfaction at least, of having our meeting house crowded to its capacity. A splendid spirit was manifested; the people were starving for spiritual food. We organized a branch with Willis Twitchell as presiding Elder.[12]

It was not too long before services were held in more commodious accommodations. A thirty-by-forty-foot log community center was constructed that came to be known as the Town Hall. This building had the first tongue-and-groove wooden floor in the area, and it was used both as a chapel and as a dance hall. The first dance was held before the building was completed and was interrupted by a playful shooting spree.[13] In 1904 Peter G. Wall, in his capacity as school trustee, purchased the hall for use as Manila's second school.

Manila Basketball Team in 1932. (Daggett County)

Two years later, the Willis Twitchell family donated a town lot for construction of an LDS chapel. A fine frame building was erected, and all seemed well until there was a prolonged wet spell. From that time on, the area around the church was known as "the swamp." Going to church often meant picking a way through mud and standing water. Planks were sometimes laid over the worst parts, and the church membership endured until the structure was eventually moved to dry ground. Andrew Loftgren also established a cooperative store called the Manila Mercantile Company in 1906.

As the area matured and more settlers moved in, irrigation water continued to be a source of conflict. Farmers were irritated by the inadequacy of the water supply and the control of their irrigation system by outsiders. In 1899 the Lucerne Land and Water Company alleviated some of the problems by divesting itself of the Sheep Creek canal system. A separate entity, the Sheep Creek Irrigation Company, was created to take control of the system and its water right. It was estimated that there were 10,000 acres that could be irrigated by the company, and 10,000 shares of stock were issued. Shares were sold in

Manila School Children. (Sweetwater County Museum)

blocks of forty; one ten-dollar share entitled the owner to irrigation water for one acre. By 1902, 1,000 water shares had been sold in the community, 1,420 were kept by the Lucerne Land and Water Company for its own farmland, and the unsold balance was held in trust by the land company but was not assessed or voted. This meant that the irrigation system had passed into the control of the irrigators, and local control was eventually achieved.[14]

Other homesteaders in the area simply refused to deal with the problems of the Sheep Creek system. Rancher Keith Smith wrote:

> Hoping to get water cheaper, a group of homesteaders started a water system of their own for the 2,000 acres at the eastern end of Lucerne Valley. This was called the People's Canal and it took water from Henry's Fork instead of from Sheep Creek. Most of the men who worked on this canal made money in winter by putting up ice in Green River for the railroad.[15]

The People's Canal Company was incorporated in 1899 by George Solomon, Edward Tolton, Marius Larsen, George Stevens, and Daniel Nelson. Other shareholders included Frank Ellison, John DeSpain, Charles Large, George Finch, Alvin Smith, and several members of the Warby family. Construction began the following year but proved more difficult than expected. The diversion ditch and canal were not completed until 1902, and water was not delivered until the next spring.[16]

During the construction process, Frank Ellison became discouraged and sold his 160-acre homestead and water right to George Solomon. Solomon envisioned the place as a townsite and paid sixty dollars to have it surveyed. Cottonwood trees, known by some as Linwoods, had been planted along the ditch banks, and Solomon named the place for them. George Solomon, however, never developed the town of Linwood. Like George Hereford, Alvin Smith, and both William and Charles Large, Solomon sold his property to an eastern family that was determined to get into the ranching business. The family's name was Smith, and young Keith Smith, a recent graduate of Yale, would stay on to become one of the area's most prominent citizens.[17]

The summer of 1901 after his junior year at Yale, Keith Smith had accompanied a friend on a hunting and fishing expedition to the wild Uinta Mountains. In September the party visited Ole Neilson's cabin on Sheep Creek and worked its way downstream looking for game. They encountered an area called the Red Bench, a terrace of land above lower Sheep Creek that showed promise as an irrigated farmsite. Young Smith was both ambitious and impressed. On his return trip to Yale, he visited his brother Sanford, and they determined to build a ranch on the Red Bench property the following year.

Keith, accompanied by his father, returned the next summer and met Sanford at Ole Neilson's. They found that the property they coveted was actually part of the recently established Uintah Forest Reserve. Attempts to have the Red Bench released for homesteading proved fruitless, and the Smiths resolved to purchase land on the Henrys Fork. Their new holdings included Uncle Jack Robinson's old cabin and George Solomon's defunct Linwood townsite.[18]

The first months of operation were spent constructing ranch buildings, building a bridge across the Henrys Fork, hunting, and digging up sagebrush. In 1903 family friend Bill Field invested in the ranch, and the business was incorporated as Smith Brothers and Field. Frank Ellison, the man who had earlier sold out in discourage-

Children in front of the Red School House built on the Wyoming-Utah State line in Linwood. (Sweetwater County Museum)

ment, arranged with the Smiths to farm his original claim on shares. The crop proved to be so good that the Smiths cleared the one thousand dollars they had paid for the land just the year before. The ranchers also began to acquire a herd of beef cattle. As the Henrys Fork deadline was still being enforced, sheep raising was out of the question.[19]

It was not long before Keith Smith was appointed the first postmaster of Linwood. Dick Son had been the local postmaster for years, and the mail was delivered to his store in what is today Washam, Wyoming. Son, however, was going blind, and he needed a replacement. Smith recalled:

> The one-time guide of Yale's Professor Marsh was now Postmaster at Lucerne, Wyoming. This is where we rode three times a week for mail. Since Dick Son was nearly blind with cataracts, we had to sort the mail for him. He could not get his post office closed until a new one was started to take its place, so I applied for the job, and October 17, 1903, I received a letter of appointment in which I was

Round Dance Hall at Linwood. (Sweetwater County Museum)

instructed to get the mailbag lock "from the Postmaster at Lucerne." We opened the new post office near our ranch, using the name that Solomon had applied to the township he had surveyed,

> "Linwood." It was at Linwood that the ranches on Lower Henry's Fork got their mail for the next 60 years though I remained the Postmaster only until 1919.[20]

This was the beginning of the Linwood community, but Linwood was not really a town in the same sense as Manila. Keith Smith's post office made Linwood a focal point for the dispersed rural community along the lower Henrys Fork, and it developed as a business district; however, it never did have a large residential population. Nevertheless, during the flourishing years of the sheep industry, especially in shearing season, Linwood was a very lively place.

A month after they were awarded the post office, Frank Smith, the father of Keith and Sanford, threw in with neighbor Marius Larsen to open the Smith and Larsen Mercantile Company. Larsen was a Danish emigrant who had first come to Lucerne Valley as an employee of the Lucerne Land and Water Company. More commonly known as M.N. Larsen, or simply M.N., he was short in stature with a well-trimmed beard and almost always dressed in a suit and tie; like the Smiths, he had a real entrepreneurial zeal.

Large sheep-ranching companies were grazing their flocks just across the deadline in the Wyoming badlands, and Larsen sensed that a store at Linwood could solve many supply problems. He interested the Smiths in his idea, and they opened their mercantile operation in a red tin building on Larsen's property. This also became the location of the post office. The partnership evidently did not work well, for within a matter of months Frank Smith bought out his partner. Keeping the name Smith and Larsen, he moved the store and post office to the bunkhouse on the Smith ranch. Larsen opened his own store, the Linwood Mercantile Company. Fortunately, there was enough business to support both enterprises.[21]

The continuing boom in the sheep business soon stimulated further development in the Linwood area. Both Marius Larsen and Keith Smith opened hostelries that were frequented, largely on weekends, by people associated with this boom. Robert Swift, who had come into the area with the John DeSpain family, opened the Bucket of Blood Saloon just across the Henrys Fork in Wyoming. Liquor, gambling, and "questionable" women were its primary attractions. Swift

Daggett County musicians. (Courtesy Pauleen Baker)

also built some tourist cabins on the Utah side of the line and connected his twin operations with a footbridge. Not to be outdone, Larsen hired two carpenters to construct an octagonal dance hall with a hardwood floor. The sheepmen liked to party hard and had money to spend, and Linwood quickly became a favorite local resort.[22]

Linwood also became the home of one of Utah's most interesting schools. In 1904, Utah's Uintah County School District Seventeen and Wyoming's Sweetwater County District Thirteen decided to cooperate to build a joint school. It was built one-half mile west of Linwood, with materials and labor volunteered by the people of both districts. The ridgepole of the building was laid right on the state boundary so that part of the structure was in each state. Painted red, the school had

The Williams family dressed up for a costume party. From left to right Paul Williams, Barbara Williams, Eleen Williams, Emmett Willliams, and Bill Williams. (Courtesy Pauleen Baker)

one room that was heated by a large wood stove; it was lighted by kerosene lamps. Enrollment reached forty students in 1907.

It has been said that, at the time, corporal punishment was not allowed in one of the two states. This, however, did not deter teachers at the Linwood School. If a student committed some grievous offense, he or she was escorted to the appropriate side of the building and given summary punishment.[23]

Charley Crouse of Browns Park was another resident caught up in the entrepreneurial fever that was gripping the region. Crouse had sold much of his Browns Park holdings to a Rock Springs partnership around 1890 and, with his partner Aaron Overholt, had opened a saloon in Vernal. A few years later, Crouse returned to the valley and settled on the Green River a couple of miles below John Jarvie's place. Here he developed Bridgeport, a small commercial center and would-be community. Crouse's operation included a combination store and saloon that also housed the local post office. He had a toll bridge constructed at the site and a canal system dug that crossed over the Green River on a flume. Still known today as the Crouse Ditch, it watered property on both sides of the river.

Competition from Crouse's Bridgeport operation worked a real hardship on John Jarvie's existing store and ferry. Jarvie closed his ferry, and sales at his store slumped. Now a widower and living alone, Jarvie managed to hold on. In a letter to a son, the aging storekeeper wrote, "So I have very little to trade, and the ferry has not run for two years, but it does not take much to keep me here." Fortunately for Jarvie, an ice flow destroyed Crouse's bridge after only a couple years of operation, and the venerable Scotsman reopened his ferry business.[24]

A small settlement also began to take root in the forested Greendale area. Greendale was originally called Lewis Allen, after the first white settler who lived in the area. Allen had purchased land in the area from Cleophus Dowd in the early 1880s for about two thousand dollars. He squatted on the land until the mid-1890s when he moved his family to Vernal. The area, known by some as the Lone Pine Ranch, was used by Allen for the grazing of livestock.[25]

About the time Allen left, William Green came into the area. Green and his family had hunted and trapped throughout the Uintas, and when talk of a railroad circulated in the middle 1890s, they determined to open a resort on a fork of Skull Creek. Green diverted a couple of small creeks and enlarged a small lake into a good-sized fishing pond. When the railroad did not materialize, the Greens changed their plans and used the water to develop a modest ranch. In 1897 the Greendale area became part of the newly created Uintah Forest Reserve, and William Green became the region's first forest guard. Oscar, Lyman, and James Swett moved over from the Vernal area and homesteaded nearby, and these families were later joined by Josiah and Vivian Arrowsmith.[26]

In Greendale and other area communities, establishment of the forest reserve ushered in new ways of doing things. The forest reserves grew out of America's growing conservation movement at the close of the nineteenth century. Alarmed by the rapid depletion of what had once seemed inexhaustible resources, professional foresters and concerned citizens urged the federal government to set aside forest and watershed areas within the public domain. Congress passed the Forest Reserve Act in 1891, and President Benjamin Harrison quickly established fifteen forest reserves totalling more

George Rassmussen with Minnie Rasmussen on the left and Mabel Adamson on the right. (Courtesy Pauleen Baker)

than 13 million acres. Most were created to protect valuable watersheds.[27]

Conservation efforts continued during the administration of President Grover Cleveland. Acting on the recommendations of a special commission, on 22 February 1897 he set aside another 21 million acres of forest in thirteen new reserves. These came to be known as the "Washington's Birthday" forests. Among them was a huge block of land in Utah's Uinta Mountains. The Uintah Forest Reserve, headquartered in Provo, was Utah's first forest reserve and included an immense amount of land.[28]

Unlike the situation in modern national forests, there was no provision for using the resources of the early forest reserves. The lands were simply withdrawn from timbering, grazing, and homesteading. It was no wonder that, especially in the West, many resource users were outraged by the government's "locking up" of vast amounts of territory. Violations of the reserves were commonplace, and, with few enforcement resources, there was little that forest administrators could do about it. To head off critics who sought to return the reserves to the public domain, conservationists in

Congress compromised to allow sustainable use of forest resources. Sometimes called the Pettigrew Amendment, this attachment to the Sundry Civil Appropriations Bill mandated that the forest reserves be managed to improve and protect the forests, protect watersheds, and provide timber. The compromise bill formed the basis of national forest management for the next sixty years.[29]

Accustomed as they were to unrestricted grazing and timbering on the public land, local residents were not happy about the new federal regulations. Many made only a token effort toward compliance. Because poor transportation limited the timber market, most of the problems concerned grazing. One forester recalled contacting a prominent rancher from the Henrys Fork country:

> I introduced myself and began to tell him of the Forest Service, its aims and part the people were expected to take in the proper use of the timber and ranges. He sat for a long time, not saying a word. Finally, he said, "Well, we don't need any Forest Service here, but when Ranger Turnbow was here, we all agreed to take some permits, and I have a permit for 50 cattle which is enough." "Well," said I, "is that all the cattle you own and run on the Forest?" He answered, "I pay taxes on 50 head."[30]

Faced with opposition from the users of the forest, the early foresters had a difficult task. Most were local men accustomed to life in the outdoors. William Anderson was appointed assistant ranger on the eastern Uintas in 1906. He recalled that:

> the distance around the country I had to oversee was about six hundred miles, all to be done with saddle horse and pack outfit. . . . I rode hard every day and during that summer I used ten saddle horses, kept my horses and myself and received a salary of $60.00 per month.[31]

The conservation movement gained momentum during the administration of President Theodore Roosevelt. Roosevelt was an avid outdoorsman and a friend of conservationist George Bird Grinnell. Grinnell had traversed the Uintas with the Marsh expedition in 1870 and had become the editor of *Field and Stream* magazine. Another of Roosevelt's friends was Gifford Pinchot, America's first professional forester.

Dr. Fay Tinker. (Daggett County)

Pinchot had been appointed head of the Department of Agriculture's Bureau of Forestry in 1898. He strongly believed that the nation's forests should be scientifically managed for sustained commodity production, and it irritated him that the forest reserves were under the jurisdiction of the rival Department of the Interior. Using his considerable political influence, in 1905 Pinchot engineered the transfer of the reserves to his agency at the Department of Agriculture. To stress that the forests would be utilized, he changed their names from "forest reserves" to "national forests." He also changed the name of the Bureau of Forestry to the United States Forest Service. Pinchot established a set of management objectives for his agency that included fire protection, sustained harvest of mature timber, watershed protection, improvement of forests, protection of the water supply, sustainable grazing use, and the improvement of range conditions.[32]

Pinchot was both an empire builder and an able administrator, and he quickly set about reorganizing the reserves into more-manageable units. The Uinta National Forest was reorganized on 1 June 1908; its eastern section became the new Ashley National Forest. The name was taken from prominent area landmarks Ashley Gorge and Ashley Creek, both named for explorer and fur trader General William H. Ashley. Forest headquarters was in Vernal, and there were seven original ranger districts. John Bennett was the first ranger for the Manila District. It was a decentralized system, and Bennett handled most important decisions dealing with timber sales and grazing allotments.[33]

One of Pinchot's goals was to professionalize the Forest Service. Toward that end, the agency began hiring graduates from eastern forestry schools. The first of these college-trained foresters arrived on the Uintas in 1907, and there was immediate friction between them and their local colleagues. William Anderson commented:

> we worked at whatever job was necessary in the routine of the day, and on several occasions, when I asked them to dig ditches, post boundaries, scale logs and build fences, they rebelled, and more than once I was told that they didn't go to school to learn how to dig ditches. Since I thought the Forest work included anything that needed to be done at the moment, I naturally didn't find much use for them.[34]

While the young easterners brought a new professionalism to forest management, their ways created tension inside and outside of the agency. There was, however, a common bond between the Forest Service and local residents. One ranger on the eastern Uintas reported that

> stock raising and farming are the leading, and in fact, the only industries in this locality; consequently, everybody in and around this Forest is vitally interested and watch very closely the management of the Forest, as they are all very well aware that to overgraze this range, or in any manner denude the drainage area of its vegetation would mean irreparable loss to them; at the same time, of course, they wish to graze as many stock on the Forest as they can get; as a consequence of all this, the public and the officers of the Forest Service are brought close together.[35]

Both local ranchers and Forest officials were vitally interested in the health of the range, but the ranchers thought they were better judges of how many animals they should run. When asked what her father Oscar Swett of Greendale thought of the Forest Service, Myrle Augusta Swett Moore answered, "He cussed them all the time. . . . The first few years . . . they got along pretty good because the rangers lived in Manila and they [the Swetts] could do as they pleased . . ."[36]

The Daggett country was growing up. Nowhere was this more apparent than in Manila, where a new school was constructed in 1912. Built by George and Adolph Hastrup, the two-story frame building had four classrooms. It featured wood paneling on the interior, a tongue-and-groove wooden floor, a large combination wood-and-coal stove for heating, and water piped in from the community tank. Grades one through six were taught on the first floor, while grades seven and eight were upstairs. Two years of high school were added to the curriculum in the school's third year of operation. The Old Hall, Manila's second school, continued to be used for a variety of civic and social functions.[37]

School organization took a leap forward in 1914. Until that time, each community in Uintah County with a school operated its own school district. District Seventeen served the Linwood area, and District Fifteen served Manila; also, a small school may have operated at Bridgeport in Browns Park, but little is known of it. In 1914 these small districts were combined under the single authority of the Uintah County School District.[38]

Both the school and the community of Linwood were starting to wind down at this time. Wyoming's Sweetwater County residents built a new school at Washam, Wyoming, in 1910 and withdrew their students from the older joint school. The wool boom that had made Linwood a bustling little mercantile and resort center was also on the wane. Overgrazing had taken a toll of both the land and the sheep industry. For the sheep ranchers who remained, the advent of the motor truck allowed their outfits to be supplied directly from the Wyoming railroad towns of Green River and Rock Springs. Linwood's hotel and entertainment establishments closed down, and, with only twenty students, the stateline school was closed in 1918. Local students were then sent to school in Washam.[39]

The decline of Linwood left Marius Larsen looking for new opportunities. He sold his Linwood Mercantile and got involved in a land-development project a few miles west of Manila. He formed the Antelope Land and Livestock Company to build irrigation works and develop a small community. The plan required diversion of water from both Burnt Fork and Beaver creeks to a reservoir in a natural basin between the two streams. A small settlement called Antelope began to form, and a school was built in 1916. M.N. Larsen, Charles Olson, Charles Terry, and a Mr. Hagerman worked with the Uintah County School District to establish the small log school on Larsen's ranch. Unfortunately, the irrigation project did not work out. The soil at the reservoir site was too porous to hold water, and the development was abandoned. The school closed in 1917 and the land reverted to ownership by Larsen.[40]

As America was on the verge of entering World War I, it was plain to those who lived along the northern slope of the Uintas that they had entered a new age. Gone were the wild days of the Outlaw Trail, widespread cattle rustling, and range wars between sheepmen and cattlemen. Frame houses were starting to replace log cabins, and a few wealthy citizens had purchased automobiles. Grazing and timber cutting in the mountain country had become regulated by officials of the Ashley National Forest. Much had changed since a handful of families had journeyed from Beaver by wagon train to start new lives in Lucerne Valley.

Despite of this progress, there was a growing dissatisfaction in the region. Residents of Linwood, Manila, Browns Park, and the surrounding country felt isolated and somewhat disaffected from their distant neighbors across the mountains in southern Uintah County. When snow was on the mountains, legal business in the county seat required a 400-mile roundabout journey by railroad and stageline to get to Vernal. North-slope communities felt neglected by the county commission and believed that they were not getting a fair return on their tax dollars. Clearly, they believed, it was time to take control of their own destiny.

ENDNOTES

1. M.N. Larsen, "History of Daggett County," 1938, unpublished manuscript in author's collection.

2. Journal History, 24 May 1892, Church of Jesus Christ of Latter-day Saints Archives, Salt Lake City, Utah.

3. *Inventory of the County Archives of Utah: No. 5. Daggett County* (Ogden, Utah: Work Projects Administration, 1939), 8.

4. Sarah Boren, ed., "Warby Family History," manuscript history in the collection of Leta Wahlquist, 25.

5. Boren, "Warby Family History," 29.

6. Richard Dunham and Vivian Dunham, *Flaming Gorge Country*, 289–90; *Inventory of County Archives*, 8.

7. J. Kent Olson, *Never Marry a Rancher* (Salt Lake City: Hiller Industries, 1979), 15.

8. Journal History, 6 December 1897.

9. Dunham and Dunham, *Flaming Gorge Country*, 290, 291; "This Was Papa," 4, unpublished anonymous manuscript history in author's collection.

10. *Inventory of County Archives*, 9.

11. John M. Baxter, *Life of John M. Baxter* (Salt Lake City: Deseret News Press, 1932), 110–11.

12. Ibid., 112–13.

13. Dunham and Dunham, *Flaming Gorge Country*, 293–94.

14. Adolph Jessen, "Operations: Lucerne Land and Water Company" (Salt Lake City: Lucerne Land and Water Co., n.d.), 14.

15. Keith Smith, "Recollections of Keith Smith of Linwood, Utah, as Told to his Daughter Susan," 1968, 14, unpublished manuscript at Utah State Historical Society.

16. Dunham and Dunham, *Flaming Gorge Country,* 302.

17. Smith, "Recollections," 14–15; Dunham and Dunham, *Flaming Gorge Country,* 302–3.

18. Smith, "Recollections," 8–13.

19. Ibid., 16–17.

20. Ibid., 18.

21. Ibid., 19; Dunham and Dunham, *Flaming Gorge Country,* 303.

22. Dunham and Dunham, *Flaming Gorge Country,* 304–5.

23. Donald Weir Baxter, "The History of Public Education in Daggett County Utah and Adjacent Areas" (Master's thesis, Brigham Young University, 1959), 50–52.

24. William L. Tennent, "The John Jarvie Ranch: A Case Study in Historic Site Development and Interpretation" (Master's thesis, Utah State University, 1980), 57–58, 104.

25. Eric G. Swedin, "The Swett Homestead: An Oral History, 1909–1970," (Master's thesis, Utah State University, 1991), 20–21.

26. Dunham and Dunham, *Flaming Gorge Country,* 316.

27. Harold K. Steen, *The U.S. Forest Service: A History* (Seattle: University of Washington Press, n.d.), 28.

28. Byron Loosle, "The Ashley National Forest," n.d., 6, paper written for the Ashley National Forest; Steen, *U.S. Forest Service,* 33.

29. Loosle, "Ashley National Forest," 6.

30. William Anderson, n.d., 8, unpublished manuscript history in the files of the Ashley National Forest.

31. Ibid., 4.

32. Samuel P. Hays, "Gifford Pinchot and the American Conservation Movement," in *Technology in America: A History of Individuals and Ideas,* Carroll W. Purcell, Jr., ed. (Cambridge, MA: MIT Press, 1989), 152, 159.

33. Loosle, "Ashley National Forest," 6; Dunham and Dunham, *Flaming Gorge Country,* 314.

34. Anderson, 10.

35. Loosle, "Ashley National Forest," 9.

36. Myrle Augusta Swett Moore, "Swett Ranch Oral History Project," 1989, 41, oral history collection, Merrill Library, Utah State University.

37. Baxter, "History of Public Education," 64.

38. Ibid., 66.

39. Ibid., 51–53; Dunham and Dunham, *Flaming Gorge Country*, 313.

40. Baxter, "History of Public Education," 58; Dunham and Dunham, *Flaming Gorge Country*, 313.

CHAPTER 8

THE CREATION AND EARLY DEVELOPMENT OF DAGGETT COUNTY

> The reason for the separation of this part into a new County was on account of the difficulty of getting to the County Seat at Vernal; the high range of mountains known as the U[i]ntahs made it almost impossible to go over . . . [in all but] four months of the year, the rest of the year a person must be under the obligation of taking the stage to some point in Wyoming on the U.P. Railroad a distance of 50 to 60 miles, then taking a journey by rail for about 400 or 500 miles, then again taking the stage for another ride of 150 miles; which made it very expensive to go to the County Seat to transact any business.
>
> —DAGGETT COUNTY COMMISSION MINUTES, 1918

Small in population and isolated from their fellow Utahns by rugged mountains, the people along the northern slope of the Uintas felt like political stepchildren. For travel and trade they looked northward toward Fort Bridger and the towns along the Union Pacific railroad line; but when Congress set the southern boundary of Wyoming at the 41st parallel, they found themselves cut off politically from their natural association. This remnant of Green River County was instead

Daniel Morgan Nielson, first Daggett County Assessor. (Daggett County)

added to Summit County in Utah Territory, and in 1880 it became part of Uintah County. A county seat in Vernal was much closer to Henrys Fork and Browns Park than one in Coalville, and Utah's lawmakers must have thought this a workable arrangement. The problem, however, was that for about eight months of each year the Uinta Mountains were choked with snow, and, for the settlers along the Uintas' north slopes, Vernal might as well have been on the moon.

In the early years this was only a limited inconvenience: each small community controlled its own schools, few people bothered to record land titles, and there was no great need for improved roads. By the early twentieth century, however, life was becoming more complex. Even in remote ranching communities, government was playing a larger role in everyday life. Land titles, water rights, and livestock ownership came increasingly under the regulation of county and state officials. The local schools were pulled together into a countywide school district in 1914, and the demands of commerce required the construction of better roadways. A long way from Vernal and with little influence in area politics, north-slope residents became increasingly disenchanted with their county government.

This sense of frustration was evident in 1907 when the people of Lucerne Valley appealed to Uintah County for road construction funds. Like residents of many outlying rural communities, they believed that unless an election was imminent county officials ignored their needs. The Manila correspondent to the *Vernal Express* wrote:

> A petition has been circulated and will be sent to the county commissioners of Uintah county, asking for money to help build a road that has been lately decided upon and also asking for the pole [*sic*] tax to be spent on this road. It is hoped that the board will hear us. You always remember us when election comes; now you can help a much needed benefit to our county.[1]

Other area communities were becoming similarly disaffected. When the Utah legislature in 1913 created a process by which parts of existing counties could detach themselves and become new counties, the western portion of Uintah County moved quickly to form itself into Duchesne County. This success was not lost on the people of Manila, Linwood, Greendale, and Browns Park.

In 1916 the Uintah County Commission refused to appropriate seventy dollars to repair mudholes on north-slope roadways, and dissatisfaction in the affected communities reached the boiling point. Peter G. Wall brought together a group of several leading citizens to discuss separation from Uintah County. They decided to initiate the process that would result in self-government. For a new county to be formed, the law required that a majority of voters throughout Uintah

Charles F. Olson, first Daggett County Attorney. (Daggett County)

County approve the separation. Wall's group traveled to Vernal to enlist support, and they found that Ashley Valley's leaders were generally favorable to the proposition.[2]

The secession movement forged ahead. According to law, petitions were circulated, and the necessary signatures were submitted in May 1917. The issue went before the voters on 31 July. As expected, the vote for the new county was overwhelmingly favorable: voters in the area to be separated were unanimous in their approval, voting 74 to 0, and citizens in the remainder of Uintah County voted more than two to one in support of the proposition the actual count being 325 in favor and 156 against.

The next hurdle to be cleared was the formation of a county government. County officers had to be elected, the county seat determined, and a name chosen. Two names were proposed for the new county: one was Finch County in honor of George Finch, the county's oldest resident; the other was Daggett County, named for Ellsworth Daggett, the former Utah surveyor general and last surviving principal of the Lucerne Land and Water Company. In a fall election, voters chose the name Daggett for their county.

On 16 November 1917, Utah Secretary of State Harden Bennion, acting in the absence of Governor Simon Bamberger, proclaimed the creation of Daggett County, effective the first Monday of January 1918. The county's boundaries were to be the Wyoming border on the north, the Colorado border on the east, the 110th meridian on the west, and the crest of the Uinta Mountains on the south. The size of the county was about 544,000 acres, and it was assigned to the Second Judicial District of Utah. In December 1917, voters approved Manila as the county seat and elected a slate of officers that had run unopposed.[3]

Daggett County officially came into existence on 7 January 1918. No one in the area was legally qualified to administer oaths of office, so the officers-elect traveled to Ogden and were sworn in by Justice Arthur E. Pratt of the District Court. The county held its first commission meeting a few days later. According to the official minutes:

> The Board of County Commissioners duly elected and qualified for the newly created County [of] Daggett, State of Utah met this 16th day of Jan. 1918 at 11 O clock A.M. in room No. 4 in Manila School House, in the town of Manila, the newly created County Seat of Daggett County Utah.
>
> Those present were, George C. Rasmussen, Niels Pallesen, M.N. Larson Commissioners, of officers, elect for said County were present A.J.B. Stewart Clerk & Recorder, Daniel M. Nelson Assessor & Treasurer, Anciel T. Twitchell Sheriff and C.F. Olsen Attorney.[4]

Niels Pallesen, one of Daggett County's first commissioners with his wife Dora. (Daggett County)

The first order of business was to choose a board chairman. George Rasmussen nominated Marius N. Larsen, and Larsen was unanimously approved. The commission then proceeded to set a reg-

Sheep Creek Civilian Conservation Corps Camp. (Utah State Historical Society)

ular time and day for monthly meetings, establish a set order for handling business, and adopt rules for bringing motions to a vote. Dr. Fay W. Tinker was appointed "County Physician and Registrar of Vital Statistics," and the commissioners decided that they would also act as the Daggett County Board of Health. Location of a state road was discussed, and five representative school-board precincts were established and representatives appointed.[5]

Eight days later, the new commissioners experienced their first real taste of democracy in action. At their meeting of 24 January they were presented:

> A petition from citizens asking for reconsideration of the question of the school, the appointing of school officers and other business of the county, and asking the County Commission to consult the wishes of the people in making appointments.[6]

With Commissioner Pallesen dissenting, Commissioners Larsen and Rasmussen voted to reconsider the matter of the schools. The representative precincts for the county school board were revised and new board members appointed according to the wishes of the people.

Furthermore, citizens in the audience made it clear they had their own ideas about the location of the state road. Commissioner Rasmussen moved that the citizens present appoint a committee of four to assist the commission in choosing the route, and all three board members voted in approval. Though they had run unopposed in the election, the new commissioners found they did not have a free rein to act as they pleased. Strong-willed and independent, the citizenry had established itself as a strong voice in Daggett County affairs.[7]

The third meeting of the county commissioners was held in the office of the county clerk. This office was most likely set up in the small log addition built on the back of the old Town Hall. It was here that the Daggett County Commission would conduct meetings for the next four years. School business was handled, and then the board turned to the assessment of property:

> The classification of real and personal property, for assessment purposes was fixed as follows.

Farm Land with water from	$18.00 to $22.00	per acre.
Farm Land without water	7.00	" "
Grazing Land	3.00	" "
Waste Land	1.00	" "
Work Horses from	$50.00 to $100.00	per head
Range Horses	20.00	" "
Milk Cows	60.00	" "
Range Cattle	20.00	" "
Blooded Horses & Cattle	according to value.[8]	

The creation of the Daggett County School District on 24 January 1918 must have been especially gratifying to the people of the north slope. All of the small Uintah County school districts had been absorbed into a countywide district in 1914, and north-slope citizens lost direct oversight of their local schools. With the establishment of the new school district, Daggett County citizens regained control of local education. Five board members were appointed by the county commission to serve until the next general election. They were: Precinct 1, Henry Twitchell; Precinct 2, Elbert E. Waite; Precinct

Ute Mountain Fire Tower. (Utah State Historical Society)

3, A.J.B. Stewart; Precinct 4, Niels Pallesen; and Precinct 5, Charles F. Olson.

At its first meeting, the Daggett County School District instructed its clerk to procure the necessary minute and account books and to obtain an official seal. Board member Elbert E. Waite was chosen to travel to Vernal and arrange the transfer of school records from the Uintah School District.[9]

The new school district board began its work with vigor. It quickly decided that the Manila School, built only six years previously, had become inadequate. Board members planned an $8,000 bond issue to build a replacement, but first they needed to obtain a certified list of registered voters from Vernal. Unfortunately, officials in Uintah County dragged their feet, and the list did not arrive before election day. Plans for a new school had to be delayed.

The board also hired Paul C. Miner to be the first district superintendent and board clerk. Miner's administrative duties were light, and he continued to work primarily as a teacher. Administrative authority remained largely with the school board.[10]

Later that year, the district faced a difficult decision. The end of the sheep boom had sent the Linwood area into decline, and enrollment at the old stateline school had dropped. This situation was aggravated when Sweetwater County, Wyoming District 13, removed its students in 1910 and opened its own school at Washam. By the 1917–18 school year, enrollment at the Linwood School had dropped to only twenty pupils, and the Daggett County School District decided that the school must be closed. Linwood area students were sent to the Washam School in 1918–19, and in subsequent years they were bused to Manila in a Model-T Ford. The old Linwood School building, which was eventually bought by Thomas Jarvie, remained intact into the 1960s. Funds were also approved for a new school in Greendale in 1919. The Greendale School, built by local residents, opened two years later.[11]

As a new county, Daggett was entitled to its own seat in the Utah House of Representatives. The legislature made Daggett County the 29th Representative District of the State of Utah, and rancher Heber C. Bennion was elected the county's first representative. A newcomer to the area, Bennion had been a high school principal in Salt Lake City. He had suffered a severe bout of ill health, and doctors had advised him to move to the country. The thirty-year-old educator became the manager of his uncle's recently acquired ranch at Birch Springs, and he soon established his own homestead nearby. One of the county's most prominent citizens, Bennion served six terms in the legislature, became Utah Secretary of State, was an LDS bishop, held many county offices, and taught school in Manila.[12]

Organizing the county required a great deal of attention; however, for many area families, the young men they had sent off to fight in World War I were of much greater concern. News of the fighting drifted in throughout 1918, and when the toll was tallied, it was learned that four Daggett County men had given their lives in the "war to end all wars." Alonzo Finch of Linwood was killed in action, George Ralph Nelson of Manila succumbed to the deadly fighting of the Argonne forest, Keith Warby was killed in France delivering a message to another platoon, and Manford W. Hayes of Manila died of heart failure in Kemmerer, Wyoming.[13]

On the home front, the question of replacing the Manila School came up again in 1920. School board members approved another bond proposal, and this time the issue went before the voters. The

Bridge across the Green River damaged by heavy ice flow. (Friend B. Slote, U.S. Bureau of Reclamation).

matter was approved. Unfortunately, no buyers could be found for the bonds, so plans for a new school were again put on hold. Two years later, a bond issue was once again approved by the voters, and the George W. Vallory Company purchased the bonds for ninety cents on the dollar. Manila's children would finally get a new school.

The Green River Lumber Company contracted to build the facility for $13,932.50, and William C. Boren was hired to dig a tunnel and pipe in water. Located a block north of the old school, the new building was of frame construction with a stucco exterior. It had plaster interior walls, tongue-and-groove wooden floors, and was heated by two coal furnaces. It also contained classrooms, an office, a library, and a large room that served as both an auditorium and a recreation room. School classes opened in the new structure on 22 December 1922.[14]

The old Manila School, built by the Hastrup brothers in 1912, was no longer of use to the school district, but it was of interest to the county. For four years the county had operated out of the small addition built on the back of the Town Hall. The school building was much more spacious, and it was certainly more fitting for use as a county courthouse. At their meeting of 6 November 1922 the Daggett County Commission approved a resolution to offer the Daggett County School District $1,600 for the purchase of the old school and two town lots. The school district accepted the offer, and the old school was remodeled and became the Daggett County Courthouse following completion of the new school.[15]

Daggett County officials settled into their new quarters and continued the day-to-day business of county government. Because it was such a small, relatively unpopulated county, some of the traditional county offices were reorganized. During the 1920s, the positions of clerk, recorder, and treasurer were combined into one office; the county attorney doubled as the county surveyor; there was a county sheriff; and there was an assessor. Much of the county commission's time was used to approve county expenditures, oversee road construction and maintenance, handle assessment problems, and provide for the indigent. It also supervised an annual rodent-control effort nicknamed "Dog Day." Each year the state provided poison for the eradication of prairie dogs, and on Dog Day Daggett County farmers brought in grain to be treated with the poison. When they returned home, the farmers were supposed to put the poisoned grain on prairie dog mounds.

One of the thorniest problems facing Daggett County in its early years was the location of the county's southern border. The boundary between Daggett and Uintah counties had been set by the legislature at the watershed divide of the Uinta Mountains; however, in the

Paul Williams and Eleen Thompson, 1938. (Courtesy Pauleen Baker)

eastern portion of the range near Diamond Mountain, the divide was difficult to determine. At issue was which county could tax the large livestock herds that grazed on the disputed land. Uintah County challenged the border as originally determined, and the controversy ended up in the hands of the state engineer. This was the beginning of more than two decades of wrangling between the two county governments. The first ruling on the disputed area favored Daggett County, and the original boundaries were essentially kept intact. Uintah County, however, did not give up, and the dilemma was submitted again to the state engineer. The matter was eventually resolved in favor of the southern county, and Uintah County received a finger of land protruding northward into eastern Daggett County. The question seemed to be settled, but location of the eastern Uinta summit and the county boundaries remained a matter of contention for many years. It was not until the legislature in 1943 proclaimed the boundary in terms of specific township and section lines that the border dispute between Uintah and Daggett counties was finally laid to rest.[16]

Though the boundary question proved difficult for the new county, crime was not considered a serious problem. Law enforcement officers generally had a hands-off attitude regarding a great deal of local behavior. Drinking and fighting, especially at dances, were an accepted part of life in this rough-and-tumble ranching community. Bootlegging of alcohol during Prohibition was commonplace. Though local communities had voted overwhelmingly in favor of the "Noble Experiment" in a 1918 election, bootlegging was generally tolerated.[17] County Attorney Charles F. Olson was a strong supporter of the Volstead Act prohibiting the manufacture and consumption of liquor, but he found his attempts at prosecution thwarted. His son later recalled:

> Violation of the law became common. . . . Usually those breaking this law were not even arrested, much less prosecuted. It was common knowledge that one particular man was manufacturing alcoholic liquor. My father had the man arrested and brought to trial. A jury was impanelled, all the paraphernalia for making liquor was presented, witnesses testified, and none of the evidence was refuted, and yet the jury came in with "not guilty." . . . Father never did win much.[18]

On another occasion, Sheriff Edward Clarke brought the problem of bootlegging before the county commission. While bound to support Prohibition, it was clear that commissioners were not interested in aggressive enforcement of liquor laws. After they discussed the situation,

> it was agreed that while the matter should of course be controlled and the law upheld, it was advisable that the officers in charge have their actions in proper order so far as legal technicalities are concerned, that there might be no ill effects on the County.[19]

Health care, another concern of county government, was ably provided by Dr. Fay W. Tinker. Originally from Morrisville, Vermont, Tinker attended Jefferson Medical College in Philadelphia, completed his residency in Salt Lake City, and began his practice in the Green River-Rock Springs, Wyoming, area. His interest in ranching may have contributed to his decision to relocate to Daggett County. Around 1911, the young doctor and his wife, Mary, moved to Linwood, where for a year he supplemented his practice by teaching at the Linwood School. Mary Tinker taught at Linwood from 1914 to 1916 and continued to teach throughout the area into the 1930s. The couple eventually started a ranch south of Manila.

As a country doctor, Tinker was called out at all hours and had to travel by horseback or buggy in all kinds of weather, often for great distances. Working conditions were often difficult. Called to Burnt Fork during a blizzard, the doctor found a young boy who required a delicate mastoid operation. Travel was out of the question, so Tinker laid the boy out on the kitchen table and performed the operation by lamplight.

For all his skill and hard work, Fay Tinker was not a wealthy man. Many of his patients had very little money, and payment was often made in butter, eggs, or meat. His greatest riches were the respect and appreciation of those he helped. Besides serving the community as a physician, he held several county offices.[20]

In 1923 Fay Tinker, Keith Smith, and other area residents started the Lucerne Creamery Company. Smith was president of the company and owned more than two-thirds of the $6,000 worth of outstanding stock. To aid the venture, Harden Bennion, owner of the Birch Springs Ranch, sold the company an acre of land with a good spring of water for ten dollars. Clifford Christensen was sent to the

Lafayette "Lafe" Potter and Bill Williams, veterans of World War II. (Courtesy Pauleen Baker)

Utah Agricultural College in Logan to learn buttermaking, and a Mr. Triplett, a retired carpenter from Burnt Fork, was engaged to construct the creamery building.

Some of the equipment came from Fort Bridger. One of old Judge Carter's sons owned a defunct creamery, and the company purchased a large churn from him. The company also bought the ice box from the old army post. Only the pasteurizer had to be purchased new.

The company then obtained a railroad carload of milk cows to stock local farms. Local farmers and ranchers, many from the McKinnon, Wyoming, area, paid for the cows by having a portion of their cream check withheld by the company. Dr. Tinker also purchased a small milking herd. Regular cream checks provided an important source of cash to rural families. Elinore Pruitt Stewart of Burnt Fork, a celebrated author and "woman homesteader," recalled that when her family was in financial difficulty

> . . . Mr. Roeshclab and another friend, Mr. Keith Smith, Linwood, Utah, further took matters in hand and made arrangements whereby we became possessed of one share of creamery stock of a creamery then being started near. And four thoroughbred Holstein cows. . . . Clyde's recovery was rapid. . . . He went out on the country road and worked until he had enough to purchase nine more cows. All Holsteins. They've all had calves and some of the original four have twice had calves. Little by little we are getting things together for a real try—I did the milking while he was on the road and until I was hurt we both milked. We milk eight cows.[21]

Keith Smith kept the books for the company and marketed the butter. Most was sold in Green River and Rock Springs; the rest was packed in ice and shipped to Los Angeles. For nineteen years, the Lucerne Creamery was an important part of the local economy. It survived the Depression and was looking forward to a profitable future. Unfortunately, in an effort to economize, the company never carried insurance. When the creamery burned in 1944 there was no money to rebuild and operations ended. Keith Smith recalled, "The only bright spot was that I was relieved of all the book work and the job of selling butter."[22]

Agriculture dominated Daggett County's economy. Farm size in the county averaged 504 acres in 1920, well above the state average farm size of 196 acres. Area livestock that year was counted at 462

Well Baby Clinic at the old courthouse in Manila. From Left to Right: Delliah Anson, Elaine Alameda, Ida Bennett, Chloe Potter, Agnes Briggs, Thelma Biorn, Phoebe Twitchell, Lena Schofield. (Daggett County)

horses, 12 mules, 2,066 cattle (63 of which were dairy cows), and 8,269 sheep. Some potatoes were planted, and there were a few orchard crops from the forty-seven fruit trees counted in the agricultural census, but , of the $94,178 value of all crops, $76,649 was in forage crops. This, though important to the county's economy, was just a tiny fraction of the state's total value of $58 million for agricultural crops in 1920.[23]

Despite a national agricultural depression in the early 1920s, the local farming economy rebounded and was robust by the end of the decade. There was an increase in the number of farms in the county—from thirty-seven in 1920 to fifty-four in 1930—and an increase in the number of acres farmed—from 18,665 acres in 1920 to 24,832 acres in 1930. The average size of county farms declined slightly to 477, but this was still more than twice the state average farm size of 206 acres.

Farmers also purchased new labor-saving machinery. Between 1920 and 1930, the value of farm implements in the county rose from $25,775 to $47,005. This modest prosperity was reflected in the county's population, which increased slightly during the 1920s from 400 to 411. In 1930 the Manila area had twenty-four farms; there were eleven farms in the Linwood area and ten farms in the Antelope area. The other sections of the county had seven farms.[24]

Though times were somewhat better, life on Daggett County's farms and ranches remained difficult. Except for the occasional dance or special occasion, there was very little recreation, organized or otherwise. Work was ongoing. Virginia Bennion Buchanan commented:

> We lived in a strange no-man's land between the past and the future. Civilization was already full-steam into the motor age, yet off the beaten path the primitive frontier still lived. . . .
>
> My father plowed the stubborn sage brush, harrowed it, piled it for burning. He dug a ditch spade-deep and spade wide from the main ditch down the hill to the farms and alfalfa fields. It was soon a small creek. He dug ditches everywhere by hand. . . . He hauled logs down from the mountain, a dangerous occupation because of the heavy loads on precarious mountain roads, and unpredictable horses. It took many loads for the house, corrals and fences, and mother always walked the floor during his 2-day mountain trips. . . .
>
> Pioneering was hardest on her. Besides the exhaustive household drudgery with no conveniences, the battle against gummy clay mud, washing on a board—in winter, melting snow water first—she suffered pioneer loneliness and isolation, being "stuck over there for months without seeing a soul but the family and hired man."[25]

Ranch work was varied, and the year was marked by large seasonal tasks. Spring was the time for calving, lambing, and sheep shearing. It was also the time to prepare ground for gardens, forage crops, and perhaps a field of potatoes. During the summer, livestock were moved up the mountain to high pastures, and ranchers turned to putting up hay for winter feed.

Haying was one of the most labor-intensive tasks on the old-time ranches. Both native grass and alfalfa were grown, and it took a crew to cut, haul, and stack the crop. Most ranchers owned a horse-drawn mowing machine. Mowers demanded a lot from a team, and green horses were often trained for work on the machines. Whether they were green or not, mowing, or any other work with horses, could be a hazardous business. In 1927 Elinore Pruitt Stewart was severely injured while driving a mower. She wrote:

July 24, 1947—the centennial of the arrival of the Mormon pioneers in Utah. Rita Twitchell, Eutona Briggs, and Reva Potter. (Courtesy Pauleen Baker)

> I had gone out with a team and a mower to cut some alfalfa for the hogs. . . . Suddenly an owl flew up from almost under the horses and struck against the head of one of them. They leaped forward and struck a small ditch with such violence that I was thrown from the seat, I held the lines, of course, and my fall jerked them so that the horses backed the mower over me. They were thoroughly frightened but they turned in the way they should have had they been mowing but that brought the eight hundred pound mower back over me and one of the horses stepped on me. . . . Three ribs broken, a cracked shoulder blade and, worse than anything a spread thorax . . . the unfeeling doctor pronounced doom when he said I could not work for a year. . . . All this is foolishness. I cannot possibly lay off for a year.[26]

After the hay was mowed, it was raked into rows, or shocks, allowed to cure for a day or two, loaded on a wagon, and hauled to the stack. Some area ranches put up hay with a wooden stacker called a "beaver slide," but most seem to have looped a rope around the load and rolled the hay off the wagon into the stack yard. Whichever method was used, haying was a big job that took its toll on both people and horses, and it could last for weeks.

Late summer and fall brought the grain harvest and threshing. Most of the farms and ranches grew a certain amount of feed grain, and it ripened in the summer heat. Grain was cut with a horse-drawn binder. This machine cut the grain, bunched it, and then tied the bunches with twine to form tight bundles. The bundles were eventually hauled by wagon and stacked to await the threshers.

In the early days, the threshing machines were powered by sweep horsepowers. Mounted on wheels so they could be pulled from farm to farm, horsepowers consisted of a large iron bull-gear mounted to a wooden frame. As many as seven wooden poles were inserted in pockets cast into the gear, and a team of horses was hitched to each pole. The driver stood in the center atop the device, and the horses walked in a circle as they provided power to the thresher. Wooden tumbling shafts and universal joints transmitted the power from the sweep horsepower to the threshing machine. In later years, steam engines or tractors powered the threshers using long rubberized canvas belts.

An enterprising individual generally purchased the threshing rig; he threshed his own grain and then sold his services to several neighbors. When the rig arrived at a farm or ranch, the threshing machine was set up between the grain stacks. Family members and neighbors provided the labor as the bundles were pitched into the thresher. The straw and chaff was blown out the back of the machine into a stack, and the grain was run out of an augur and put into sacks.

The approach of cold weather brought the fall roundup. Livestock was gathered on the mountains and driven back down to the lower pastures. During winter, the cattle were fed from the stacked hay, and repairs might be made on harnesses and machinery. It was often a time for cutting and hauling fence poles and posts.

There were also a myriad of other jobs that were fit in as work allowed. Fences had to be built and mended, there were ditches to be dug and maintained, firewood needed to be cut and hauled, and corrals and buildings had to be repaired and constructed. In addition, ranchers often took jobs to bring in extra cash. They might hire out to a nearby ranch, teach school, use their wagons to haul freight, or work on the county roads. A few owned small sawmill operations that marketed lumber to the local community. When men were away

Two young girls in pioneer dress in front of the Manila School during the 1947 Pioneer Centennial Celebration. (Courtesy Pauleen Baker)

at work, women and children were expected to take care of the ranch in addition to their regular chores.

Life could also be hard for those who lived in town, but it had more conveniences and there was more social life. Besides a school and an LDS chapel, Manila boasted of a store and a gas station by the late 1920s. The old Town Hall, where the store was housed, continued to be the social center of the community. Willard Schofield had purchased the structure from Peter G. Wall, and he operated a number of enterprises within its walls. His grandson wrote:

> On the east side, which was a lean-to structure of some proportions, Willard had a store which supplied groceries, hardware, harnesses, candy, etc. In one end of the store was the post office with Willard as postmaster and in an adjoining room on the southwest corner was the barbershop with Willard's son-in-law Edward Boren, as barber.
>
> Along the barbershop wall on the north side of the room were several pool tables for the entertainment of the customers, operated by Bill Potter. The remainder of the Town Hall was utilized

as a large dance hall with a small triangular bandstand in the southeast corner.[27]

Schofield freighted his own merchandise to the store and also traded in various farm commodities and livestock. For a time in the mid-1920s, William Grothe showed movies in the Town Hall with a hand-cranked projector. These were the first motion pictures to be shown in Manila.[28]

As the 1920s ended and the 1930s began, life, which had always been difficult in Daggett County, got even harder. On 3 December 1929 the Daggett County Clerk was instructed to report that "at the present time there were almost no unemployed in this County owing to heavy crops, and belated road work." However, by 1931 the effects of the Great Depression were beginning to be felt throughout the region. J. Kent Olson, who had been living in Evanston, Wyoming, lost his job on the Union Pacific Railroad. He recalled that:

> During this time, no one paid taxes, principle, interest or any other liabilities. Everything was stagnant, and at a standstill. Money almost stopped circulating. No one could borrow any money. No one would lend any.[29]

Under such adverse economic conditions, country folk fared somewhat better than their city cousins. On a ranch or farm in Daggett County, a family could at least raise its own food and cut timber and firewood on the public land. J. Kent Olson was able to trade his house in town for the old family ranch near Antelope, and he and his young bride moved back to the land.

During these dark days, work on the county roads became a form of government assistance. Daggett County wages for road work were raised to three dollars per day for a man and five dollars per day for a man and a team. In December, L.W. Beason, district engineer for the Utah State Road Commission, met with the Daggett County Commission to discuss road work for the unemployed. He suggested that the local committee of unemployment give a list of the unemployed to the road supervisor and that work be distributed evenly among those in need.[30]

There was only so much road work that could be done. Those who had borrowed money or had purchased machinery on credit

Beaver pelts being prepared by Paul, Emmett and Barbara Williams in 1947. (Courtesy Pauleen Baker)

suffered severe losses. Remembering the Depression, the daughter of Heber Bennion wrote about it and about her father:

> There came a day when the sheep herd was gone, along with the cattle and horses. The beautiful red thresher, stacker, binder, and tractor were taken away. That fall of 1932 he walked off the homestead and joined us in Salt Lake. He helped organize a self-help group which saw us and many others through the winter.[31]

In addition to the county's economic woes, it also lost its only doctor. Fay W. Tinker had become sick and was no longer able to practice. He was eventually taken to the hospital in Rock Springs, where he succumbed, at age forty-nine, after a long illness. Funeral services were held in Manila on 20 June 1933.[32]

The year 1933 also saw the inauguration of Franklin D. Roosevelt as president of the United States. Though Daggett County had gone against the national trend and voted an almost straight Republican ticket, Roosevelt and his fellow Democrats had swept the 1932 elections. They had a clear mandate to take strong governmental action against the economic woes being caused by the Great Depression. During its first few months in office, hoping to alleviate the nation's problems, the Roosevelt administration pushed through a number of new programs. Roosevelt's massive reform movement, the New Deal, not only provided relief for millions from immediate suffering but also attempted to remedy the underlying causes that had brought on the Depression. A myriad of new government agencies sprang into existence.[33]

The New Deal came to Daggett County later that year. Federal loans were made available to the people of the county, and the county commission recommended that Marius Larsen, already the chairman of the Daggett County Unemployment Committee, become agent for the new programs. Not long after, the commission discussed the establishment of a school-lunch program. According to the minutes, "Mr. Norton met with the Board at this time taking up the matter of serving foods to the school children, and stated that there were a number of the students in need of added nourishment." The school home economics teacher and class were instructed to prepare and serve hot soup and milk to the children, and funding was provided by the governor's Committee on Relief and State Welfare and administered by the Daggett County Relief Commission.[34]

Despite the beginning of widespread government relief programs, even harder times came in 1934. The early 1930s had been dry years, but drought hit especially hard in 1934. Rancher J. Kent Olson wrote:

> That winter [of 1933–34] came and went and left us with little or no moisture. The summer that followed was also dry. This was the year of the dryest this country had ever seen. This year was also the depth of the Great Depression. . . . In that year, a ton of hay was worth more than a cow, so we sold our hay instead of buying any cows.[35]

While the Olsons were mastering the art of living without money, Heber Bennion and his family were fighting to rebuild their ranch. In bad health and without any assets, Bennion had hitched a ride back from Salt Lake City in the spring of 1933. According to his daughter, "The neighbors, shocked at his appearance, said 'Heber Bennion has come back to die;' but he had come back to live." Bennion repaired a broken tractor and started plowing. His wife won fifty dollars in a quilt contest, and that was enough to buy seventeen

The Biorn Sawmill on Carter Creek, 1960. (Daggett County)

old ewes—the beginning of a new flock. With grit, determination, and a little luck, the Bennions began to put their lives back together.[36]

If there was good news for the people of Daggett County in 1934, it was the establishment of Manila Camp DF-35 of the Civilian Conservation Corps (CCC). This federal program was a quasi-military operation that enlisted unemployed young men throughout the nation for work on conservation projects, generally on public land. Many who served at the Manila camp were from Daggett County and the three-corners region. The camp, located along Sheep Creek, was occupied by Company 1965 on 13 October 1934. Camp buildings and walkways were arranged to form the shape of a pine tree. Captain Vernon Peterson, an officer in the U.S. Cavalry Reserve, commanded the camp, John S. Bennett was the work superintendent, and First Lieutenant Martin Leichter, another reserve officer, was camp surgeon.

The young corpsmen enlisted for six-month periods, and could subsequently reenlist. Besides room and board at the various camps, they were paid a monthly wage of thirty dollars, twenty-five of which was sent home to their families. The remaining five dollars a month was theirs to spend for personal items and recreation, and this spending was of great economic benefit to merchants in towns near the camps. In addition, a number of older residents of the areas, called "local experienced men" (LEMs), were often hired to help direct and supervise various projects.

Throughout the first winter and into 1935, the Manila camp's men were engaged in a number of work projects on the Ashley National Forest. They built a ranger station at Summit Springs, worked on roads and trails, built telephone lines, and improved their own camp. One of their larger projects was the construction of a suspension bridge over the Green River. Six feet wide with a 252-foot span, the structure was made of creosoted timber and could carry twenty-five head of cattle at a time.[37]

The greatest contribution of the CCC men was in the area of forest road construction. Theirs was the task of constructing the scenic road up Sheep Creek Canyon to Summit Springs. When completed, this gravel road supplanted the perilous switchbacks on the Manila-Vernal highway. Such heavy construction work, however, could be dangerous, and two young men were killed building a road west of the Green River. In March 1935, a CCC crew from the Manila camp was working on the Hideout road project in the Ashley National Forest. Without warning, an overhead rock ledge gave way and crushed Edward Bailey of Ferron, Utah, and O'Dell Thomas of Salt Lake City. Miraculously, several other enrollees working nearby escaped serious injury. An investigation determined that the ledge had been gradually undermined by erosion and probably had been loosened by nearby blasting. The bodies of the young men were taken to a mortuary in Rock Springs and shipped home by railroad.[38]

Life in the CCC was not all work and danger. The camp had extensive recreational programs for off-duty enrollees. There were pool tables, table tennis, a camp newspaper, occasional beer parties, and a regular schedule of movies. Basketball and baseball teams from the camp traveled throughout the area to compete against teams from neighboring communities.

One of the most important of the camp officials was the camp surgeon, Lieutenant Martin Leichter. He handled the camp's sick and injured, regularly gave medical advice in the camp newspaper, and

The Daggett County Courthouse, 1997. (Allan Kent Powell)

provided medical services throughout the county. Leichter and his successors assisted in the births of several Daggett County residents during the 1930s. With the exception of Daggett County public health nurse Mabel Philbrick, who was appointed in 1935, the doctor at the CCC camp was the only medical practitioner between the Uinta Mountains and the Union Pacific Railroad. When the Manila CCC Camp finally closed in 1940, the *Salt Lake Tribune* ran an article with the headline, "Manila Faces Grim Winter, With Doctor 50 Miles Away."[39] Emergency treatment and minor care were all that was available locally, and most serious illnesses were treated at the hospital in Rock Springs, Wyoming, as were births to area residents, who tried to prepare by traveling to the hospital when the delivery date drew near.

The men of Manila Camp DF-35 of the Civilian Conservation Corps did a great deal of good for Daggett County and the Ashley National Forest in the camp's more than five years of operation. Not only did they construct numerous roads, ranger stations, and other facilities, they improved themselves through hard work and discipline, and the money they sent home was a godsend to their

Depression-stricken families. In an edition of the Manila Camp newspaper, one enrollee offered his assessment of the CCC:

> From the practical standpoint, who knows how many men have been saved their self-respect . . . ; how many men who have had leanings to Communism have been made to see the advantages of good government; or how many have actually been saved from crime as a means of providing for their loved ones. The C.C.C. is an institution of which the United States may well be proud.[40]

As the 1930s progressed, New Deal programs had an even greater effect on life in the county. During the twenty-eight-month period from October 1933 to February 1936, fresh apples (1,000 pounds), canned beef, mutton, and veal (2,687 pounds), butter, cheese, flour, evaporated milk, smoked pork, rice, and other foodstuffs were distributed in the county. In addition, in the same period, nineteen blankets, twenty-eight comforters, twelve mattresses, ninety-six hand towels, and sixty-nine wool coats were distributed. From August 1932 to February 1936 the county received $86.17 per capita in federal aid, which was above the state average assistance per person of $67.32.[41]

The entire second floor of the county courthouse was eventually occupied by New Deal welfare and public-works programs. The Works Progress Administration (WPA), the Civil Works Administration (CWA), and the Federal Emergency Relief Agency (FERA) were all active in the area. In Manila, these agencies developed two new water tunnels and laid water pipe through town. They also graded and graveled local streets, laid out a park, and planted trees as windbreaks.[42]

The Taylor Grazing Act of 1934 brought change to Daggett County's ranch lands. The act promulgated regulations and fees for grazing on the public domain, much like those already in place on the national forests. Unreserved public lands were finally closed to settlement, and grazing rights were leased to stockmen under a system of permits and fees. Local grazing boards, made up of area ranchers, oversaw the administration of the system. Rancher Keith Smith commented:

> In 1936 Helen and I drove together to a number of meetings concerning the U.S. Bureau of Land Management which was being

> formed by the Secretary of the Interior to protect the range against overgrazing. I became a member of the Advisory Board for our district, and along with Am Nebeker, represented the sheep men in Daggett County. The regular meetings were held in Vernal and were followed two weeks later by an appeal meeting. I suggested that we change the chairman each year, alternating from a sheep-man to a cattleman to keep the board as fair as possible, and this was adopted.[43]

Daggett County and the nation gradually rebounded from the devastating effects of the Great Depression. By the late 1930s, Manila was the home of two new stores, two service stations, and a hotel; and a new school had been opened at Bridgeport. Improved roads had enabled the establishment of daily mail service. Ranchers began to ship livestock by truck, eliminating long drives to the railroad. Improved roads also facilitated growth in the timber industry.[44]

Improved roads and the development of the truck made it possible to ship lumber from the Uinta Mountains to the railroad towns of Green River and Rock Springs. This opened new markets for Daggett County timber. In 1938, Lawrence Biorn and Ren South moved their families and small sawmill operation from Idaho to the Manila area. A year or so later, the South family moved on, but the Biorn family stayed. For almost twenty years, their sawmill provided props and wedges for the Union Pacific coal mines at Rock Springs.[45]

Natural gas production also began about this time in the county's northeastern corner at Clay Basin. The field had been discovered on the Keith Smith ranch in 1927 by geologist Glen Mathew Ruby, and a test well found gas in the Frontier Formation at a depth of 5,375 feet. Commercial production, however, did not occur until Mountain Fuel Supply Company took over the field and found much more gas some 250 feet deeper in the Dakota Formation. A workers camp grew around the site, production began in 1937, and gas royalties were soon being paid to the Smith family. By 1940, tents and tarpaper shacks at the camp had been replaced by frame houses, and a small elementary school had been opened by the Daggett County School District.[46]

In addition, the 1930s saw the beginnings of the M & L Homemakers Club. This longstanding organization was rooted in efforts of Wyoming's Sweetwater County Extension Agent Ray B. Noondyke to develop girls' sewing and cooking clubs in the Washam-Linwood area. His work resulted in the establishment of local 4-H activities and the inauguration of women's homemaking clubs. With members in both the Manila and Linwood areas, it was named the M & L Extension Homemakers Club. Meetings were held on the first Friday of each month.

By 1933, the club was firmly established with a strong membership. Programs touched on all areas of home management, including such topics as sanitation in the home, control of flies and bacteria, "The Charming Hostess," and "Cleaning and Repairing of Furniture." In 1939 the M & L club joined five similar clubs to form the Sweetwater County Council of Homemakers Clubs. Though based in Utah, the club continued to affiliate itself with its Wyoming neighbors and remained under the auspices of the University of Wyoming Extension Service.[47]

The spirit of civic improvement continued as the Manila LDS Ward began renovation of its chapel. After years of dealing with mud and water, the membership decided to move the building out of "the swamp" and remodel it. The chapel was painstakingly lifted off its foundation and moved two blocks to drier ground. Additions were made, and on 10 July 1938 Apostle Melvin J. Ballard dedicated the remodeled structure. According to local tradition, some members in attendance claimed to have heard a "heavenly choir" singing during the service. After Ballard returned from his trip to Manila, the *Salt Lake Telegram* reported:

> Melvin J. Ballard, member of the council of twelve apostles of the L.D.S. church, Wednesday returned from Manila, Utah-which he termed as "one of the most out of the way places I have ever seen"—where he officiated at the dedication of a $20,000 chapel, which he said was paid for by members and non-members of the church.[48]

Daggett County also finally was able to experience the wonders of electricity. Nels Philbrick installed a diesel generator to run equipment in his garage. Wires were strung, and Philbrick was soon providing power to the Manila School and other nearby buildings.

Although the CCC camp and a few other places in the county also had small electric light plants, Philbrick was the first to supply electricity to the public.[49]

As the 1930s neared their close, the effects of New Deal programs and the outbreak of war in Europe with its increased demand for U.S. goods and farm products brought the Great Depression to an end. Hard work, a bit of luck, and federal assistance had helped county residents rebuild their lives and businesses. In fact, by the end of the decade, federal projects had left Daggett County a much better place to live. Parks, water systems, and streets had been built, and the CCC had constructed roads and other facilities in the national forest. County population in 1940 was 546 people, up substantially from the 411 counted in the 1930 census. The Rural Electrification Administration, another federal program started as part of the New Deal, eventually aided in the extension of power lines to Daggett County in the early 1950s. All in all, Franklin D. Roosevelt's Depression-era programs left a very valuable legacy for the people of Daggett County.

Unlike the previous decade, the onset of the 1940s promised prosperity. However, it was not long until the Japanese sneak attack on Pearl Harbor embroiled the nation in World War II. Many Daggett County men enlisted, and other county residents moved away to work in Wyoming's mines or at defense plants in California. Keith Smith, chairman of the county's draft board, recalled drafting fifty-five men into the nation's armed forces, and sixty-one (about one-third of the county's total able-bodied men) reportedly served in the war, three of whom—Roy Nelson, William Pallesen, and Lafayette Potter—were killed.[50]

With so many people called away, a labor shortage developed, and local men and women had to work even harder on the county's ranches and businesses. Higher farm profits did facilitate the purchase of tractors and other labor-saving machinery. Although the war years did bring some increased material prosperity, surprisingly, the county population actually declined by over one-third during the decade—from 546 to 350.

County residents, like other Americans, coped with the hardships of war, including rationing of foods and other commodities. Jokes were even made about some of the allotments officially prescribed to the sparsely populated county, one example being when a ration of half a tire was allotted.

In Daggett County and elsewhere in rural America, World War II ushered in another round of agricultural consolidation. Many rural people moved to new higher-paying jobs in the cities. With tractors and other machinery, those who stayed on the land became more productive and enlarged their holdings. The result in Daggett County was a smaller but more prosperous population.

In spite of the Great Depression and World War II, life in the county remained largely unchanged. Agriculture continued to be the mainstay of the local economy. As LDS apostle Melvin Ballard had stated, the county was still a very out-of-the-way place. It hosted few visitors, and most residents liked it that way.

However, as the war ended and the world entered the atomic age, a revolution was on the horizon. The federal government was once again ready to turn its energies toward the development of western resources. Engineers and bureaucrats dusted off old reports that had been shelved during the war and renewed plans to harness the giant Colorado River system. Their efforts would eventually alter the landscape of the three-corners region and bring fundamental changes to the lives of Daggett County's people.

ENDNOTES

1. *The Vernal Express,* 2 March 1907.

2. Dick Dunham and Vivian Dunham, *Flaming Gorge Country,* 318–19.

3. *Inventory of the County Archives of Utah, no.5 Daggett County,* 11; Daggett County Commission Minutes, 7 January 1918, Daggett County Offices, Manila, Utah.

4. Daggett County Commission Minutes, 16 January 1918.

5. Ibid., 16 January 1918.

6. Ibid., 24 January 1918.

7. Ibid.

8. Ibid., 4 February 1918.

9. Donald Weir Baxter, "The History of Public Education in Daggett County," 67.

10. Ibid., 68, 69.

11. Ibid., 50, 59, 68.

12. "Homesteading in the 1920s was Rugged, Too," *Kansas City Times*, 31 May 1962.

13. Journal History, Church of Jesus Christ of Latter-day Saints, 13 June 1920, LDS Church Archives.

14. Baxter, "Public Education in Daggett County," 69.

15. Daggett County Commission Minutes, 6 November 1922.

16. Ibid., 18 September 1924; Dunham and Dunham, *Flaming Gorge Country*, 320; Journal History, 13 June 1920.

17. Utah Secretary of State Election Papers, 1918 Election Returns, Series 00364, microfilm, Utah State Archives, Salt Lake City.

18. J. Kent Olson, *Never Marry a Rancher*, 33.

19. Daggett County Commission Minutes, 4 August 1931.

20. *Salt Lake Tribune*, 25 June 1933; Dunham and Dunham, *Flaming Gorge Country*, 311–12; Baxter, "Public Education in Daggett County," 52, 55.

21. Susanne K. George, *The Adventures of the Woman Homesteader: The Life and Letters of Elinore Pruitt Stewart* (Lincoln: University of Nebraska Press, 1992), 130, 131.

22. Keith Smith, "Recollections," 45.

23. Department of Commerce, Bureau of the Census, *Fourteenth Census of the United States: 1920, Agriculture* vol. 1, 1920 (Washington, D.C.: Department of Interior, 1924), 54–55, 60.

24. Ibid., 12; Department of Commerce, Bureau of the Census, *Fifteenth Census of the United States: 1930, Agriculture* (Washington, D.C.: U.S. Government Printing Office, 1931), 1:633. Statistically, Daggett County was one of fifteen counties in the state that experienced an increase in the number of farms during the decade of the 1920s. The county led the state with the highest percentage increase in the number of farms.

25. "Homesteading," *Kansas City Times*, 31 May 1962.

26. George, *Adventures of Eleanor Pruitt Stewart*, 128–29.

27. Kerry Ross Boren, "Manila's Old Town Hall," unidentified news clipping in author's collection.

28. Boren, "Manila's Town Hall"; Ora Schofield Iverson, journal excerpt in author's collection.

29. Daggett County Commission Minutes, 3 December 1929; Olson, *Never Marry a Rancher*, 50.

30. Daggett County Commission Minutes, 1 December 1931.

31. "Homesteading," *Kansas City Times,* 31 May 1962.

32. "Fay W. Tinker," *Salt Lake Tribune,* 25 June 1933.

33. Utah Secretary of State Election Papers, Series 000364, microfilm, Utah State Archives.

34. Daggett County Commission Minutes, 7 November 1933, 13 November 1933.

35. Olson, *Never Marry a Rancher,* 60.

36. "Homesteading," *Kansas City Times,* 31 May 1962.

37. "Pinon O Pinon," news bulletin of CCC Company 1965, 21 December 1934, Utah State Historical Society Library.

38. "Pinon O Pinon," 23 March 1935.

39. *Salt Lake Tribune,* 17 November 1940.

40. "Pinon O Pinon," 21 December 1934.

41. Engineering Department, Works Division, Utah Emergency Relief Program, "Statistical Summary of Expenditures and Accomplishments, Utah Emergency Relief Program, 1936," 10, Utah State Historical Society. Tooele County received $92.33 per capita, the highest in the state, and Box Elder County received $37.20 per capita, the lowest in the state.

42. M.N. Larsen, "History of Daggett County," manuscript, Utah State Historical Society), 5; *Inventory of County Archives, Daggett County,* 10.

43. Smith, "Recollections," 51.

44. *Inventory of County Archives, Daggett County,* 9–10; Baxter, "History of Public Education," 37; Kouris, *Brown's Park,* 233–34.

45. Thelma Biorn, "History of Lawrence Paul Biorn and Thelma Edgington Biorn," manuscript in author's collection.

46. Smith, "Recollections," 45; Baxter, "History of Public Education," 41; "A Look at Clay Basin," typescript in author's collection.

47. Mary J. Ruble, "Our Club is Born," manuscript in author's collection.

48. Journal History, 10 July 1938.

49. Dunham and Dunham, *Flaming Gorge Country,* 326; *Inventory of County Archives, Daggett County,* 10.

50. Dunham and Dunham, *Flaming Gorge Country,* 329.

CHAPTER 9

FLAMING GORGE DAM AND RESERVOIR

> Like most battles over the environment, there were no winners or losers, only bargainers. In order to save Echo Park and, by extension, the national park system, another canyon had to be sacrificed . . . the only loss in the case of the Flaming Gorge Dam, it seemed, was to a few ranchers, farmers, and sheepmen.
>
> —ROY WEBB

Flaming Gorge Dam redefined life in Daggett County. To some it is an engineering miracle that transformed a remote corner of the West into a national playground. Others mourn the loss of the freeflowing Green River and its beautiful canyons, and a few still bristle over the federal taking of homes and ranches. For good or ill, this massive project has changed the landscape, economy, and way of life in the three-corners area. Its story is a complex tale of power politics, the national parks, and America's growing preservation movement. If any number of things had happened differently, the dam might never have been built.

Flaming Gorge Dam, like most of the great western water projects, traces its origins to the Newlands Reclamation Act of 1902.

An artist's rendering of the completed Flaming Gorge Dam. (Utah State Historical Society)

Sponsored by Representative Francis G. Newlands of Nevada, the act was a concession to angry westerners who, incensed by growing regulation of the public lands, wanted federal lands given to the states. Instead, Newlands proposed that funds generated by the sale of public lands be put into a revolving fund for construction of "reclamation projects to irrigate the arid lands."[1] The act was passed by Congress, and it mollified western interests.

A few weeks after the passage of the Newlands Act, the Reclamation Service was established as a division of the U.S. Geological Survey. In its first few years of existence, the service moved quickly to survey potential western dam sites. It proposed the construction of a dam about a half mile below the mouth of Henrys Fork in 1904. Three years later, its engineers also surveyed the Gates of Lodore for a dam that, had it been built, would have flooded Browns Park. Work continued in 1914 and 1915 as Reclamation Service crews took drill samples at the Henrys Fork location and at a site near the mouth of Horseshoe Canyon.[2]

Aerial View of Dutch John while Flaming Gorge Dam was under construction. (United States Bureau of Reclamation)

Private industry also showed interest in developing the Green River. Utah Power and Light Company sent an expedition down the river in 1917 to study streamflow and possible dam sites.[3] It identified Flaming Gorge as one of several potential dam locations, and it received a preliminary permit from the Federal Power Commission (FPC) to further investigate the site.[4] When the company attempted to secure a permanent permit for a dam at Flaming Gorge, interstate rivalries over the division of Colorado River water halted the process. The FPC was precluded from issuing the permit until the seven basin states ratified an agreement allocating the streamflow. Even Utah's governor reluctantly opposed issuance of the permit. Appearing before a U.S. Senate committee in 1925, Governor George H. Dern stated:

> The Utah Power and Light Co. is ready, willing, and anxious to build a great dam at Flaming Gorge. We want that sort of development. It means plenty of electrical power for all our present

Dutch John Family Store and Post Office, c. 1960. (United States Bureau of Reclamation)

> needs, and it will develop a remote section of our state and increase our taxable wealth. And yet we are opposed to that development until we are assured that the water impounded at Flaming Gorge . . . can not be permanently annexed by somebody on the lower river.[5]

Since the end of World War I, the states sharing the drainage system of the Colorado River—Wyoming, Colorado, Utah, Arizona, Nevada, New Mexico, and California—had been feuding over the division of water from the river. California prompted the debate when it sought federal funding for a storage project on the Colorado River. The river had been used to irrigate several hundred thousand acres in the Palo Verde and Imperial valleys prior to World War I, and Californians were eager to put even more irrigated land into production.[6] Fearing that extensive California development, under the legal practice of prior appropriation (first in time, first in right), would give California a vested right in Colorado River water, the other Colorado River Basin states opposed the project.

In November 1922, after extensive state and local debate, representatives of the seven states met in Santa Fe, New Mexico. Their task

Barracks Buildings at Dutch John, c. 1960. (United States Bureau of Reclamation)

was to work out an equitable agreement that would divide the flow of the Colorado River system. The agreement, known as the Colorado River Compact, split the river's flow equally between the upper-basin states of Wyoming, Colorado, Utah, and New Mexico and the lower-basin states of Nevada, Arizona, and California. Each basin received a right to beneficially develop 7,500,000 acre-feet of water. The Colorado River Compact and the resultant Colorado River Commission were heralded as a major advance in interstate cooperation that would "remove causes of present and future controversies."[7]

The representatives at the Santa Fe conference, however, found little cooperation when they submitted the compact to their respective state legislatures for ratification. The allocation of Colorado River waters remained locked in controversy, and it was not until 1940 that all seven of the affected states finally approved the agreement. In the interim, Utah, Wyoming, Colorado, and New Mexico held preliminary discussions toward the formation of a compact among the upper-basin states.

Reclamation plans were sidetracked during World War II; but, in

Mrs. H. C. (Duke) Miller hanging her washing at the base of the canyon wall that became the abutment for Flaming Gorge Dam. The Millers lived in the trailer while Duke Miller was in charge of drilling tunnels for the dam. March 1959. (Friend B. Slote, United States Bureau of Reclamation).

March 1946 the Bureau of Reclamation submitted a report on Colorado River development to the affected states and various federal agencies. In 1947 Secretary of the Interior J.A. Krug transmitted the report to Congress. The Krug Report contained the basic features

Carol Ann Rosling, the three and a half year-old daughter of Mr. and Mrs. Arnold H. Rosling, sweeps snow away from their home in Dutch John in February 1959. (Friend B. Slote, United States Bureau of Reclamation)

of what would become the Colorado River Storage Project (CRSP), but it did not recommend congressional approval of specific projects. Instead, it suggested that the states settle their differences and proceed to determine their respective water rights.[8]

Utah and the other upper-basin states took the initiative by reviving earlier efforts to negotiate a water-allocation compact. Created in

Members of the Bureau of Reclamation Police Force at Dutch John. (Friend B. Slote, United States Bureau of Reclamation)

October 1948, the Upper Colorado River Basin Compact was approved by Congress in 1949. The agreement permitted Utah to divert 1,322,000 acre-feet of the annual yield of the upper basin. With this new compact in place, planning for the proposed Colorado River Storage Project could continue.

Not everyone was ecstatic over the Colorado River Storage Project. Considerable opposition developed among the lower-basin states of the Colorado River Commission, and conflicts between Arizona and California further complicated the situation. There was also disagreement, particularly in California and Nevada, over water granted to Mexico in 1944.[9]

Squabbles between the states over the Mexican claim were only part of the story. Additional opposition to the CRSP came from the United States Army Corps of Engineers. The corps, another dam-building agency responsible for the development of navigable waterways, had a longstanding political rivalry with the Bureau of Reclamation. Chief of the Army Corps of Engineers Major General Lewis A. Pick first questioned the economic feasibility of the project during 1951 congressional hearings. Pick questioned the practicality of building large, expensive dams and reservoirs when there was little hope that subsequently developed irrigated agricultural lands would be able to repay the construction costs. He called attention to the fact that there was "unrestricted subsidization of irrigation projects by power revenues."[10] This, coupled with the fact that the water resources to be developed by the project might not be utilized by the upper-basin states for seventy-five years, made Pick less than enthusiastic.

Congressmen and senators whose states did not directly benefit from the CRSP also questioned certain parts of the project. Perturbed by the reluctance of their colleagues and the Interior Department's "foot-dragging" over the CRSP Report, Utah Senators Wallace Bennett and Arthur V. Watkins co-sponsored legislation to move the project forward. Nevertheless, unresolved concerns, especially over the location of some of the dam sites, doomed the bill to a quiet death in committee.

Flaming Gorge Dam was one of many projects proposed under the CRSP, but it was by no means the highest priority. In 1949 the Bureau of Reclamation made preliminary studies of three dam sites in the general region—at Echo Park, at Horseshoe Canyon, and at Red Canyon in Daggett County. The favored location for a dam on the Green River was the Echo Park site at the confluence of the Green and Yampa rivers in northwestern Colorado. This site offered engineering advantages that made it the clear favorite of the dam builders; however, the reservoir that would be created by the dam's construction would inundate a large portion of Dinosaur National Monument.

This famous dinosaur fossil quarry was given national monument status in October 1915. Geologist Earl Douglass noted during the late 1920s that "a rich quarry like this with such complete and satisfactory material has never been found before in any part of the world."[11] In 1938 the National Park Service proposed that the boundaries of the park be greatly enlarged to protect the nearby scenic canyons of the Green River. Dinosaur National Monument administrator David H. Madsen conducted hearings at Vernal, Utah, and Craig, Colorado, prior to the enlargement, and in an affidavit he stated that when local citizens raised questions concerning

The Flaming Gorge Dam site photographed by Stan Rasmussen for the United States Bureau of Reclamation in June 1957. (Utah State Historical Society)

grazing rights, irrigation, and power development, assurances were given by the National Park Service that the enlargement of Dinosaur National Monument "would not interfere with such development."[12] President Roosevelt approved the expansion of the monument that year.

The failed Bennett and Watkins bill for authorization of the CRSP had included the recommendation that one of the first two dams constructed in the upper basin be at Echo Park. The second recommended project, a dam at Glen Canyon, was also liable to impact the national monument at Rainbow Bridge. In 1953 the National Park Service came out decidedly against the proposal. One of the National Park Service's publications noted that:

> The greatest Peril to the parks from the dam proposals comes from the plans and programs of the governmental dam building agencies themselves and the pressures which their activities generate in the various sections of the country.[13]

The Williams Ranch in Linwood before construction of Flaming Gorge Reservoir. (Courtesy Pauleen Baker)

Most advocates for the development of the Upper Colorado River Basin considered the Echo Park site essential. Referred to as "the workhorse of the Colorado River Project," one official within the Interior Department quipped that eliminating Echo Park was like "taking the pistons out of an engine."[14] Officials in Utah maintained that Echo Park was the only site which could be constructed at a sufficiently high elevation to enable the state to consumptively utilize the waters of the upper Colorado River Basin for irrigation and municipal water supplies. Furthermore, water engineers within the Interior Department continuously claimed that only the Echo Park site, with its deep, narrow canyons, provided the necessary safeguards against evaporation losses. Nevertheless, David Brower of the Sierra Club questioned the Interior Department's figures concerning evaporation losses.

The Sierra Club played an integral role in the Echo Park controversy. Since the construction in 1913 of the Hetch Hetchy Dam in

Ranch buildings being removed to make way for the Flaming Gorge Reservoir. (Friend B. Slote, United States Bureau of Reclamation)

northern California which encroached on Yosemite National Park, the Sierra Club had actively promoted the sanctity of national parks and monuments. The Hetch Hetchy conflict had defined the boundaries between conservationists such as Gifford Pinchot, who came to favor the construction of Hetch Hetchy Dam, and preservationists such as John Muir, founder of the Sierra Club, who opposed the dam's construction. Although the Sierra Club lost the decade-long battle to preserve the Hetch Hetchy Valley, the organization learned valuable lessons which would be used to great effect during the Echo Park conflict. Coming "out of the campaign much wiser politically than they had entered it," wrote author Holway R. Jones, Sierra Club officials saw a need "for greater coordination in preserving the wilderness and natural scenic areas of America."[15]

Following the loss at Hetch Hetchy, preservationists mounted a campaign to organize individuals and groups at the local level. Although he was by far the most vocal opponent of dam construction during the Echo Park debate, David Brower was not alone in his opposition to the dam. Appearing before the House Subcommittee on Irrigation and Reclamation, retired chief engineer of the United

Burning of Linwood buildings before the area is inundated by the waters of Flaming Gorge Reservoir. (Courtesy Pauleen Baker)

States Army Corps of Engineers General U.S. Grant III explained how a series of dams built at White River, Cross Mountain, and Flaming Gorge would store more water for less money, while at the same time decreasing evaporation.[16] Though Grant's claims were later refuted by project advocates, the Red Canyon site (which came to be known as Flaming Gorge after the upstream canyon that would be largely flooded by the dam's waters) began to be viewed more positively as a viable alternative to Echo Park. In 1954 David Brower again testified, this time before the Senate Subcommittee on Irrigation and Reclamation. Brower proposed that Flaming Gorge, in conjunction with other dams, would provide adequate storage for the upper basin and be considerably less expensive than the Echo Park/Glen Canyon combination.[17]

Opposing Brower and the preservationists, Carl J. Christensen, Dean of the College of Mines and Mineral Industries at the University of Utah, stated:

> I am completely at a loss to understand the thinking back of the opposition which has arisen in the name of *conservation*. Not to

The Linwood area after all buildings were removed or burned. (Friend B. Slote, United States Bureau of Reclamation)

> develop the upper Colorado River in the manner outlined by the Bureau of Reclamation is to waste—(fail to conserve)—a tremendous natural resource.[18]

In order to counter the opposition to an Echo Park dam and other projects, the four upper-basin states organized a "grass roots" coalition. Calling themselves "aqualantes," one such group, the Upper Colorado River Grass Roots, Inc., pledged its members to "combat" what they perceived as the widespread misinformation being spread by project opponents. A brochure of the organization noted how they considered themselves "water vigilantes, pledged to back the Colorado River Storage Project. . . . Aqualantes . . . serve the cause of progress," the report concluded.[19]

George D. Clyde, avowed "aqualante" and Commissioner of Interstate Streams for Utah, summarized the history of the Echo Park proposal and its relation to Dinosaur National Monument. Clyde, who later became governor of the state, noted that the proposed dam was to be located in the "expanded" boundaries of the park, some twenty miles upstream from the original eighty-acre parcel containing the dinosaur bones. He continued by mentioning that power and

Heavy equipment working on the access road at the south face of Dutch John Gap. September 1957. (Friend B. Slote, United States Bureau of Reclamation)

irrigation withdrawals from both the Yampa and Green rivers had been made as early as 1910 and that twelve power and irrigation sites had been withdrawn and reserved by 1925. The 1938 expansion of Dinosaur National Monument increased the monument's size from eighty acres to 203,885 acres. Clyde noted that although the National Park Service had requested that the Federal Power Commission relinquish the sites on the Yampa and Green rivers the commission, "in the Public interest," Clyde added, had refused. Clyde closed his summation by stating that a denial "for the construction of the Echo Park Dam on the grounds that it is in a National Monument would be a breach of faith on the part of the United States Government."[20]

The "aqualantes" presented a number of experts who favored the construction of an Echo Park dam and reservoir. Many engineers, state and local officials, and other professionals testified in favor of the project. They were, however, up-staged in the quantity of support they could generate. It was reported to the House Committee on

Powdermen use a wooden tamping rod to assure that sticks of dynamite are in place prior to blasting on the power plant service road. November 1958. (Friend B. Slote, United States Bureau of Reclamation)

Interior and Insular Affairs that of the more than 4,700 letters received concerning Echo Park, only fifty-three were in favor of the project.[21] By the mid-1950s, the general mood of the American public had begun to shift away from development towards preservation. More and more people, in large part because of the successful cam-

Early construction work on the Cart Creek Bridge. (P. D. Smart, United States Bureau of Reclamation)

paign carried forward by organizations like the Sierra Club, were looking at projects such as the proposed dam at Echo Park as being invasive and exploitive. A *Salt Lake Tribune* editorial noted that the "opponents of the upper basin plan have the advantage of time, numbers, years of canny propaganda, and vast financial resources."[22]

By 1955, project advocates, fearing that public opposition might jeopardize the entirety of the CRSP, began downplaying the importance of the Echo Park site. Once resolute in his support of Echo Park, Commissioner of Reclamation Wilbur Dexheimer now claimed that Echo Park's elimination from consideration as a dam site would not make the CRSP unfeasible, it would mean only that the upper basin could not be fully developed. With support for the Echo Park site slowly eroding, David Brower again seized the moment by suggesting that dams should be built only when a demonstrated need for additional water was present. Brower did allow that the first dam which would be needed would be at Red Canyon—Flaming Gorge.[23]

A huge dump truck places earth and rock in the coffer dam at Flaming Gorge. (Friend B. Slote, United States Bureau of Reclamation)

Few of the project's advocates placed much stock in Brower's suggestion, but the construction of a dam at Flaming Gorge gradually became the preferred alternative to one at Echo Park. The scenery that would be inundated by Flaming Gorge Reservoir at Horseshoe and Red canyons was no less spectacular than that above the Echo Park dam site, but Flaming Gorge was outside the boundaries of a national park or monument area. It is now evident that Flaming Gorge was offered as a sacrificial lamb by conservation groups in the hopes of preserving the integrity of the national monument at Echo Canyon. Significantly, Glen Canyon became the second victim. Dean E. Mann wrote:

> The intensity of the opposition by the conservationists reflected their protective concerns for Echo Park, but it also reflected their concern for the sanctity of national parks. The invasion of the Monument, if

> successful, was considered a harbinger of future invasions when the magical goal of economic development was used as justification. . . . The battle to save Echo Park became the struggle of the generation to save a part of America's hallowed heritage.[24]

Despite intense opposition from the environmental community, on 21 April 1955 the U.S. Senate narrowly passed a CRSP bill that included Echo Park on the list of approved projects.[25] The Senate, however, was merely passing the final decision back to the House of Representatives. Later in the year, CRSP proponents met in Denver to consider their options. While the meeting was in progress, a full-page advertisement, paid for by conservationists, appeared in the *Denver Post.* The ad suggested that if the Echo Park dam was eliminated from the proposal the conservation community would not attempt to obstruct the remainder of the CRSP and would support dams at Flaming Gorge and Glen Canyon.[26]

Sensing that an Echo Park dam had become a stumbling block, Congressman Wayne Aspinall of Colorado had previously introduced CRSP legislation that did not include the controversial project.[27] When the attendees of the Denver conference, including the Utah delegation, realized the futility of pursuing the Echo Park location, they decided to abandon the "workhorse of the Colorado River Project" and throw their support behind Aspinall's bill. The deletion, noted the *Salt Lake Tribune,* was made in order to "reduce opposition from various organizations and areas of the nation."[28]

The elimination of Echo Park opened the way for construction to begin on Flaming Gorge. Once the CRSP bill passed Congress and was signed into law by President Dwight D. Eisenhower on 11 April 1956 the Echo Park controversy disappeared almost as if it had never existed. The dam at Flaming Gorge became the favored project of the upper-basin states, and it, like the proposed Echo Park dam before it, continued to hold the promise of grand economic development.

At the time, the defeat of the Echo Park dam and the substitution of the Flaming Gorge project seemed like a great victory for the conservationists. It reversed the precedent set by the earlier Hetch Hetchy Dam controversy, and it demonstrated strong political support for the preservation of the national park system. Ironically, the decision

Drilling and grouting operations in the Flaming Gorge Dam diversion tunnel. 1959. (Friend B. Slote, United States Bureau of Reclamation)

to sacrifice Flaming Gorge and Glen Canyon drove a wedge between the preservationist wing of the conservation movement and its more traditional elements. Angered by their own complicity in the compromise, preservationist forces vowed a new militancy, split with their former resource-conservation and sportsmen allies, and became the core of a new environmental movement.

Although the Sierra Club and other environmental organizations came to regret their compromise over the Colorado River Storage Project, the CRSP moved ahead. Bids for building Flaming Gorge Dam were let on 10 June 1958 at the high school in Manila.[29] The prime contract for the dam and powerhouse was awarded to Arch Dam Constructors, a joint venture consisting of Peter Kiewit Sons' Company, Morrison-Knudsen Company, Mid-Valley Utility Constructors, and Coker Construction Company.[30] Construction commenced in July 1958, and the estimated construction cost of the dam was $83.1 million.[31]

Few opponents of CRSP ever questioned the economic legitimacy of the dam. Some, such as syndicated columnist Raymond Moley, questioned the economics of the whole of the CRSP, but once the project passed muster in the U.S. Congress, no one came forward to challenge the price of the dam at Flaming Gorge. "The reasons seem clear," noted Dean E. Mann:

> irrigation projects financed by federal funds were part of the *expected* or *accepted* output of the political system . . . there remained an aura about irrigation as an almost mystical technological and sociological process that led to economic development, to opening up the frontier, and to further opportunities for the small farmer. [32]

Specifications for the structure called for a dam 502 feet high from the lowest part of the foundation, having a crest length of 1,180 feet and a base thickness of 130 feet.[33] Before any concrete could be poured, however, construction crews first had to re-route the Green River. This was accomplished by drilling a twenty-three-foot-diameter diversion tunnel for a length of 1,100 feet through the right abutment rock. The entire tunnel was then lined with concrete to protect it against erosion. The diversion tunnel was completed by March 1959.

Construction of such a dam required painstaking attention to detail and rigorous adherence to specifications, but it also demanded that engineers and supervisors be sensitive to unexpected situations. Securing adequate material for the making of concrete proved to be a major problem. Aggregate near Henrys Fork which was to be used in the concrete was found to contain unsuitable lightweight material. Engineers discovered that if they placed the aggregate in a slurry mix with a high specific gravity, they could float the unsuitable material over a weir and retain the heavier elements. This process was implemented by the contractor on a large scale, and the first concrete was poured in September 1960.[34]

Grouting also proved more difficult than originally planned. When first laid out on paper, the specifications required that only the upstream portions of the dam be grouted. After construction began, it became evident that further strengthening would be necessary. Construction crews performed the process of grouting from a series

The last bucket of concrete is readied for delivery. (Friend B. Slote, United States Bureau of Reclamation)

of traverse adits (tunnels) inside of the dam. Each section was grouted after the initial mass of concrete was poured.

Workers encountered other problems not necessarily related to the dam itself. Severe winters hampered construction crews, and concrete could only be poured for about five months out of the year. In

The last bucket of concrete for the Flaming Gorge Dam is unloaded high above the waters of the Green River. 15 November 1962. (Friend B. Slote, United States Bureau of Reclamation)

1961, for example, the construction site closed down on 9 November.[35]

Housing was another issue that had to be dealt with; a new town near the construction site had to be constructed for the workers. The resulting town, Dutch John, not only became the newest but also the largest town in Daggett County. It was built at Dutch John Flat, a desolate bench on the river's north side named after John Honselena, an early settler originally from Schleswig, Germany. In 1957 the Bureau of Reclamation moved in eight transit houses and twenty-five trailers. Arch Construction Company later moved in additional trailers and built "a bunkhouse for 300 men, a cookhouse and mess hall."[36] A large sixty-foot trailer was used for a hospital. It was directed by nurse Melanie Ylincheta, and for a time it contained the only bath in town.[37] Additional trailers served as the post office and fire station. Permanent buildings were constructed between 1960 and 1963 to house the fire station, hospital, and the Bureau of Reclamation office. A number of homes were also built. Some 3,500 workers reportedly lived at Dutch John at the peak of construction activity.

With the influx of so many construction workers and families, Daggett County experienced an unprecedented population explosion and consequent crowding of its educational system. In 1940 the average school attendance in the county was 121 students, and the figure had declined to 96 in 1950 and 98 by 1955; yet, in 1959, average attendance had soared to 232 pupils and enrollment was almost 300 students, 205 of whom were in grades one through eight.[38] A new elementary school was constructed by the federal government for workers' children at Dutch John. Older students attended secondary school in Manila, but county residents balked at covering the cost of the increased high school enrollment; they had just completed an expensive remodeling and expansion of the Manila School in 1955 and were unwilling to take on further debt. Citizens voted on a $50,000 school bond issue in May 1958 that would have paid for adding classroom and laboratory facilities. Local taxpayers maintained that they could not afford the sudden growth, and the school district members became only the fourth such group of voters in the state ever to vote down a school building bond issue.[39]

The town of Manila also suffered growing pains from the dam's construction. Bill Steinaker and Duane Lamb both opened trailer parks to house workers associated with the Flaming Gorge project, and the sudden increase in population created water and sewage-disposal problems. To obtain funds for new water and sewage systems,

President John F. Kennedy presses a telegraph key at the Salt Lake City Municipal Airport on 27 September 1963 to give the signal to begin power generation at Flaming Gorge Dam. United States Senator Frank Moss, standing, and W. I. Palmer look on. (Mel Davis, United States Bureau of Reclamation)

the town, which had been incorporated for a time in the 1930s and 1940s, had to reincorporate. This was accomplished; and Kay Palmer, Kenneth Reed, and Elbert Steinaker were elected to the town council, with Nels Philbrick as town president and WaNeta Lamb town clerk. Thus ended Daggett County's distinction of being the only county in the United States with no incorporated towns.[40]

Outside of these problems of providing infrastructure and services for the increased population, the large influx of construction workers appears to have disrupted the county relatively little. Other boom areas of the western United States have experienced significant problems with housing shortages and increased crime, but little social disruption took place within Daggett County.[41] In part, this was because most construction workers lived in the remote construction town of Dutch John, where Bureau of Reclamation police took care of the law enforcement problems. Furthermore, the remoteness of the construction site and the seasonal nature of the work prompted many workers to leave the area during the winter.

The building of the dam did lead to the creation of Daggett County's first newspaper. In 1959 Manila schoolteacher Hartwell Goodrich published the first issue of the *Daggett County Record* on 8 September. Subscription rates were three dollars a year for the newspaper; however, that first issue was the only one ever published. A longer-lived institution was founded in 1958 with the chartering of the Daggett County Lions Club on 29 March, with Tom Welch elected president. Twenty-eight members constituted the original group, which since that time has taken over management of the annual Manila rodeo as well as sponsering and promoting many social and civic-improvemnt activities in the county.[42]

The isolation of the dam construction site also made transportation difficult. Access to the dam site was from Green River, Wyoming, sixty-three miles to the north, and Green River was also the closest railhead. Once the reservoir began filling, however, the Green River Bridge would be inundated, and the dam site then could only be accessed from Vernal, Utah, forty-five miles to the south. Plans were considered to either rebuild the bridge at Green River once the reservoir filled or provide a new access road on the east side of the reservoir.

During construction, a temporary bridge connecting Dutch John to Vernal to the south was installed at Cart Creek. After the dam was topped out in November 1962, the top of the dam itself became the roadway to the south side of the river and the improved roads to

Vernal and Manila. The reservoir was then allowed to rise to the level of the outlet pipes. Engineers employed a stoplog mechanism to temporarily seal the diversion tunnel and then installed a sixty-two-foot concrete plug keyed from twenty-nine feet at the upstream end down to twenty-three feet within the tunnel.[43]

The first of three massive generators was installed in 1963, and on 17 September of that year President John F. Kennedy threw a switch in Salt Lake City that energized it. Two more generating units were installed, and the entire dam and reservoir were dedicated by Ladybird Johnson, wife of President Lyndon Baines Johnson, on 17 August 1964.[44]

Flaming Gorge Dam, at the time of its construction, was the seventh-highest concrete dam in the United States.[45] It was built at a cost of $65 million. The reservoir created by the dam, at capacity, extends upstream some ninety-one miles and contains only slightly less than 3,800,000 acre-feet of water. The dam's spillway is tunneled through the canyon wall above the left abutment for a distance of 650 feet. The spillway tunnel has an upstream portal more than twenty-six feet in diameter, narrowing to eighteen feet at the tunnel outlet, capable of carrying 28,800 cubic feet of water per second (cfs). The spillway, coupled with two seventy-two-inch river outlet pipes running through the dam, provides for flood protection up to a maximum run-off of 76,000 cfs, or a total discharge of 1,084,000 acre-feet of water over a fifteen-day period.[46]

Embedded within the center of the dam itself are three penstocks designed to serve the hydroelectric plant below. Each penstock is ten feet in diameter and serves a 50,000-horsepower turbine. Water from each penstock drops approximately 250 feet before entering the turbines. Each generator produces 36,000 kilowatts of electrical power. Electrical power generated at Flaming Gorge is carried over a 138-kilovolt power line to Rangely, Colorado.[47] The transmission lines were constructed by Irby Construction Company of Jackson, Mississippi, operating out of Vernal, Utah.[48]

Following the completion of Flaming Gorge Dam, the temporary trailers and workers' housing at Dutch John were moved out. The Bureau of Reclamation offices were remodeled and are currently (1998) used by the Forest Service. The LDS church purchased another of the permanent buildings to use for its services. The Bureau of Reclamation moved its permanent office location to the dam. With limited shopping, an elementary school, and government services, the town has become a welcome convenience for residents in the eastern end of Daggett County. About seventy-five families currently live in Dutch John; most are employed by either the U.S. Forest Service or the Bureau of Reclamation. The transient nature of federal employment, where one usually has to move frequently to advance in an agency, has made it difficult for Dutch John residents to put down roots and become full participants in the mainstream of county life.[49]

Completion of Flaming Gorge Dam was a bittersweet event for many residents of Daggett County. The community of Linwood had been doomed by the rising waters of the lake, and federal regulations specified that all reservoir sites below the water level had to be stripped clean. This included the Williams Brothers Ranch at Henrys Fork, Keith Smith's sheep operation at Linwood, the Smith and Larsen Mercantile store, and homes in the vicinity.[50]

The Williams brothers "put up their last hay in 1958" wrote local historian Richard Dunham.[51] They moved their home, originally part of the old Driskell-Finch Ranch, to Manila, where, "standing on a low bluff as the home of Nels and Mabel Philbrick, it commands much the same view of the Ballies and Richards Peak it formerly did."[52] The old Linwood School, which straddled the state line with Wyoming, was also moved to save it from the rising reservoir waters.

The Bureau of Reclamation also tore down and burned the old mercantile run by George and Minnie Rasmussen. George Rasmussen reportedly never quite got over the loss and died shortly after the store's destruction. When government officials informed Minnie that she must abandon her house, she genteelly invited the men in for tea. As the officials drove away, Minnie put a torch to her home rather than turn it over to the Bureau of Reclamation.[53] For many Daggett County residents, Minnie Rasmusen's burning home has become a symbol of defiance to bureaucratic authority and the many changes wrought by Flaming Gorge Dam.

In the years that have followed, it has become clear that Flaming Gorge Dam has left a mixed legacy for the people of Daggett County and the nation. As part of the original Flaming Gorge Dam and Reservoir proposal, the Bureau of Reclamation retained a right to 500,000 acre-feet of water from Flaming Gorge. This was to be diverted through the Flaming Gorge Aqueduct, a project proposed as part of the Central Utah Project.[54] This massive interbasin replumbing project is yet to be built. The main contributions of the dam so far have been power generation, water storage, flood control, and recreation possibilities; it provides no irrigation water to lands in Daggett County.

Flaming Gorge Dam has also had a significant effect on archaeological resources. It is difficult to know for certain the number of archaeological sites that are covered by the waters of the reservoir. Federal researchers noted in 1979 that the area may have been part of the territory of the Clovis culture, a Paleo-Indian culture from about 13,000 years ago. Archaeological evidence appears to support this contention and certainly supports the claim that the area was utilized by later Indian groups of the Fremont culture.[55] Very little archaeological field work was carried out before the impoundment of water at Flaming Gorge Reservoir, and recent discoveries seem to indicate that there was significant prehistoric use along this section of the Green River.[56] Valuable information certainly was lost due to the construction of the dam and reservoir.

The impoundment and release of Flaming Gorge waters has also decimated the native fishery of the Green River. Research carried out by K.G. Seethaler showed that indigenous fish such as the Colorado squawfish and the humpback chub had been eliminated in the Green River below Flaming Gorge "by colder water temperatures and altered flow patterns."[57]

In addition, the native fishery suffered due to unwise use of the highly toxic fish poison rotenone. In 1961, fish and game departments from Utah and Wyoming made plans to treat the Green River above Flaming Gorge Dam. The treatment was meant to poison so-called "trash" fish and facilitate the introduction of game fish in the new reservoir. To protect fish populations downstream, the treatment was scheduled for September 1962 to coincide with the closing of the dam gates. The treated water would then be contained by the dam, and the downstream fishery would be protected.

When officials learned that the dam would not be completed on time, they asked the Bureau of Reclamation to seal the diversion tunnel so that the treatment could go on as planned. Bureau officials, however, declined to do this because they feared the dam was not ready for closure. Although they knew that the rotenone treatment would prove deadly for endangered fish species downstream, the state agencies decided to implement the treatment anyway. The Utah and Wyoming fish and game departments pressed forward and actually moved up the treatment date. Opposition from conservation and environmental groups mounted because of the possible eradication of endangered Colorado squawfish, humpback chub, and humpback suckers that flourished below the dam. Although the agencies claimed that an attempt would be made to "insure prepetuation of native fish species," rotenone was released into the river in January 1962.[58] It is impossible to know if the indigenous fish were affected more by the rotenone treatment or the cooling of the water following the closing of Flaming Gorge Dam. Whatever the case, only a few individuals of these endangered species exist in that section of the river today.

In the aftermath, the State of Utah decided to create a trout fishery in the cool river below the dam. The stocked trout did well during the 1960s, but in the late 1970s they began to die off and failed to reproduce. It was decided that the coldness of the water and its lack of oxygen was causing the problem, and in 1979 an expensive shutter system was added to the dam's facilities. This system mixes warmer water from the top of the lake with colder bottom water exiting the power plant. Though the dam's discharge is still much cooler than the water of the historic fishery, schools of lunker trout now swimming below the dam seem to indicate the success of the $5 million project.[59]

Not only is the river below the dam much cooler than it once was, streamflows have been dramatically altered. The massive flows of spring runoff have been minimized, and the extreme low water that once was characteristic of late summer and fall is a rarity. This evening-out of the flow has made it possible to run the river at any time of the year, and commercial rafting companies have flourished. Unfortunately, the wild springtime rides of yesteryear now only occur in rare times of extreme runoff. The once fearsome rapids of Lodore are now considered tame by most river runners.[60]

Despite the costs to taxpayers, the people of Linwood, and the environment, the development of Flaming Gorge Dam and Reservoir has provided a wealth of recreational opportunities and relatively inexpensive hydroelectric power for the people of the Intermountain West. For citizens of Daggett County, the dam has brought improvements in the county's infrastructure and economic development. Older county residents look back to a time before the tourists came and remember when Daggett County was a tightknit homogenous community where people left their doors unlocked. They sometimes think that the dam was the worst thing that has happened to the region, but younger residents who make their living from motels, RV storage, gas stations, or boat rentals might disagree.

In Daggett County and the rest of the West, the verdict on the overall benefit of the Flaming Gorge project is still a matter of contention. Many county residents and thousands of boaters, waterskiers, and fishermen would give an enthusiastic "yes" if the question was put to them. However, some older county residents and a growing number of environmentalists would offer a resounding "no" in answer to the question. There is no consensus; there is only the reality that this tour de force of concrete and steel has irrevocably changed the course of Daggett County history.

ENDNOTES

1. Paul W. Gates, *History of Public Land Law Development* (Washington, D.C.: Government Printing Office, 1968), 28–29.

2. Ralf R. Woolley, *The Green River and Its Utilization,* USGS Water Supply Paper 618 (Washington, D.C.: Government Printing Office, 1930), xi.

3. Roy Webb, *If We Had a Boat: Green River Explorers, Adventurers, and Runners,* 125.

4. Woolley, *The Green River and Its Utilization,* 110.

5. George H. Dern, Utah's Interest in the Colorado River: Statement of the Hon. George H. Dern, Governor of the State of Utah, Salt Lake City, Utah at the Hearings Before the Committee on Irrigation and Reclamation, U.S. Senate, 17 December 1925, in *The Colorado River* (Colorado Springs, CO: n.p., 1926).

6. Dean E. Mann, "Legal-Political History of Water Resource Development in the Upper Colorado River Basin," *Lake Powell Research Project Bulletin* 4 (September 1974): 5.

7. Reuel Leslie Olson, *The Colorado River Compact* (n.p., 1926), 18.

8. Mann, "Legal-Political History of Water Resource Development," 7.

9. The 1922 Colorado River Compact provided no guarantees of water to Mexico. Rather, the compact intimated that if the United States decided to recognize Mexican rights to water that any such water would come from surplus and the water would be provided equally by the upper and lower basins. The original compact, however, overestimated the amount of flow in the Colorado River system. Only once between 1933 and 1976 did the river flow in excess of the 7,500,000 acre feet allotted to each of the two basins. As long as it flowed uninterrupted, the Colorado River continued to provide Mexico with irrigation water. But planned development in the upper basin would restrict the flow of the river and possibly damage the relationship between Mexico and the United States. Congress, therefore, recognized Mexico's right to Colorado River water in 1944, allocating 1.5 million acre-feet of water annually to the southern nation.

The question of where the 1,500,000 acre-feet of water for Mexico would come from was essentially left unanswered, however. The lower-basin states were already using the lion's share of their appropriation, and the upper-basin states, poised to begin a development project which would allow them to utilize their share, were not about to volunteer any of their portion to Mexico. Passage of the CRSP by Congress in 1956 absolved the Colorado River Basin states from any obligation to Mexico; rather, the act obligated the entirety of the United States to honor the agreement with Mexico. The act stated "that the satisfaction of the requirements of the Mexican Water Treaty from the Colorado River constitutes a national obligation." Political scientist Dean E. Mann noted that the method whereby the United States would meet this national obligation was unclear: "What does seem clear is that the taxpayers and the beneficiaries of the waters of the Colorado River . . . will be largely relieved of their obligations and that the taxpayers of the United States will assume them instead. Domestic distributive politics appears now to have an international hitching post." See Mann, "Legal-Political History of Water Resource Development," 42–43.

10. *Colorado River Storage Project: Letter from Assistant Secretary of the Interior Transmitting a Report on the Colorado River Storage Project and Participating Projects, Providing for the Development and Utilization of the Water and Related Resources of the Upper Colorado River Basin, Pursuant to the Federal Reclamation Laws* (Washington: Government Printing Office, 1954), 321.

11. Woolley, *The Green River and Its Utilization,* 66.

12. *Utah Water News* 1 (March 1954): 1.

13. Mann, "Legal-Political History of Water Resource Development," 9.

14. Ibid., 11.

15. Holway R. Jones, *John Muir and the Sierra Club: The Battle for Yosemite* (San Francisco: Sierra Club, 1965), 168–69.

16. Mann, "Legal-Political History of Water Resource Development," 11.

17. Ibid., 13.

18. Carl J. Christensen to A. Ray Olpin, 15 January 1954, in *Statement of George D. Clyde, Commissioner of Interstate Streams for Utah, Representing the State of Utah, Presented at the Congressional Hearings on H.R. 4449, In Support of the Colorado River Storage Project and Participating Projects, January 1954* (Washington, D.C.: Government Printing Office, 1954).

19. *The Colorado River Storage Project: A Project to Benefit All Americans.* book collection 38, no. 23, pamphlet in Special Collections and Archives, Merrill Library, Utah State University, Logan, Utah.

20. George D. Clyde, "The Case of the Upper Colorado River Storage Project and Participating Projects," (September 1954), 3, typescript, Special Collections and Archives, Merrill Library, Utah State University.

21. Mann, "Legal-Political History of Water Resource Development," 11.

22. *Salt Lake Tribune,* 12 December 1954, in Papers of B.H. Stringham, Ms. 48, Scrapbook 1, Special Collections and Archives, Merrill Library, Utah State University (hereafter referred to as Stringham).

23. Mann, "Legal-Political History of Water Resource Development," 15.

24. Ibid., 31.

25. Stringham, *Salt Lake Tribune,* 21 April 1955.

26. Mann, "Legal-Political History of Water Resource Development," 37.

27. Ibid.

28. Stringham, *Salt Lake Tribune,* 2 March 1956.

29. *Salt Lake Tribune,* 1 June 1958.

30. *Max Ford,* "Design of Flaming Gorge Dam," paper presented at ASCE Convention, Phoenix, Arizona, April 1961, 2.

31. Mann, "Legal-Political History of Water Resource Development," 41.

32. Ibid., 32.

33. Ford, "Design of Flaming Gorge Dam," 2.

34. Ibid., 7; Dunham and Dunham, *Flaming Gorge Country,* 333.

35. Ford, "Design of Flaming Gorge Dam," 22.

36. Dunham and Dunham, *Flaming Gorge Country,* 335.

37. Ibid.

38. *Statistical Review of Utah's Economy* (1960), 25, 26.

39. *Salt Lake Tribune,* 17 November 1958; Donald Weir Baxter, "The History of Public Education in Daggett County, Utah and Adjacent Areas," 88.

40. Clara Robinson, "Life Story of Clara Geneva Ruble Robinson," manuscript history in author's collection.

41. Writing about Evanston, Wyoming, in 1979, the *Salt Lake Tribune* noted: "like a slow-moving but unstoppable glacier, the drilling crews are moving along the geologic overthrust belt. . . . Evanston has been the easiest place to see this impact. Mobile homes are crammed into every square foot of open space." *Salt Lake Tribune,* 23 July 1979, 7.

42. Dunham and Dunham, *Flaming Gorge Country,* 330–31.

43. Ford, "Design of Flaming Gorge Dam," 12.

44. Dunham and Dunham, *Flaming Gorge Country,* 333.

45. *Salt Lake Tribune,* 1 June 1958.

46. Ford, "Design of Flaming Gorge Dam," 19–20.

47. Ibid.

48. *Salt Lake Tribune,* 2 August 1961.

49. Dunham and Dunham, *Flaming Gorge Country,* 335.

50. Dunham and Dunham, F*laming Gorge Country,* 335–36.

51. Ibid., 337; William Tennent, "Birthday at Minnie's Gap," unidentified newsclipping in author's collection.

52. Inventory of Water Rights: Upperent, "Birthday at Minnie's Gap," unidentified newsclipping in author's collection.

53. Inventory of Water Rights: Upper Colorado River Basin, Utah (Salt Lake City: Utah Division of Water Rights, *1974), 2.*

54. *Utah Statistical Abstract, 1983, xv-14.*

55. *Draft Wild and Scenic River Study, Green and Yampa Riverstement: Green and Yampa Rivers, Colorado/Utah* (Denver: National Park Service, 1979), 66.

56. The only pre-impoundment study carried out at Flaming Gorge was William M. Purdy, *An Outline of the History of the Flaming Gorge Area*

(Salt Lake City; University of Utah Press, 1957); Byron Loosle, interview with author, 12 November 1993, notes in author's collection.

57. *Draft Wild and Scenic River Study, Green and Yampa Rivers,* 19.

58. *The Planning, Operation, and Analysis of the Green River Fish Control Project: A Joint Report of the Utah State Department of Fish and Game, [and] Wyoming Game and Fish Department* (Salt Lake City, UT, and Cheyenne, WY: Utah State Department of Fish and Game/Wyoming Game and Fish Department, n.d.), 3–4.

59. Webb, *If We Had a Boat,* 141.

60. Ibid., 141–42.

CHAPTER 10

KEITH SMITH AND DAGGETT COUNTY TRANSPORTATION

> Close calls were inevitable when driving the dirt roads in winter. She had to 'make a run at' a muddy hill four or five times. In a spring storm, the old bridge was not only heaving sideways but also up and down, wind had blown some of the boards off . . . and she abruptly brought the car to a halt.
>
> —DIANA ALLEN KOURIS

The people of the Daggett country have always been travelers. Indians traveled to trade and hunt, trappers roamed in search of beaver, and ranch families journeyed to distant towns to sell livestock or buy supplies. Modern residents think nothing of making a one-hundred-mile round-trip to visit the doctor or go shopping. It is a country of vast distances where taking a child to school can turn into an adventure. It is also a tortured landscape of snowcapped mountains, rugged canyons, spring mud, and sudden storms. By foot, horseback, boat, or automobile, travel has never been easy.

Moving people, parcels, livestock, and lumber has been an ongoing challenge that continues to shape the region.[1] The distance from markets and the cost of bringing in supplies have limited the regional economy. Ironically, it is this isolation that many residents have found appealing. They find freedom in the empty spaces, and they have toughened to the hardships of travel. Though long lonely roads and sometimes perilous conditions may drive away the feint-of-heart, they breed a sense of confidence, self reliance, and community among those who are willing to meet the challenge.

Merchant, rancher, sportsman, and public servant, Keith Smith not only met the challenge—he thrived on it. He visited the country on an outing in 1901 and returned to put down roots. Over seven decades, Smith walked Indian trails, floated the Green River, roamed on horseback, cajoled his Model-T Ford over dirt roads, and sped along paved state highways. His memoirs are filled with interesting stories of travel, and they present a fascinating perspective on area transportation from 1901 to 1964.[2] Smith's reminiscences offer rare insight into the changing nature of human mobility, but they also show that in spite of advances, travel in Daggett County continues to be a struggle between people and the forces of nature.

Born in Cincinnati in 1878, Keith Smith first visited the Utah's Daggett region in 1901. Smith was a promising young college student at Yale University and ready to enter his senior year. In the company of a classmate's family, he spent an adventurous summer hunting and fishing in the Uinta Mountains.

They found that travel in this remote region had changed little since Ute and Shoshoni Indians had first traversed the country on horseback. The military and settlers had scratched a few rough tracks across the landscape that were barely suitable for light wagons. Winter snows or spring mud kept these impassable a fair share of the time. A stagecoach line connected Rock Springs, Wyoming, and Vernal, Utah, by way of Brown's Park, but most people preferred to ride the narrow mountain trails on trusty cow ponies. To the Yale men, this was, indeed, a wilderness.

The group assembled their equipment at Vernal and began the trip to "a camp at Fish Lake west of Leidy Peak."[3] The northwestwardly journey offered fantastic scenery and revealed changes in vegetation as the party's wagons ascended "Taylor

Mountain on and old army road."[4] They were traveling the

The Ole Neilson Cabin on Sheep Creek. Keith Smith is in the 1902 sweater. George Finch, on the extreme right, had just arrived with the news of President William McKinley's assassination. Other individuals include Ole Neilson, his wife, and children. (Daggett County)

Carter Military Road completed in 1883 between Fort Thornburgh, Utah, and Fort Bridger, Wyoming. Only eighteen years old when Smith encountered it, the harsh alpine climate and lack of maintenance had left the road in miserable condition.

The Carter Military Road, referred to in its day as the Fort Thornburgh Road, owes its origins to the climate of fear generated by the infamous Meeker Massacre and the ambitions of Judge William A. Carter to secure lucrative military freighting contracts. In 1879, the White River Utes in Colorado rebelled against agent Nathan Meeker's harsh and misguided attempts to turn them into farmers. Meeker called in troops from Fort Fred Steele, and the Utes killed Meeker and ambushed the military column. Major Thomas Thornburgh, in command of the soldiers, died during the struggle.

After the army regained control of the situation, citizens of Colorado pressured the government to remove the White River Utes to a reservation in Utah. This solution eased the minds of Coloradans, but it only increased fears among the few white settlers in eastern Utah. To calm the settlers and keep a watchful eye on the Utes, Fort Thornburgh was located near the site of present-day Vernal in 1881. The post, however, was quite isolated and difficult to supply.

Judge Carter had a solution. Ever the entrepreneur, Carter had made abundant profit as a provisioner for the Army. Settling at Fort Bridger in 1858, Carter soon was involved in a wide range of trading activity. He increased his profits, became postmaster, probate judge, and ventured into the businesses of cattle, mining, and lumber. His profits declined when troops abandoned Fort Bridger twenty years later. In the wake of the Meeker Massacre, Carter exploited the climate of fear and used his political influence to secure the return of troops to Fort Bridger. He also obtained the contract to freight supplies to the newly established Fort Thornburgh. This would require the location and building of a wagon road from Carter Station on the Union Pacific Railroad over the Uinta Mountains to the Ashley Valley.

General George Crook inspected and approved the route in the summer of 1881. It followed the Fort Bridger-Brown's Park military road that Major Noyes Baldwin's Nevada Volunteers had roughed out in 1865. At the base of the eastern Uintas, it left this road and crossed the mountain on an old Indian path known as the Lodgepole Trail. This was the shortest of the prospective routes and was favored by Carter. Work quickly began on the road.[5]

Carter hurried to complete construction and personally supervised the operation; the decision may have cost him his life. Overcome by cold and exposure, Carter died at home at Fort Bridger in November of 1881. His son, Willie, hastened west from his studies at Cornell University and took up his father's task.

Willie's description of the first season of building show the haste with which the work progressed:

> The winter of 1881–82 was approaching: there was no time for surveys; streams had to be bridged; marshes corduroyed; a roadway cleared through timbered sections; and two long and difficult dugways were to be constructed.[6]

Road-building continued the following spring, and by May Willie Carter was ready to take the first supply train of more than twenty wagons over the road. The trip started badly and only got worse as the teams and vehicles struggled across the Uintas:

> It soon became evident that from the character of the past winter at Fort Bridger, we had very erroneous conceptions of what we would encounter in attempting to freight through the mountains

Building the Steamboat Comet. (Sweetwater County Museum)

> so early in spring. The dug-way between Sand Canyon and Lodgepole was blocked with snow and ice . . . hills so soft that all the teams we could hook up were often required to pull a single wagon to the top . . . in one locality a separate road had to be cut through the timber for each wagon. The ground at this place appeared dry and firm, but each wagon broke through a thin crust into a quicksand beneath, making the road impassable for the next team.[7]

Despite these seemingly insurmountable obstacles, the supply train arrived at Fort Thornburgh in three weeks. The journey had taken its toll. The return trip was postponed for two weeks while blacksmiths at the post repaired the wagons.

It was understood by all that work on the road would have to be ongoing. The summer of 1882 brought military work crews to the wagon track. Major construction, particularly the corduroying of road sections, moving of large rocks, cutting, and filling, was done by the army the following summer. Work continued in 1883, but it was becoming evident that the road's high altitude conditions and short travel season made it costly and undependable. Fort Thornburgh was abandoned in 1884, and completion of the Rio Grande Western Railroad to Price opened a better supply line for the Ashley Valley communities.

Even so, the rough track continued to be used by local residents when the snow was off the high country. Ranching families along the north slope of the Uintas rode horseback or took light wagons over it to do business in Vernal. Many traversed it to take care of legal matters at the county seat or to buy fresh fruit. Copper ore from the Dyer Mine, located on the southern slope of the mountains, was freighted out over the road during the 1890s.

Such was the state of this road when Keith Smith passed a pleasurable summer of mountain camping and trout fishing along it during 1901. There was a place near Sheep Creek that particularly caught his attention:

> I had never seen such stretches of empty country, but I wrote home saying, "I am looking about . . . and see some possibility for the dim future. This place is immensely fertile by nature, but a desert on account of water. Miles of land are now absolutely desolate, which might, under the latest irrigation laws, be obtained for a nominal sum and made into the best of farming land."[8]

When it was time to head back to Vernal, the party's return trip over the Carter Road was reminiscent of earlier struggles by Willie Carter's freighters. The wagons were stopped by the seven mile grade of the Young Springs Dugway, and it was necessary to double-team them to the summit. Smith continued alone on horseback, got lost in the heavy timber, and was surprised by an early snowstorm. Sizing up the situation, the plucky lad built a fire and survived the night. He regained his way the following morning and, quite luckily, met his friends on the road. The trip to Vernal continued on horseback.

Summer vacation was ending, and it was time to return to Yale. Smith bought passage on the stagecoach that went to the railroad in Price. The vehicle accelerated dangerously as it descended a long canyon, and the "increasingly drunk driver curbed our speed by forcing the wheels into the inner bank."[9] Arriving safely, Smith was happy to catch an eastbound train. Stopping in Grand Junction, Colorado, to see friends, he told them of the "Red Bench land which attracted me in Utah" and of his plans to return the following summer after graduation.[10]

True to his word, in July of 1902, Smith and his father headed west with work—not fishing and camping—in mind. They purchased "$500 worth of ranching supplies including a ton of wire fencing" at the Montgomery Ward store in Chicago and from there continued the trip by rail to Green River where they met their friends.[11] From here, Smith was to experience another of the interesting modes of travel in the Daggett country.

This year the journey to Sheep Creek would be from another direction and in an

> eight by sixteen foot boat made of half inch redwood boards. It has sides two feet high so it was like a cigar box. After waiting two days for our supplies to arrive, we loaded the boat . . . and started down the Green River for the Red Bench.[12]

Smith's voyage presents a vivid picture of travel on the Green River in the early twentieth century. The two young friends were experienced river travelers while the elder Smith was a "complete tenderfoot and sat in the rear as a passenger."[13] Keith, however, felt confident enough in his ability to handle one of a pair of "two-by-fours for and oar."[14]

Navigating the unwieldy craft was quite a problem. "Once we warded the boat off an overhanging cliff with our two-by-fours."[15] On the third day of the trip, as the crew passed just below the mouth of Henry's Fork, they "hit a rock which sprang a leak in the boat, but by bailing"[16] they kept the vessel afloat and were fortunate to continue down the river. Late that evening they beached opposite the Red Bench where they were to spend the summer. The Smiths' intention was to homestead. The land, however, was within the boundaries of the Uintah Forest Reserve. Here they waited while a special permission petition was presented for them at the land office in Vernal.

During the summer of 1902, the Smiths made several trips by wagon to Green River, Wyoming. The incidents that occurred on these journeys reveal much about the roads, terrain, and general travel conditions in the area. On one trip, for example, while nearing Sheep Creek, the grade of the last ridge was too steep for the horses to

The Vernal-Manila Road near Sheep Creek in 1931. (Daggett County)

pull until the wagon load was lightened. The jettisoned cargo was carried to the top of the hill by hand. Coming down the reverse slope was no easier. The horses were difficult to control and Smith was forced to unharness them and walk them home. Returning the next day with the team, Keith secured the hind wheel with logging chains. Only then could the wagon safely descend the hill.

By the fall of 1902, the Smiths had not yet received permission to homestead the Red Bench. The decision was made to leave Sheep Creek and purchase a ranch near the mouth of the Henry's Fork. From this new site, Keith Smith's diverse experiences in travel and transportation in the Daggett country continued.

The Smith ranch progressed nicely. Buildings were repaired and built and various livestock purchased. In conjunction with neighbor Marius Larsen, the family opened the Smith and Larsen Mercantile Company in 1903. Larsen's interest was soon bought out, but the company name was kept. Supplying the store proved a difficult task. As a boy, J. Kent Olson helped his father freight supplies for Smith and Larsen. He remembered:

> Our wagon was a "Wynona [*sic*]." It was a wagon to be proud of. The main difference between Wynona and others lay in the hubs. The Wynona had steel clad hubs. It hauled the logs for our house, the wood to heat the house and in the winter, hauled merchandise from Green River, Wyoming for the Smith and Larsen Merc. Co. I had gone with father on one or two of these freighting trips. It took two days to drive into Green River and three to return. This required four nights camping. I can still hear the horses munching their oats and hay as we lay in bed near the wagon where they were tied. We were up and traveling before daylight with the wheels squeaking along in the cold snow. I had to walk a lot of the time to keep my feet warm. To pull a wagon loaded with freight, the horses had to plod along slow and steady, about the speed that one would walk. On a steep hill the team had to be rested at intervals according to the judgement of the driver. If the horses knew they would be rested when it was necessary for them to get their wind, confidence grew between horses and driver so that when the word was given to proceed farther up the hill, they were ready to do their best. If, on the other hand, they didn't know they would be rested, they possibly would balk for fear of dropping from exhaustion.[17]

After a brief trip east to be married in December of 1905, Keith Smith returned with his bride to the ranch. With the exception of blacksmithing, the essential repair work concomitant with ranching was done on site. In 1908, however, Smith had the opportunity to hire a blacksmith. A blacksmith could repair wagons and farm

Sheep crossing the Green River on the Swinging Bridge. (Daggett County)

machinery for the ranch and the growing Linwood community. A shop was constructed; a forge and other equipment were ordered in April but did not arrive until July. The tools and accoutrements finally came down the river "on the maiden and only [*sic*] voyage of a steamboat called the *Comet*."[18] Once again, Smith provides an introduction to one of the most fascinating stories in the region's transportation history.

The steamboat *Comet* was the product of a group of Sweetwater County, Wyoming, and Linwood, Utah, businessman who had formed the Green River Navigation Company on March 18, 1908 for

> the carrying on and conduct of a general transportation business by water in all its manners and details upon the Green River, a tributary of the Colorado River, rising in the state of Wyoming, and flowing through the states of Wyoming, Colorado and Utah; including the carrying for hire of passengers and freight of all descriptions between various places upon said river by boats run by steam, gasoline and other power.[19]

Fortuitously, one of the stockholders, Marius Larsen, had a brother who was a steamboat builder. Holger Larsen traveled from

Germany, made an inspection of the river, found the concept of steamboat navigation to be a feasible one, and agreed to construct the required vessel. Necessary equipment, boiler and engine, for example, were purchased in Chicago and a boat building yard was established on the water's edge in Green River.

Construction proceeded, and the $25,000 craft was christened on 4 July 1908. The ceremonies for this "first boat for commercial purposes that ever floated the waters of the Green River" were impressive.[20] The traditional bottle of champagne was broken on the bow, bands played, and speeches were made praising the contributions to industry and progress that the *Comet* and the navigation of the Green River would bring.

The vessel "was a 60-foot, 40-ton stern-wheeler, with a 60-horsepower boiler and a pair of 20-horsepower engines."[21] The *Comet* undertook her maiden voyage on 7 July 1908. Round-trip tickets for the excursion to Linwood were $5.00. The trip to Linwood required eight hours, but the passengers were entertained with news of William Jennings Bryan's Democratic Party presidential nomination, delicious meals, and plenty of beer.

The return to Green River, however, was no party. Over a thirty-three hour period the *Comet* ran aground, was winched over sandbars, and ran out of fuel many times. Passengers had to help lighten the boat's load to get it across the sandbars and wait while additional coal was carried from ranches and farms along the river. Plans for coaling stations along the route were formulated. The *Comet* made another voyage to Linwood, but problems continued. Smith noted that the *Comet* "unfortunately could not carry enough fuel for the round trip."[22] The company tried operating short excursions, but by the fall of 1908 it was evident that steamboating on the Green River was impractical. The boat was stripped and eventually sank. As the *Comet* dropped beneath the water's surface, the region's aspirations for commercial river navigation disappeared with her.

The Smith memoirs also provide valuable insight into other methods of traveling over and on rivers in the Daggett country. Keith Smith constructed bridges and ferries on his ranch that were similar to others built throughout the area. In the winter of 1902, for example, Smith spanned the Henry's Fork with a bridge "built of log cribs filled with rocks on top of which heavy timbers were laid."[23] This bridge and a replacement were washed out by floods. High water took its toll on other bridges, too. In March of 1906, the Black's Fork bridge was destroyed by rushing torrents "carrying blocks of ice and was not rebuilt for two years."[24] Fording the river at lower water was not accomplished until April. A summer storm in July 1910 swept away the reconstructed bridge. In a hurry to reach Green River, Smith made a dangerous high-water fording of the river:

> I wired the singletrees to the traces and then we perched on the backs of the buggy seats. The horses had to swim and water came over the seats. The buggy wobbled from side to side but miraculously did not turn over.[25]

As mentioned above, the Smiths were also involved with the construction and operation of ferries. Their first ferryboat was built "by a Scot from Brown's Park" in 1912.[26]

> The ferry was attached at both ends by a trolley to a cable. The current pushed it in either direction, depending on which end of the ferry was winched upstream. It was a long process to transport a herd of two thousand sheep who neither wanted to get on or get off. We replaced the ferry twice. Each ferry lasted six years.[27]

The Green and other rivers provided an alternate, albeit seasonal, avenue of regional transportation. When frozen, the water's surface became a viable—though dangerous—bridge and roadway. During the very hard winter of 1904–05, Smith remembered that he and his wife

> crossed the river at Badger Bottom. The river was frozen but so slippery that the horses skidded when they tried to cross it. I unharnessed the team and Effie and I walked across with the horses resting their heads on our shoulders. We returned to the other side and pulled the buggy across.[28]

The greatest advancement in Daggett County transportation was the introduction of the automobile. These vehicles appeared on the local transportation scene in the second decade of the twentieth century, and Keith Smith became an early proponent. On a trip in 1911 to pick up visiting friends, he had planned to rent cars in Green River to make the journey back to the ranch more comfortable. Smith set out on horseback followed by a freight wagon to carry the party's luggage. At the foot of Green River Canyon he "met two carloads [of the friends] driven by the Gaenssler brothers who owned cars and had generously volunteered their services."[29] For the return trip to Green River after the visit Smith

> assembled three automobiles to carry the family. . . . A buckboard was used for the luggage. One rented car got four flat tires and had to be left on the road. Another got one flat tire at the top of the Green River Canyon, but came down it. Dunton's car, in which I had been riding, arrived intact.[30]

In 1914, the Smiths purchased their first automobile, a Model-T Ford:

> On "The Long Way [To] Tipperary," the road between town [Green River, Wyoming] and the ranch [Linwood, Utah] we always breathed a sigh of relief when we got the midway 'point of no return,' for at least there would be less than a twenty-five mile walk for help.[31]

After his ranch at Linwood became part of Daggett County in 1917 (and the population had grown to four hundred), Keith Smith became a county commissioner. Often acting as chairman of a three-man commission, Smith served for more than eighteen years.[32] Much of the commission's time was spent in improving roads.

In 1918, Sweetwater County, Wyoming, graded an automobile road from Green River to the state line at Linwood. With a new substantial bridge over the Black's Fork, it provided a much more reliable connection to the Union Pacific Railroad. About the same time, Daggett County residents successfully lobbied the Utah Highway Commission to extend this road from Linwood through Manila and westward to connect with the Burnt Fork road.[33]

The county also cooperated with the Ashley National Forest to build a system of forest roads in the 1920s. In his memoirs, Keith Smith revealed that he was particularly proud that he helped "bring

A truck partially submerged when the ice on the Green River gave way. (Daggett County)

about the construction of a road from lower Sheep Creek to Carter Creek."[34] Prior to 1923

> the only way to get on the mountain by car or by wagon was by going west as far as Connor Basin, and then traversing the old army road. Our new piece of road joined the army road farther east . . . There were about ten miles of road, five of which were switchbacks with a ten percent grade. The county put up $10,000 and the Forestry Service gave the same amount [35]

Under the supervision of John Bennett, the U.S. Forest Service began construction of a dependable road through the mountains that would connect Manila and Vernal. Daggett County constructed the section between Manila and the forest boundary. The route went through South Valley, Sheep Creek Gap, switchbacked up the mountain, and headed east to Green's Lakes and Allen Creek. Completed in 1926, it connected with another forest road that went south over the mountain toward Vernal. This route finally supplanted the perilous old Carter Military Road for travel across the Uintas.[36]

Despite such improvements, harsh winter conditions could still make the roads impassable, and travelers continued to use the ice-covered Green River as a thoroughfare. The winter of 1928/29 was a hard one and the feed supply at the Smith ranch was getting quite low:

> The frozen river had less drifted snow on it than the road so we finally resorted to hauling out corn on the ice. We used our truck to haul feed between Rock Springs and Green River . . . and then shifted the corn to a four-horse bobsled as the ice below this point was not strong enough for a truck.[37]

That same winter presented particular problems to the region's mail delivery service. On a normal postal route, for example, the

> mail left the Manila post office each Monday, Wednesday, and Friday at 7 A.M. The first stop was Linwood, the ranches of Brinegar, Buckboard and Holmes and on to Green River. Over roads that were mere cow trails, this round trip took all day by truck.[38]

After Christmas the heavy snow caused the same trip to take two days. The weather then deteriorated to the point that mail drivers Clay and Reed Benson were forced to abandon the truck and begin delivering the mail by bobsled, extending the round trip to four days. On another delivery, while Clay was driving the frozen Green River, "the ice gave way and his truck sank nearly out of sight in the water."[39]

In 1930, Smith and his wife Helen designed and built a bridge over the Green River so that their sheep could cross to the west side of the river for shearing:

> Engineers told us it was impossible to build a bridge for the price we could afford to pay. The Mountain Fuel Supply Company, however donated to us some very heavy cable. Helen and I planned the bridge with large cement "deadmen" buried on each side of the river to hold the cables. The bridge had a wooden floor and wire sides with wooden supports and rails. It was wide enough to lead a horse across. Dogs did not like the bridge because it swayed, but when the sheep once started on it, in spite of the motion, they continued across.[40]

This suspension bridge remained serviceable for thirty years; it was removed at the beginning of construction on the Flaming Gorge

Dam. It was very similar to a bridge constructed across the Green River in 1927 at Brown's Park by Stanley Crouse.[41]

New road building in Daggett County continued as did efforts to improve and maintain existing routes. During the Great Depression, the Civilian Conservation Corps built a scenic highway up Sheep Creek that bypassed the difficult switchbacks. It constructed a new road from Summit Springs to the old Carter Road and then rebuilt that road down Birch Creek toward McKinnon. To improve maintenance, Daggett County received a motorized truck and grader in 1938. This machinery replaced five teams that had previously powered the road working equipment.[42]

Even so, automobile travel could still be an adventure. On his way to visit the Smith ranch in 1935, Frank Zeigler wrote:

> First day to Gosling Ranch over the river. Car hauled across by Roy Twitchell with horse-team wagon (coming back water came in through the door). Water got in the clutch, making it take up harshly as Hell. Got stuck several times on "road"—short terrifically steep hills, a bridge caved in (which we repaired with cedar wood and rocks).[43]

Ranch wife Marie Allen also dealt with hazardous driving conditions. On her way from Rock Springs to Brown's Park during the mid-1940s, she encountered Stanley Crouse's old bridge. As the car rolled onto the swinging suspension, she noticed a "gaping space."[44] Getting out of the car

> she got down on her hands and knees beside the car, then crawled behind it. In the red aura of the taillights she jerked three flat boards from the old bridge, dragged them to the front of the car, crawled to the hole and laid the boards across it.[45]

Marie scrambled back to the car and carefully maneuvered the automobile across the bridge and out of danger. In a land of sudden storms with miles of backcountry roads, she—and other area drivers—would have many close calls over the years.

In 1947 Daggett County saw its first paved road. The state highway traversing the county through Manila and Linwood was blacktopped, and the connecting Wyoming road to Green River was paved shortly thereafter. To prepare for the construction of Flaming Gorge Dam, paving and upgrading the highway over the mountains to Vernal began in 1956. Daggett County now had reliable all-weather roads to the north and south. Journeys that had once taken two days could now be completed in a couple of hours.[46]

In the fall of 1960, Keith Smith, "at the sprightly age of eighty," was elected Daggett County Representative to the Utah Legislature where he was a member of the Highway Committee.[47] In the summer of 1962, Smith was notified that, to make way for the rising waters of Lake Flaming Gorge, everything would have to be removed from his ranch by the end of the year. Some parts of the old house, including material from Uncle Jack Robinson's historic cabin, were moved and incorporated into a new house at Greendale. This new family homestead was quite affectionately named "High Linwood."[48]

Keith Smith dictated the story of his long and interesting life in the middle 1960s. His chronicle covered more than sixty years of change in the three-corners region, and nowhere had changes been more dramatic than in the field of transportation. He experienced the evolving nature of travel from horseback to Model-T to the modern highway. He saw the speed of transportation literally go from six miles per hour to sixty miles per hour, and his experiences mirror those of so many others who traversed the region during its long history. At the end of his story, travel was much quicker, safer, and more convenient, but the hazards of the old days were not entirely gone. When blizzards come roaring across the badlands, sub-zero temperatures set in, or heavy rains cause washouts and rockslides, the most routine of trips can still become a struggle for survival.

ENDNOTES

1. Patricia Nelson Limerick, Clyde A. Milner, and Charles E. Rankin, eds., *Trails: Towards A New Western History.* (University of Kansas Press, 1991), 155.

2. Keith Smith, "Reflections of Linwood, Utah," (Typescript at Utah State Historical Society, c. 1965).

3. Smith, "Reflections of Linwood," 8.

4. Smith, "Reflections of Linwood," 8.

5. "The "Carter Military Road," U.S. Forest Service, Ashley National

Forest Brochure, 1993; C.G. Coutant, *History of Wyoming and the Far West,* vol.II (New York: Argonaut Press, 1966), 666; Richard Dunham and Vivian Dunham, *Flaming Gorge Country* (Denver, Co: Eastwood Printing and Publishing, 1978), 197.

6. William A. Carter, "The Fort Thornburgh Road" (copy at Ashley National Forest Office, Vernal, Utah), 1.

7. Carter, "Thornburgh Road," 2.

8. Smith, "Reflections of Linwood," 8.

9. Smith, "Reflections of Linwood," 9.

10. Smith, "Reflections of Linwood," 10.

11. Smith, "Reflections of Linwood," 10.

12. Smith, "Reflections of Linwood," 10.

13. Smith, "Reflections of Linwood," 10.

14. Smith, "Reflections of Linwood," 10.

15. Smith, "Reflections of Linwood," 10.

16. Smith, "Reflections of Linwood," 10.

17. J. Kent Olson, *Never Marry a Rancher* (Hiller Industries, 1979), 28.

18. Smith, "Reflections of Linwood," 33.

19. "Article II, Certificate of Incorporation of Green River Navigation Company," State of Wyoming, County of Sweetwater,

1908, 1.

20. "Steamboat Christened." *Green River Star,* Supplement,

July 10, 1908, 1.

21. "Green River Dreamboat Hits Rocky Sailing In 1908 Venture,"

Sweetwater County Guide, Tuesday, 25 August 1987, 8.

22. Smith, "Reflections of Linwood," 33.

23. Smith, "Reflections of Linwood," 15.

24. Smith, "Reflections of Linwood," 29.

25. Smith, "Reflections of Linwood," 36.

26. Smith, "Reflections of Linwood," 39.

27. Smith, "Reflections of Linwood," 39.

28. Smith, "Reflections of Linwood," 23.

29. Smith, "Reflections of Linwood," 37.

30. Smith, "Reflections of Linwood," 37.

31. Smith, "Reflections of Linwood," 41.

32. Smith, "Reflections of Linwood," 46.

33. Dunham, *Flaming Gorge Country,* 320.

34. Smith, “Reflections of Linwood,” 46, and “Notes from meetings of the County Board of

Equalization,” Manila, Daggett County, Utah, 21 May and 24 June 1923, 67.

35. Smith, “Reflections of Linwood,” 48.

36. Dunham, *Flaming Gorge Country,* 321.

37. Smith, “Reflections of Linwood,” 49.

38. Mary E. Tinker, “No Wonder Mail Was Late,” Salt Lake

City, 14 April 1963, 5.

39. Tinker, “Mail Was Late,” 6.

40. Smith, “Reflections of Linwood,” 39–40.

41. Harold Calder, “Bridges of Brown’s Park, Bountiful, Utah, notes and photographs on bridge construction, 1984.

42. “Daggett County Gets Road Aids,” *The Salt Lake Tribune,* 16 October, 1938; Dunham, *Flaming Gorge Country,* 321,322.

43. Smith, “Reflections of Linwood,” 51.

44. Diana Allen Kouris, *The Romantic and Notorious History of Brown’s Park.* (Greybull, Wyoming: The Wolverine Gallery), 261.

45. Kouris, *Brown’s Park,* 264.

46. Dunham, *Flaming Gorge Country,* 322.

47. Smith, “Reflections of Linwood,” 56.

48. Smith, “Reflections of Linwood,” 56.

CHAPTER 11

A RECREATIONAL ECONOMY

> Welcome to Flaming Gorge Country. . . . Only primitive roads lay across the eastern Uintas when construction of Flaming Gorge Dam began in 1957. Dam construction, the development of the recreation area, and construction of highways have ushered in the modern era for this ageless country.
>
> PROMOTIONAL BROCHURE

In Daggett County and many other areas of the American West, the decades following World War II have brought tremendous change. Agriculture and extractive industries, the West's traditional economic base, have declined in importance. With the aid of massive water-development projects, it has been the West's cities that have boomed in the postwar era. Manufacturing, defense, electronics and the growing service sectors have brought millions of new jobs to budding Western metropolises. A spiralling urban population has enjoyed unprecedented gains in both spendable income and leisure time, and recreation and tourism have become one of the region's biggest industries.

In terms of human history, tourism as we know it is a fairly recent phenomenon. It grew out of the industrial revolution and the

The Manila LDS Church, 1997. (Allan Kent Powell)

emergence of the middle class. According to historian John Opie: "Beginning with the New York-New England 'Grand Tour' taken by Manhattanites in the 1830s, and the traditional middle class 'summer vacation' first by train and later by automobile, tourism became an intrinsic feature of American life."[1]

It was the railroads that made the first concerted efforts to develop the western tourism industry. In an effort to stimulate passenger business, railroads supported the establishment of national parks and built spur lines to many of these sites. They also developed lodges and transportation systems in the parks. Glowing accounts of scenic wonders, exotic landscapes, and colorful native people appeared in railroad brochures, lending an aura of adventure to western travel. At places like Yellowstone and Yosemite, the fledgling industry began to flourish; however, in isolated areas where the railroads did not run, the country remained the province of rugged homesteaders and wild animals.

For the rugged homesteaders in the early days of the Daggett country, recreation, if it could be called that, was generally of a practical nature. Hunting and fishing, for instance, may be viewed as

The Dutch John LDS Church, 1997. (Allan Kent Powell)

recreational in today's society, but in the early days of settlement along the Green River they were also necessities of survival. Early settlers to the Green River basin subsisted in part on the "wild game, ducks, [and] geese, which were plentiful around the river bottom."[2] In addition to these, and venison taken in the mountains and forests, settlers found fish plentiful in the Green River, especially "large white fish," and early communities even made sport of annual seining parties along the river.[3]

Amusements such as dances or holiday celebrations were an exceptional activity. Work was ongoing, and evenings usually were a quiet time. Wilda Swett Irish remembered:

> You worked pretty long days. After dinner, we would go out on the big porch that's on that house there, and just rest, talk a little. People would probably be terribly bored to do what we did, because we just sat there. . . . And then pretty soon Dad would get up and pull his pocket watch out and he'd say, "Well, the old Waterbury say's its time to go to bed."[4]

The area's scenic attractions, however, made it likely that someday Daggett County would attract a national reputation as a scenic wonderland. A 1902 promotional brochure from the Lucerne Land and Water Company called attention to the country's remarkable scenery and wildlife by noting that it

> would be a famous summer resort if scenery galore, such as snow-clad summits, large forests, picturesque canyons, sylvan lakes, and grassy meadows, alone could make it so, for these things are all there in great abundance . . . but easy access, good accommodations and judicious advertising are only conspicuous by their absence.[5]

Although the three-corners region had great recreational potential, the fulfillment of its promise was still years in the future. The creation of national parks, such as Yellowstone in 1872 and Yosemite in 1890, increased the nation's recreational interest. Other national parks followed in the wake of Yosemite, and, by the turn of the century, six areas, containing over 4 million acres, had been set apart as national public parks.

In addition, the federal government also began reserving large areas of forest land. During the 1890s, presidents Benjamin Harrison and Grover Cleveland withdrew over 17 million acres of forest lands from possible homestead entry.[6] The Uintah Forest Reserve, from which the Ashley National Forest was created, was set aside in 1897. A few years later, the administration of President Theodore Roosevelt greatly expanded the national forest system. Nevertheless, recreation constituted a very small percentage of public use on the early national forests. Most who utilized the resources of the Ashley National Forest, for example, were ranchers and lumbermen who had been using the area long before the creation of the forest reserve.

Parley Pratt Peterson, Jr., who served as a ranger on the Ashley from 1917 to 1919, spent most of his time dealing with permit holders—ranchers and loggers. Only once during those years did he note in his work journal any recreationists on the forest. In August 1917 he wrote: "Sunday did not work except walk up to the Hole-in-the-Rock Gap with a party of excursionists from Ogden[.] Park Wherry and J.H. Rushmer and families[,] 10 in number in two Hudson autos. I showed them a wonderfully beautiful camping place."[7]

The proliferation of automobiles during the 1920s made it much

Manila High School, 1997. (Allan Kent Powell)

easier for Americans to pursue recreation in national parks and forests, but access to Daggett County remained quite limited. As late as 1937 there was not a single oiled road in the county. An unimproved gravel road linked Manila to Green River, Wyoming, and a bituminous surfaced road linked Manila to Vernal.[8]

Despite the difficulty of access, a fledgling tourism industry began to develop in Daggett County during the 1930s and 1940s. A small fishing resort was opened at Greens Lakes near Greendale, and the Schofield family opened a lodge at Spirit Lake. Manila had a hotel and two gasoline stations to serve the traveling public.

Recreationists were also showing interest in boating the spectacular canyons of the Green River. Early whitewater enthusiasts of the twentieth century, like Nathaniel Galloway, Julius Stone, and brothers Emery and Ellsworth Kolb, traveled the rapids and canyons of the Green River in relative isolation. According to historian Roy Webb, they formed the vanguard of things to come:

> They were there for the adventure, for the thrill of doing something that few others had done. They were pleasure boaters, tourists. . . . Stone and the Kolbs represent a transition point in the

Dutch John Elementary School, 1997. (Allan Kent Powell)

> history of the human use of the river, when people came not to exploit, but to experience.[9]

Gradually, the river-running business developed out of this sport. Bus Hatch of Vernal, Utah, is often credited as the first to commercialize the activity. In fact, Hatch's ideas eventually came to define the profession. His pioneering efforts on the Green River at Flaming Gorge, Red Canyon, and Lodore awakened many to the prospects of commercial river running. Hatch's river business augmented his income as a carpenter during the Depression, but the small "Galloway"-style boats of the period could only accommodate a boatman and one or two passengers; trips were not particularly lucrative.[10] In addition, most people could not afford the high cost of $6.50 a day for recreation.

Interest in river running dissipated with the arrival of World War II, but technological advances during the war provided Hatch and his competitors with a vastly improved form of whitewater boat. The first rubberized-canvas rafts began appearing at military surplus stores shortly after the end of hostilities. They could be purchased for as little as twenty-five dollars, and they held as many as ten passengers. Hatch and others soon took advantage of this windfall.[11]

Although he shunned the use of rubber rafts, or "baloney boats," as he called them, A.K. Reynolds ventured into the river-running business following World War II. Preferring wooden boats of a design created by Norm Nevills, Reynolds ran excursions from Green River, Wyoming, through Flaming Gorge, and on into Browns Park.[12] With his partners Mike Hallacy, and G.G. "Lug" Larson, he guided excursionists down the Green River until the filling of Flaming Gorge Reservoir. Reynolds told the *Salt Lake Tribune* that the summer of 1958 would be the last time "vacationists [would] be able to explore the rapids and cataracts of Red Canyon." Although he admitted that "Flaming Gorge Lake . . . [would] be one of the most scenic lakes in the entire nation," he noted with sadness that the construction of the dam would put an end to the "complete run through all of Red Canyon and Little Hole to the Brown's Park country."[13]

Increased recreational interest in post-war America was a boon for commercial outfitters like Reynolds and Bus Hatch. U.S. economic expansion created unprecedented prosperity for the nation's middle class. American wage-earners were the beneficiaries of new discretionary income and increased leisure time. Not only could working people generally afford housing, automobiles, and other consumer items, a portion of their income and leisure time could also be spent on recreation. By 1952, according to historian Earl Pomeroy, "ninety-five percent of labor-management agreements provided for vacations with pay," and most wage-earners had three weeks vacation or more.[14]

The result of this development was a skyrocketing demand for recreation, and Americans were continually on the lookout for new adventures and scenery. Coincidentally, the controversy over the proposed Echo Park Dam created a good deal of free publicity for the Green River country. Dam opponents publicized the spectacular scenery and exciting cataracts that would be inundated by the dam, and proponents touted the recreational opportunities that the dam would create. Regardless of the political question, the dam controversy brought the Green River country to the attention of the public.[15] One source claims that during the height of the debate overall

Flaming Gorge. (Allan Kent Powell)

visitation to nearby Dinosaur National Monument increased two hundred percent.[16]

As recreational opportunities in the region were expanding, opportunities in agriculture, the traditional mainstay of the Daggett

Flaming Gorge Reservoir with the Cart Bridge in the distance. (Allan Kent Powell)

County economy, were declining. Science and technology had increased the productivity of American factory workers, and mechanization, agricultural chemicals, and new scientific farming methods were doing the same thing on American farms and ranches. The trend was spurred by government policies aimed at providing inexpensive and abundant food. Farmers and ranchers who purchased new equipment needed more land to get the most out their investment, and the process of farm consolidation that began in World War II continued at an accelerated pace in the postwar era. In the 1930s there were more than eighty farms and ranches in Daggett County; by 1960 the number had dropped to forty-nine. The result was fewer available jobs in local agriculture. Sons and daughters of ranching families moved from the area to find new opportunities in the cities, and their aging parents often sold out to larger operators.[17]

When Flaming Gorge Dam was proposed as an alternative to the controversial Echo Park site, its construction promised economic development to a region that could not provide many jobs for its young people. The dam, and the tourism associated with it, would certainly pump a great deal of money into the Daggett County economy, and it hopefully would allow many of the county's young men and women to make a living without leaving home. During the dam's construction during the late 1950s and early 1960s, the construction boom and the promise of a dynamic new tourist industry began to remake the local area.

Two trailer parks were built in Manila, and Norman "Sonny" Larsen opened a movie theater called the Flame. Stores and cafes sprang up, and the Manila Ward of the LDS church constructed a new chapel. This rapid growth brought water shortages and sewage problems. Manila became an incorporated town and constructed new water and sewer systems in 1963.

Public safety took an important step forward when the town of Manila organized a volunteer fire department in 1965. With funds provided by the Daggett County Lions Club, a used fire engine was purchased, and a quonset hut was erected by volunteers for use as a fire station. The *Vernal Express* reported that, "Now that the new firehouse is nearing completion and Manila can depend upon a fire truck and a good hydrant system, residents can breathe much easier, especially those who remember the "bucket brigade" of not so long ago."[18]

Spurred by recreational development, Manila's growth continued, and so did its water and sewer problems. By December 1966,

Flaming Gorge Reservoir and the top of Flaming Gorge Dam. (Allan Kent Powell)

bids were being accepted for construction of enlarged sewage lagoons. A new well was also developed at Birch Springs. Unfortunately, the well did not produce as much water as expected, and water shortages continued.

Big changes also came to the unincorporated areas of the county. Property values began rising as developers and speculators bought up land that they believed had recreational or commercial value. Lewis Lyman Swett, son of Oscar Swett, had hoped to buy his father's ranch at Greendale. Orson Burton and Sylvan Arrowsmith had both sold out in the 1950s, and Oscar Swett was the last of the old Greendale ranchers. Lewis Swett commented: "Well, at one time I was in hopes to buy the place to live. But it was so high it wasn't adjustable for farming. When the value of the property went up that much you couldn't farm it and come out."[19] Oscar Swett eventually sold his 397 acres to a developer for $500 an acre. The same developer had also acquired other property in Greendale. Ironically, much of the land was later condemned by the U.S. Forest Service.[20]

Another developer, the Flaming Gorge Recreation Company,

The Green River below Flaming Gorge Dam. (Allan Kent Powell)

started a subdivision at Taylor Flats in Browns Park. Brochures portrayed the area as an outdoor paradise for hunters and fishermen, and an unimproved 10,000-square-foot lot sold at the time for $299. Like so many 1960s land-development schemes, the Taylor Flats subdivision developer went out of business before utilities and other amenities were provided. Property owners eventually got together and arranged for Moon Lake Power Company to extend electric lines to their homesites.[21]

Government agencies were also interested in Browns Park property. The U.S. Fish and Wildlife Service decided that the sheltered valley would make an excellent addition to its system of wildlife refuges, and it set about purchasing most of the valley's ranches. The government threatened use of its eminent domain powers, and ranchers were forced to give in. Some may have been happy to get the money, but other ranch families found it a traumatic experience.

Bill and Marie Allen, owners of the Park Livestock Ranch, did not want to sell, but they acquiesced when the government threatened to invoke its powers of eminent domain. The "Park Live" had a long and rich history, and the Allens' roots had sunk deep into the land. Diana Allen Kouris poignantly remembered:

> One afternoon, when time at the Park Live was growing short, Marie put on her familiar gold-colored cowboy hat and she and Diana walked halfway up the side of the nearby rocky hill. . . . When they reached the corral fence, Marie climbed halfway up the grayish white poles. She gazed across the corrals where Charlie Crouse, Albert Williams, Butch Cassidy, Ford DeJournette, her own family, and so many others had made plans and worked stock. A tear soaked into the weathered wood as Marie slowly took off her hat and hung it on the top of the post. Arm in arm, mother and daughter walked away.[22]

In July 1965 the United States government established the 14,500-acre Browns Park National Wildlife Refuge. The Utah Division of Wildlife Resources gained control of another 1,500 acres that became the Browns Park Waterfowl Management Area. In efforts to clear refuge property, numerous ranch buildings and structures were razed without consideration of their historic value. The Allen family eventually moved back to Browns Park and purchased the Red Creek Ranch. This ranch and the Radosevich Ranch on Willow Creek became the last two working ranches on the Utah side of Browns Park.[23]

Trout fishing in the Uinta Mountains. (Frank Jensen)

In 1968 other familiar faces returned to Browns Park. Longtime area schoolteacher Esther Campbell and her husband, Duward,

A fisherman follows a well-worn path through Little Hole along the Green River. (Frank Jensen)

retired to the old John Jarvie property. "Miss Esther" had taught at the old Lodore School and other country schools in Colorado and

Utah. The Campbells acquired the property through a trade with the Allen family. They raised palomino horses and had about one hundred head of cattle. After her husband's death, Esther Campbell remained and turned the old Jarvie store into a private museum. She later moved to Maeser, and the thirty-five-acre Jarvie property was bought by the Nature Conservancy, which, in turn, sold it to the Bureau of Land Management. It is now preserved as an important cultural resource.[24]

At Flaming Gorge, both the U.S Forest Service and the National Park Service were busy constructing marinas and campgrounds. The National Park Service was charged with construction and maintenance of most of the facilities along the lakeshore. It was to administer the area north of the national forest boundary, and the Forest Service was responsible for development within the Ashley National Forest. This division of responsibility led to interagency rivalry and what some thought was an unnecessary duplication of visitor facilities.

In 1963 Harold Crane, director of the Utah State Fish and Game Department, noted that the "dark cloud of inter and intra-agency competition instead of cooperation still hangs heavily overhead." This duplication of effort was most noticeable at Flaming Gorge. Crane stated:

> The National Park Service is planning to spend in excess of $8 million by June, 1969 for recreation development; whereas, the U.S. Forest Service, in turn, is spending $2 million for similar developments. In this case two agencies are building five boat launching facilities with the accompanying camp ground and picnic areas on approximately 32 miles of reservoir.[25]

The U.S. Congress finally resolved these issues in September 1968. In an effort to stem interagency rivalry, cut administrative costs, and curtail duplication of services, the entire Flaming Gorge region was made a National Recreational Area (NRA). Administrative responsibility for the 196,000-acre Flaming Gorge NRA was given to the United States Forest Service on 1 January 1969. The area included camping and boating facilities plus sixty-six square miles of water surface behind Flaming Gorge Dam. The act that created

Fishing from a boat on the Green River just below Flaming Gorge Dam. (Allan Kent Powell)

the NRA directed the Forest Service, under the supervision of the Secretary of Agriculture, to conserve scenic, scientific, and historic areas; promote public outdoor recreation; and initiate "such management, utilization, and disposal of natural resources as in his

Horseback riding is a popular recreational activity in Daggett County. (Frank Jensen)

judgement will promote or [be] compatible with, and not significantly impair the purposes for which the recreation area is established." Responsibility for operating the dam remained with the Bureau of Reclamation.[26]

Thus ended the rivalry between the National Park Service and the U.S. Forest Service—at least at Flaming Gorge. In retrospect, the duplication of recreational facilities around the lake was probably a good thing. Improved access from Interstate 80 in Wyoming soon made the area extremely popular. The Forest Service estimated that only a few hundred people visited Flaming Gorge in 1957; in 1969, however, it figured that 500,000 visitor days had been spent there.[27]

Daggett County by 1970 was well on its way to becoming a playground for the Intermountain West. New subdivisions and summer homes were popping up throughout the county, resorts and motels were being built, and a number of businesses had opened to serve the traveling public. Author Richard Dunham commented that:

> from being an isolated ranching community, Manila has become tourist oriented, with new restaurants, motels, campgrounds, and trailer courts. Steinaker's store has turned into a supermarket.

> Service stations now cater as much to boats as they do autos. And a significant change is that young people no longer have to go elsewhere to make a living, but can make a living right here, either with the government or with the various tourist businesses.[28]

Dunham went on to note that some visitors had become residents. Whereas the population of the county had been only 350 in 1950, it had increased to 666 by 1970. Increased business outlets and a larger population meant an increased tax base, and both Daggett County and the Town of Manila were able to provide improved facilities and services to their citizens.[29]

In 1972 county officials began to think of building a new courthouse. The old frame courthouse, originally built as the Manila School early in the century, was no longer adequate for the needs of a growing area. In that year, the county began saving federal Revenue Sharing funds for construction purposes. In 1977 a Capital Project Fund was created, and the accumulated Revenue Sharing money was added to in lieu tax funds. With the overwhelming passage of a $250,000 bond election on 21 March 1978, the funding package was completed. Construction began in May on the site of the old courthouse.

The new Daggett County Courthouse was dedicated on 19 December 1978. This 10,000-square-foot facility is a one-story building of brick and block construction. It contains a spacious courtroom, jail holding cells, all county offices, and a meeting room for the Daggett County Commission. Fortunately, the old courthouse was not torn down; the historic structure was moved about a block to the south where it now is part of a motel complex.

A few years later, the county received a grant and started an emergency medical program. An ambulance was purchased and more than twenty local residents were trained as Emergency Medical Technicians (EMTs). Without a doctor in the county, and with the closest hospital some fifty miles away, county residents found this to be a major step forward in local medical care.[30]

Meanwhile, Manila continued to struggle with its water system. Mayor Charles Willis hoped that a new well at Cedar Hollow would finally solve the problem. Unfortunately, that was not the case. Clara

The rodeo grounds in Manila. (Allan Kent Powell)

Robinson remembered that, "Mr. Willis was able to get funding from Water Resources to drill a big well at Cedar Hollow, which seemed to be the answer, but if there was a leak anywhere there would be an air block afterward and people on the upper end of the line would be out of water."[31]

When Blaine Tuttle created a new subdivision within the town, Manila's water problems worsened. The town explored the possibility of working with the Sheep Creek Irrigation Company and government agencies on a reservoir project in Longs Park. Town officials eventually decided that it would cost too much to purify the water. They dropped out of the project and arranged to purchase water from a well owned by the Pallesen family.[32]

It was not until the 1980s, during the administration of Mayor Carole Scott, that Manila finally achieved a dramatic improvement in its water-delivery system. Town workers found that the cast-iron water lines laid in 1963 had suffered greatly from an electrolytic reaction with the soil. A newspaper correspondent reported that, "the last ten years there has been serious leaks causing the town to be drained

The historic Swett Ranch, administered by the United States Forest Service, is a popular stop for summertime visitors to Daggett County. Here are the three homes built by Oscar Swett—the 1912 one-log cabin on the left, the 1919 two-room log house on the right, and the 1929 five-room lumber house in the center. (Allan Kent Powell)

in a very short time. Some winters there has been two or three of these breaks. This past year a whole section had to be replaced."[33]

A $56,000 bid to replace 6,000 feet of six-inch pipe and 1,000 feet of two-inch pipe was accepted from a Mapleton construction company on 24 October 1982. Work began later that month. A series of valves was installed to maintain water pressure in the higher areas of the system, and new fire hydrants were located throughout the town.[34]

In 1986 Mayor Scott also oversaw construction of a new city building. The structure was built with both paid and volunteer labor adjacent to the existing senior citizens center, and Merle Young of the *Vernal Express* wrote:

> The real frosting on the cake is the completion of a new town hall with offices, meeting rooms, and an attached triple garage. Housed within the garage are the town's fast response unit and fire engine and Daggett County's ambulance which is kept there at no cost to

> the county. On the other end of the complex is the Senior Citizens Center which has been totally remodeled, a kitchen added and the structure tied into the newly built town building.[35]

Clearly, Flaming Gorge Dam had brought a wave of development to Daggett County; but not all the changes were considered positive. The filling of the reservoir and the building of recreational facilities had destroyed the community of Linwood, flooded spring pastures, and closed off other areas to livestock grazing. The creation of wildlife refuges in Browns Park had dislocated ranch families. Furthermore, increased property values tempted many ranchers to sell out, and their land became recreational property. A longtime Manila resident commented, "We used to have a lot of little farms and ranches, but they have been bought up by people with money. Only one or two families live on ranches where there used to be many families."[36]

Statistics tell the story. In the middle 1930s there were eighty-one farms and a farm population of 323 people in Daggett County. A government report at the time stated that, "The resources of the county principally are agricultural." By 1970 there were only twenty-six farms in the county, and total personal farm income was listed as $83,000. In comparison, nonfarm personal income was reported at $1,483,000, and personal income from government employment was $1,231,000. The importance of agriculture in the county economy had plummeted.[37]

Not only had the dam disrupted traditional economic patterns, it brought increased public safety problems. For some tourists, Daggett County was still the "Wild West" where there were no rules. Drownings, drunk driving, drug use, fireworks violations, and petty theft became quite common. Search-and-rescue activities and emergency medical calls began to strain county resources. The Daggett County Sheriff's Office reported the following statistics for April 1983:

> 56 calls were answered, 41 warnings were issued, 40 citations were issued and 8 arrests were made. 5 for DUI, 1 public intoxication, 2 possession of a controlled substance. Assistance was given 35 times to motorists and other law enforcement agencies; 3 thefts were

These buildings, just to the west of the Oscar Swett homes, were an important part of the ranch operation. (Allan Kent Powell)

> investigated; a rape-kidnapping originating in Salt Lake City was investigated. Several domestic disturbances were investigated, the issuance of bad checks were investigated and a report of dogs bothering livestock was handled. Total April ticket money was $2,431.[38]

In the midst of all these changes, many county residents began working to preserve their disappearing heritage. The Daggett County Historical Society was organized in December 1969, and the first organizational meeting was held at the Manila Elementary School. Kerry Ross Boren displayed some two hundred items from his considerable collection of Western Americana, and Dr. Charles Peterson and Allan Kent Powell of the Utah State Historical Society conducted the meeting. Peterson led a discussion covering aspects of area history, the marking of historical sites, the preservation of collections and records, and the publishing of history books and articles. Not long after, Kerry Boren, WaNeta Lamb, Timothy Potter, and Delores Redden came together as a committee to draft a constitution and bylaws for the local society.[39]

Many of the society's programs featured talks by some of the county's longtime residents. Mabel Philbrick presented a program on the medical history of the county, George Walkup remembered his days as one of the area's first forest rangers, and Minnie Rasmussen took members on a field trip to historic sites in Browns Park. Stories of early settlers, the Outlaw Trail, rustling, and mysterious killings were favorite topics for discussion.

In the 1970s, author and retired university professor Richard Dunham revisited Daggett County to write his comprehensive local history, *Flaming Gorge Country.* Looking for "Old West" adventure, Dick and Vivian Dunham had moved to Daggett County in 1947. He was a scholar and she was a concert pianist, and they had come to the area to live out some of their fantasies. They stayed a couple of years before returning to the world of academia; but they wrote and published a small booklet on Daggett County history entitled *Our Strip of Land.*

Decades later, the Daggett County Lions Club persuaded Dunham to revise and expand the booklet. Vivian had died, and Dick Dunham welcomed the project. The result was more than a revision—it was a greatly expanded work. Dunham combed mountains of historical material dealing with every aspect of regional history. The result was a volume of almost 400 pages that delves deeply into the history and lore of the entire three-corners area. Loving a good story, Dunham included numerous yarns, some of which may be more lore than fact. It is unfortunate that Dunham did not cite his sources in any detail; still, his 1977 work was a milestone in the preservation of Daggett County history. Dick Dunham's contacts with some of the region's pioneers gave him insights that later historians will never be able to duplicate. Those who follow are forever in his debt.

Another milestone in Daggett County history was marked on 6 October 1992 when the Flaming Gorge National Recreation Area celebrated its twenty-fifth anniversary. Only a handful of visitors and government employees were present as District Ranger Steve Sams and Bureau of Reclamation Manager Tom Welsted served up birthday cake donated by the Flaming Gorge Natural History Association. During this anniversary year, more than 2 million visitors had come to the Flaming Gorge National Recreation Area. In addition to promoting traditional recreational activities like boating and fishing, the U.S. Forest Service had started to promote hiking, mountain biking, and cross-country skiing. The old Oscar Swett Ranch at Greendale had been opened as an historic site, and commercial whitewater trips from the dam to Browns Park had become popular.[40]

Plans were also underway to privatize the government housing area at Dutch John. Since the early days of the national parks and forests, the federal government had provided low-cost housing for its employees in remote areas. This policy began to change during the administration of President Ronald Reagan. The conservative "Reagan Revolution" administrators considered such employee benefits expensive and no longer warranted, and the government began to pull out of the housing business. Various alternatives eventually were presented to make Dutch John a private recreational development or a retirement community. Plans bogged down amid disagreements between various levels of government, and the privatization of Daggett County's second-largest town began to face an uncertain future.

In the county, residents had also begun to realize that despite many improvements in government services, transportation, and business services, the recreational economy brought about by Lake Flaming Gorge had serious limitations. It was, first of all, a highly seasonal economy that was concentrated between Memorial Day and Labor Day. Tourist-oriented businesses had a long, unprofitable off-season, and many employees were laid off for much of the year. Furthermore, many of the jobs in these service businesses were minimum-wage positions—not the kind of jobs that support families and keep young people from moving to the cities.

Empty commercial buildings on Manila's main street also revealed that although gross motel rents in the county had skyrocketed from $188,200 in 1984 to $1,022,600 in 1994, there was still a high mortality rate for local businesses. This was due, at least in part, to the fact that many visitors bring much of their food, gasoline, and other supplies with them and that many of the campground and marina facilities they use are owned by the government.[41]

Most recreational facilities for camping and boating in close proximity to the reservoir are part of the NRA and are not privately owned commercial ventures. In 1986 the Forest Service recommended management plans for the Northern Desert Area, the Conifer Forest Canyon Area, and the Green River Management Area within the Flaming Gorge NRA. The Forest Service's proposed management plan did not encourage private commercial development, as the management decision noted:

> Private use of NRA lands under special use permits will be considered only if there are no other practical means to provide the services and they are needed and not just desired for convenience.[42]

Even in areas where private property existed, such as the Greendale Unit, the management plan suggested that private landowners be encouraged to only make improvements that would "maintain or enhance the values of the surrounding NRA lands."[43] Such policies were traditional approaches to public-land management, but they restricted development in Daggett County's private sector.

A less obvious result of the growth in outdoor recreation, but nonetheless an important one, is the fact that urban recreationists are now major participants in the decision-making process regarding remote public lands. In a county where 92 percent of all lands are either owned by the federal or state governments, this change may significantly affect future development. Environmental opposition has already been directed at oil and gas exploration in the western Uintas, and timber sales and forest road development may come under increased scrutiny.

Even the management of Flaming Gorge Dam may change because of political pressure from the nation's environmental and conservation movements. For many years, environmental and wildlife groups have worked to change the way large hydroelectric dams are operated. Traditionally, Bureau of Reclamation managers have run such dams to maximize power revenue, and the degradation of downstream environments has not been a consideration. At times of low power demand, for example, only one of Flaming Gorge's generators may be on line, and the flow below the dam will be very low. However, on a hot summer evening when lights and air conditioners create peak power demands, the other two units may be brought on line, and the flow below the dam will suddenly increase greatly. Huge fluctuations in water releases have been common during a twenty-four-hour period, and the result has been beach erosion and habitat degradation for native plants and fish.

At Glen Canyon Dam, where environmental groups have focused much of their opposition, the Department of the Interior ordered the Bureau of Reclamation to alter its management practices in order to reduce and repair environmental degradation. Not only will fluctuations in water releases and power output be restricted, massive spring water releases also may become commonplace to mimic the spring floods that were once common on the wild river. In the spring of 1996 a large experimental release of water from Glen Canyon Dam was tried for the first time. Preliminary data seems to indicate that the manmade flood did much to restore beaches and fish habitat downstream in Marble and Grand canyons. Because of this success, Secretary of the Interior Bruce Babbitt has indicated that such practices may become standard procedure at Flaming Gorge and other large hydroelectric dams. If this change occurs, it will in great part be the result of environmental activism, a movement that has been directly connected to the growth of outdoor recreation.

The year of Glen Canyon's manmade flood, 1996, also marked Utah's centennial of statehood, and, like people all across Utah, Daggett County residents took time to reflect on their heritage and the changes they had experienced. For those who had grown up during the Great Depression and World War II, the change from an agricultural to a recreational economy was dramatic and not always welcome. These people had been born into an insular community composed mainly of small farmers and ranchers. It was a tightknit group, and outsiders were a rarity. These residents remember the earlier simplicity and close personal relationships, and they tend to forget the drudgery, danger, poverty, and loneliness that were once so commonplace in the county.

But whether the dam had been built or not, the world in which they had grown up could not last. Changes in agricultural markets hastened by World War II, technological advancements, and government policies in large part doomed small farms and ranches. Between 1940 and 1950, the county population had declined to 350 people.

Farm mechanization and consolidation, coupled with the lure of high-paying jobs in the growing cities of the West, were driving people off the land. Like so many communities in other parts of rural America, Daggett County was in decline and Manila might have become a ghost town.

Flaming Gorge Dam brought new life to the area when it was very much needed. It brought high-speed roads that vastly improved transportation, and it brought new jobs and business opportunities in recreation and tourism. It also brought the problems of growth, crime, economic insecurity, and social tension that are all part of life in the modern West.

Younger residents who grew up with Flaming Gorge Dam, now the majority of the county population, are more accepting of the changes that have accompanied it. Directly or indirectly, most owe their jobs to the dam and the tourism it has generated. Even those who commute to mining jobs near Green River, Wyoming, depend on the highways that resulted from the massive reclamation project.

Daggett County has indeed changed greatly during the last half of the twentieth century. Manila has gone from a tiny agricultural village to a tourist town of convenience stores, RV parks, and motels. Linwood is gone entirely beneath the waters of Flaming Gorge Reservoir. Dutch John has arisen it its place, but it is still more a federal employee housing area than a real town. Greendale has changed from a community of small ranches to a resort, and Browns Park now sees more bird-watchers and river rafters than cowboys and outlaws. And, on a busy summer weekend, there now may be more tourists in the county than there are residents.

Yet there is much about the county that remains the same. The rugged Uinta Mountains continue to dominate the scenery, there is still a large amount of farm and ranch land, and the annual Cow Country Rodeo continues to be the major social event of the year. With fewer than one thousand permanent residents, the population density remains less than two people per square mile. There continues to be no bank, doctor, or newspaper. People still must travel to Green River, Rock Springs, or Vernal for most of their health care, shopping, and entertainment needs.

In many ways, Daggett County residents now have the best of both the Old West and the modern era. They can enjoy a friendly small-town atmosphere and great stretches of undeveloped backcountry. Good roads, however, have made amenities in Vernal and Sweetwater County, Wyoming much more accessible. Television, telephones, and the computer internet have done much to end the feeling of isolation. More importantly, residents now have many of the basic services that larger communities take for granted.

The people of Daggett County are no different from other Americans in following news, sports, and cultural events. County youth participate in organized sports through their schools and other community programs, and adults participate in a variety of sports and activities. Residents cheer the Utah Jazz professional basketball team and county youngsters participate in Junior Jazz programs. Despite the small student body, Manila High Schools boys' and girls' basketball teams have enjoyed great success in the mid-1990s, and enthusiastic community support along with the coaching skills of Robert Anderson and school principal Bruce Northcutt have helped to make this possible.[44]

Success has also been noted in the classroom. Honors have been bestowed upon many students, including a national champion, Josh Keller, in the school's Future Farmers of America program, and state champions in the Future Business Leaders of America program. Many students have to travel forty miles to class, and the dedication that they and other community residents display in support of school and community endeavors is noteworthy.[45] County residents definitely feel part of society's mainstream even though they are tucked away in a relatively quiet corner of the state.

Such is the paradox of Daggett County. As it looks to life in a new century, it continues as a small rural community isolated by mountains and badlands; yet modern roads, services, and communications technology have enriched the lives of its citizens. Compared to Denver or the Wasatch Front, Daggett County may still be the western frontier—but it is a frontier with waterskiing, an airstrip, and satellite television.

ENDNOTES

1. John Opie, "Environmental History in the West," in *The Twentieth Century West: Historical Interpretations,* Gerald D. Nash and Richard Etulain, eds. (Albuquerque: University of New Mexico Press, 1989), 217.

2. *Builders of Uintah: A Centennial History of Uintah County, 1872 to 1947* (Springville, UT: Daughters of Utah Pioneers, 1947), 65.

3. Ibid.

4. Eric Swedin, "Wilda Swett Irish," *Swett Ranch Oral History Project* (Logan: Mountain West Center for Regional Studies/Ashley National Forest, 1989), 8.

5. "Operations of the Lucerne Land and Water Company," promotional brochure, Harold B. Lee Library, Brigham Young University, 23–24.

6. Paul W. Gates, *History of Public Land Law Development* (Washington, D.C.: Government Printing Office, 1968), 567.

7. Parley Pratt Peterson, work journals, 1917–1919, Special Collections and Archives, Merrill Library, Utah State University.

8. State Road Commission of Utah, General Highway Map, 1937. Special Collections and Archives, Merrill Library, Utah State University.

9. Roy Webb, *If We Had A Boat,* 101.

10. The Galloway style boat takes its name from Nathaniel Galloway, who designed the craft; see Webb, *If We Had a Boat,* 10.

11. Webb, *If We Had a Boat,* 148–49.

12. Nevills spent most of his time running the San Juan River in southeastern Utah and the Colorado River through Grand Canyon, but he did spend some time on the Green River. His cataract boats became well known on western rivers. His acquaintance with A.K. Reynolds's father, Adrian Reynolds of Green River, Wyoming, influenced A.K. to become interested in river running. See Webb, *If We Had A Boat,* 150, 154.

13. Bryant Stringham, *Salt Lake Tribune,* (n.d.), scrapbook, MSS. 48, Special Collections and Archives, Merrill Library, Utah State University.

14. Earl Pomeroy, *In Search of the Golden West: The Tourist in Western America* (New York: Alfred A. Knopf, 1957), 216.

15. Webb, *If We Had A Boat,* 137.

16. Pomeroy, *In Search of the Golden West,* 198.

17. *Daggett County: Basic Data of Economic Activities and Resources* (Salt Lake City: Utah State Planning Board, 1940), 11; *A Statistical Review of Utah's Economy* (Salt Lake City: University of Utah College of Business, 1960), 110.

18. *Vernal Express,* 25 November 1965.

19. Lewis Lyman Swett, "Swett Ranch Oral History Project," 6.

20. Ibid., 42–43.

21. "The Flaming Gorge Recreation Company," n.d., brochure at the Utah State Historical Society Library.

22. Diana Allen Kouris, *The Romantic and Notorious History of Brown's Park,* 274.

23. Dunham and Dunham, *Flaming Gorge Country,* 340; Kouris, *Brown's Park,* 275, 276.

24. Esther Campbell and Carole L. Jackson, *Visit "Miss Esther" Campbell* (Vernal, UT: Carol Jackson, 1995), 59–61; Kouris, *Brown's Park,* 276–77; "John Jarvie Historic Property," n.d., Bureau of Land Management brochure in author's collection.

25. Harold S. Crane, "States Views on Federal Recreation Programs," 6–7, typescript in Special Collections and Archives, Utah State University.

26. *Flaming Gorge National Recreation Area, Ashley National Forest, Forest Service, U.S. Dept. of Agriculture: Multiple Use Management Guide and Recreation Management Plan,* (Washington, D.C.: U.S. Forest Service, 1970), 1.

27. Ibid., 13.

28. Dunham and Dunham, *Flaming Gorge Country,* 340.

29. Ibid.

30. "Manila," *Vernal Express,* advertising supplement, 18 May 1983.

31. "Manila News," *Vernal Express,* 1 December 1966; Clara Robinson, "Life Story of Clara Geneva Ruble Robinson," manuscript history in author's collection, 20.

32. "Clara Robinson," 21.

33. "Manila," *Vernal Express,* advertising supplement, 20 October 1982.

34. Ibid.; "Clara Robinson," 21; *Vernal Express,* 23 July 1986.

35. *Vernal Express,* 23 July 1986.

36. Ibid.

37. *Inventory of the County Archives of Utah: Daggett County,* 13; *Daggett County: Basic Data,* 10, 11; *Utah Statistical Abstract, 1976* (Salt Lake City: University of Utah College of Business, 1976), XV-11, XV-16.

38. *Vernal Express,* 18 May 1983.

39. *Vernal Express,* 11 December 1969.

40. The Swett Ranch is currently one of five Daggett County historic sites listed on the National Register of Historic Places. The others are the John Jarvie Ranch, Dr. John Parson's cabin, petroglyphs near Manila, and the Ute Mountain fire tower.

41. *Statistical Abstract of Utah: 1996,* 497.

42. *Final Environmental Impact Statement for the Ashley National Forest: Forest Plan for Land and Resource Management Plan* (Washington, D.C.: U.S. Forest Service, 1986), A26–A46. The Northern Desert Area included the units at Antelope Flat, Firehole, Buckboard, Squaw Hollow, Lucerne, and Linwood Bay; the Conifer Forest Canyon Area included the Scenic Highways Unit, Boat Camps Unit, Undeveloped Areas Unit, Greendale Unit, Cedar Springs–Bootleg-Mustang Unit, Red Canyon Unit, and the Sheep Creek Unit; and the Green River Management Area included the Green River Corridor Unit, Dutch John Unit, and Undeveloped Areas Unit.

43. Ibid., A39.

44. *Salt Lake Tribune,* 22 December 1997, C1.

45. Ibid.

EPILOGUE

> Since the creation of Daggett County, we have seen prosperity to a certain extent, we have seen drought and depression to its full extent, we have seen people and families come and go, but the sturdy, never give ups, are still here.
>
> —MARIUS N. LARSEN

There was almost no snow at all in Daggett County during the winter of 1976–77. A warm, dry fall had been followed by a very dry winter—the driest since the terrible drought year of 1934. But, unlike 1934, this winter brought strong southeast winds that tore at the soil and ripped the grass. On Daggett County's ranches, it was becoming clear that there would be very little feed in the spring. One elderly rancher began a desperate search for pasture in order to save his cattle. He found that his neighbors had also suffered, and there simply was no pasture available.

The options were not good. The cattle could be sold in a depressed market, but that would not provide enough income to meet expenses. With nothing left to do, the rancher and his wife telephoned their children, explaining the situation and asking for their

This 1997 aerial view of Dutch John shows the outline of the temporary housing area in the fore ground. (Edward Lennon—United States Bureau of Reclamation)

prayers. The family pulled together with offers of money and support.

Still, it was hard to keep up the fight. Even before the drought, the ranch had been losing money and the family had been borrowing on their assets. If they sold out, they would at least get something for the place, and the constant worries about weather, markets, and cattle would no longer trouble them. There were feelings of defeat.

An abandoned house near Birch Creek on the Jon Wilde Ranch. (Daggett County)

Yet there was also the barn that had been built in 1934 with logs hauled down from the mountains. It was as solid as ever. There were some thirty miles of six-wire fences in good repair, and one could still look out over the hayfields and stackyards that had been there for generations. The house that the old rancher and his father had built long ago, the house where eight children had been raised, still stood straight and proud.

A few years previously, the ranch had been made into a family corporation, and the regular annual meeting was held that July. Selling the ranch became the primary topic of business. Though the prospects were grim, nobody was ready to make a decision—there were too many memories and emotions tied up in the land. When another meeting was held the following month, the family members made a firm choice: the ranch would not be sold.

Somehow they got through the year, but the ranch was still in danger, and there was no real solution on the horizon. Christmas was

As the twentieth century draws to a close, ranching and western traditions remain an important part of life in Daggett County. (Frank Jensen)

coming. Children and grandchildren came home to visit, and the old rancher was once again asked to sing "O Holy Night" at the family Christmas program. His heart was not in it, but he agreed anyhow. The singing improved his spirits. He looked back at a year that had been filled with so many frustrations, and he counted his blessings:

> It certainly would be a sin not to be happy. Many of the numerous things I possessed to make me happy, the Lord blessed me with, and had come my way, and I had received unwittingly, not knowing the Lord's way was better than mine. I could not have planned it that good.[1]

Such faith and optimism, with a good measure of courage and a great amount of hard work, enabled early settlers of Daggett County to establish a human hold on the land. Though times and situations are changing, altering the relation of humans to much of the land in Daggett County, Utah, and throughout the West, it is that mixture of faith and determined hard work that will allow residents of the country to continue to live in this land that they have come to love.

ENDNOTE

1. J. Kent Olson, *Never Marry a Rancher,* 127–32.

Appendix 1

Daggett County Commissioners

1918
George C. Rasmussen
Niels Pallesen
M. N. Larsen

1919–1920
Niels Pallesen
George C. Rasmussen
Henry Twitchell

1921–1922
Niels Pallesen
John Bennett
S A. Green

1923–1924
John S. Bennett
F. W. Tinker
Keith Smith

1925–1926
Keith Smith
E. W. Tinker
W. W. Tinker

1927–1928
Keith Smith
Ammon Nebeker
Heber Bennion

1929–1930
Keith Smith
Ammon Nebeker
Willard Schofield

1931–1932
Ammon Nebeker
Keith Smith
Willard Schofield

1933–1934
Keith Smith
John Green
W. L. Russell

1935–1936
W. L. Russell
Buell Bennett
Marion F. Twitchell

1937–1938
Buell Bennett
W. L. Russell
Marion Campbell

1940–1941
Walker Russell
Peter G. Wall/Keith Smith
Marion Campbell

1942–1943
Walker Russell
Keith Smith
Marion Campbell

1944–1945
Walker Russell
Keith Smith
Marion Campbell

1946–1947
Marion Campbell/Joseph Steinaker
Keith Smith
Walker Russell

1948–1949
Walker Russell
Keith Smith
Joseph Steinaker

1950–1951
Keith Smith/Levi Reed
John Tinker
Nels Philbrick/John Ylincheta

1952–1953
John Tinker/William Allen
John Ylincheta
Levi Reed

1954–1955
Levi Reed
John Ylincheta/Dixon Christensen/
Albert Neff (appt. 5-3-55)
William Allen

1956–1957
Levi Reed
Albert Neff
Wiliam Allen/Harvard Lee Redden

1958–1959
Albert Neff
Levi Reed/Lawrence Biorn/Jack
Buckley (appt. 11/18/59)
Harvard L. Redden/A. K. Reynolds

1960–1961
Albert Neff/John Ylincheta
A. K. Reynolds
Jack H. Buckley

1962–1963
A. K. Reynolds
John Tinker/Harvard L. Redden
John Ylincheta

1964–1965
John Ylincheta/J. D. Harper
Harvard L. Redden/V. Nelson
A. K. Reynolds

1966–1967
J. D. Harper
Vernon Nelson
A. K. Reynolds/Albert Neff

1968–1969
Albert H. Neff
Vernon Nelson/Levi Reed
J. D. Harper/Burnell Lamb

1970–1971
Albert H. Neff
Burnell Lamb/Milton Beck
Levi Reed, Jr./Forrest Pallesen

1972–1973
Albert Neff
Milton Beck
Forrest Pallesen/Carl Collett

1974–1975
Carl S. Collett
Milton Beck
Albert H. Neff

1976–1977
Carl S. Collett/Vance Grubb (appt. 10-5-77)
Milton Beck/Laray Sadlier
Albert H. Neff

1978–1979
Vance Grubb
Laray Sadlier
Albert H. Neff/George Ellsworth

1980–1981
Laray Sadlier
George Ellsworth
Vance Grubb/Jerry Taylor

1982–1983
Carl S. Collett
Laray Sadlier
Jerry N. Taylor

1984–1985
Laray Sadlier
Jerry N. Taylor/E. J. Steinaker
Carl S. Collett/Duane Lamb

1986–1987
Laray Sadlier
Elbert J. Steinaker, Jr.
Duane Lamb

1988–1989
Laray Sadlier
Elbert Steinaker, Jr.
Duane Lamb/Dick Bennett

1990–1991
Laray Sadlier/Bruce Christensen
Elbert J. Steinaker, Jr.
Dick Bennett

1992–1993
Elbert J. Steinaker, Jr.
James M. Briggs
Dick Bennett/Sharon Walters

1994–1995
Elbert J. Steinaker/Chad L. Reed
James M. Briggs
Sharon P. Walters

1996–1997
Sharon Walters
Chad L. Reed
James M. Briggs

APPENDIX 2

Daggett School District School Board Members

1918
Henry Twitchell
Elbert E. Waite
A.J.B. Stewart
Niels Pallesen
Charles F. Olson

1919
Charles Olson
A.J.B. Stewart
P.G. Wall
F.W. Tinker
A.T. Twitchell

1920
A. T. Twitchell
F.W. Tinker
Charles F. Olson
Marion Twitchell
John Tolton

1921
George Walkup
Heber Bennion, Jr.
Charles F. Olson
Leo B. Stewart
Marion Campbell

1922
Elizabeth Allen
Vern Hardy
Charles F. Olson
George Walkup
Leo B. Stewart

1923
Elizabeth Allen
Vern Hardy
Charles F. Olson
P.G. Wall
Leo B. Stewart

1924
Elizabeth Stanton
Oscar Swett
J.L. Wade
Vern Hardy
A.J.B. Stewart

1926
Elizabeth Stanton
Oscar Swett
J.L. Wade
M. N. Larsen
John Bennett

1927
Niels Pallesen
Elizabeth Stanton
Oscar Swett
M. N. Larsen
John Bennett

1928
P. G. Wall
Archie Lamb
Eli Briggs
Niels Pallesen
John Bennett

1929–30
A. T. Twitchell
Mark Anson
J. S. Bennett
P.G. Wall
Oscar Swett

1931
A. T. Twitchell
Mark Anson
John S. Bennett
Leland A. Mayers
John C. Allen

1932–34
A. T. Twitchell
Silver Licht
John S. Bennett
Leland A. Mayers
John C. Allen

1935
A. T. Twitchell
Silver Licht
Martin Schwab
Leland A. Mayers
John C. Allen

1936–37
Kenneth Reed
Silver Licht
Frank J. Scofield
Leland A. Mayers
John C. Allen

1938–39
Kenneth Reed
Silver Licht
Frank J. Scofield
Leland A . Mayers
John C. Allen

1940
Kenneth Reed
John Allen
Archie Lamb
Leland Mayers
Frank Scofield

1941
Kenneth Reed
John Allen
Archie Lamb
Lemand Mayers
C.A. Christensen

1942
L.A. Meyers
Kenneth Reed
C.A. Christensen
Vernon Nelson
Archie Lamb

1943
M. N. Larsen
Kenneth Reed
C.A. Christensen
Vernon Nelson
Archie Lamb

1944–45
M. N. Larsen
Kenneth Reed
C.A. Christensen
Paul Williams
Archie Lamb

1946
M.N. Larsen
Paul Williams
Claude Jones
Howard Iverson
C.A. Christensen

1947
M. N. Larsen
Paul Williams
Vernon Nelson
Howard Iverson
C.A. Christensen

1948
Vernon Nelson
C.A. Christensen
Howard Iverson
M.N. Larsen

1949
Gene Campbell
Vernon Nelson
John Yincheta
M..N. Larsen
C.A. Christensen

1950–51
C.A. Christensen
Kenneth Reed
M. N. Larsen
John Yincheta
Gene Campbell

1952
Kenneth Reed
John Yincheta
M. N. Larsen
Dick Bennett
C.A. Christensen

1953
Gene Campbell
John Yincheta
Dick Bennett
Alton Beck
Kenneth Reed

1954
Kenneth Reed
Dick Bennett
Gene Campbell
John Yincheta
Alton Beck

1955–56
Dick Bennett
Gene Campbell
John Yincheta
Tom Christensen
Alton Beck

1957
Tom Christensen
John Yincheta
Alton Beck
William Robinson
Dick Bennett

1958
Tom Christensen
John Yincheta
William Robinson
Muerl Larsen
Dick Bennett

1959–60
Frederick O'Regan
John Tinker
Merlin Schofield
Muerl Larsen
William Robinson

1961
Frederick O'Regan
John Tinker
Albert Neff
William Robinson
Merlin Scofield

1962–63
Frederick O'Regan
John Tinker
Albert Neff
William Robinson
Merliln Scofield

1964
William Robinson
George Swan
Albert Neff
Hillis Steinaker
Richard Taylor

1965
William Robinson
Dick Bennett
Jon Wilde
Hillis Steinaker
Richard Taylor

1966
Dick Bennett
Jon Wilde
Hillis Steinaker
Dixon Christensen
Gene Briggs

1967
Jon Wilde
Dick Bennett
Maxie Smith
Weldon Potter
Rex Masters
John Tinker

1968
Jon Wilde
Dick Bennett
Maxie Smith
John Tinker
Rex Masters
Richard Webster

1969
Jon Wilde
Dick Bennett
Maxie Smith
Richard Webster
Peggy B. George

1970–71
Jon C. Wilde
Dick Bennett
Peggy George
Richard Webster
John Tinker

1971–72
Jon C. Wilde
Dick Bennett
Richard Webster
John Tinker
Terry Hopson
Peggy George

1972–73
Jon C. Wilde
Peggy George
Dixie Grubb
Richard Webster
John Tinker

1973–74
Jon C. Wilde
John Tinker
Peggy George
Dixie Grubb
Richard Webster
Gene Briggs

1974–75
John Tinker
Jon Wilde
Dixie Grubb
Harry Opfar
Leslie Schofield

1975–76
John Tinker
Jon Wilde
Dixie Grubb
Harry Opfar
Leslie Schofield
Stephen Thompson

1976–77
John Tinker
Dixie Grubb
Jon C. Wilde
Leslie Schofield
Stephen Thompson

1977–78
John Tinker
Dixie Grubb
Jon C. Wilde
Leslie Schofield
Levi Reed, Jr.

1978–79
John Tinker
Dixie Grubb
Levie Reed, Jr.
Jon C. Wilde
Stephen Thompson

1979–80
Jon Wilde
Dixie Grubb
Levi Reed, Jr.
Stephen Thompson
John Tinker

1980–81
Levi Reed, Jr.
Stephen Thompson
John Tinker
Agnes Briggs
James Olson

1981–82
Stephen Thompson
John Tinker
Levi Reed, Jr.
Agnes Briggs
James Olson

1982–83
James Olsen
Agnes Briggs
Rusty Muir
Joe Johnson
Lee Skabelund

1983–84/84–85
Agnes Briggs
Joe Johnson
Rusty Muir
Lee Skabelund
James Olson

1984–85/85–86
Dixie Grubb
Joe Johnson
Rusty Muir
Lee Skabelund
Bryan Tinker

1986–87/87–88
Rusty Muir
Lee Skabelund
Craig Collett
Bryan Tinker
Dixie Grubb

1988–89/89–90
Rusty Muir
Bryan Tinker
Dixie Grubb
Craig Collett
Lee Skabelund
Bill Taylor

1990–91/91–92
Bryan Tinker
Dixie Grubb
Craig Collett
Lee David
Monica Solawetz
Bud Rogers

1992–93/93–94
Bryan Tinker
Craig Collett
Bud Rogers
Leona Davis
Pat Asbill

1994–95/95–96
Craig Collett
Pat Asbill
Bryan Tinker
Penny Muir
Anne Steen

1996–97/97–98
Craig Collett
Pat Asbill
Penny Muir
Anne Steen
Clyde Slaugh

Bibliographical Essay

Though isolated and small in population, Daggett County has attracted a great deal of literary attention. Much of this can be attributed to the colorful nature of the county's history. Long after most of the country had settled down, the remote Daggett region was a surviving bastion of the "Old West." At the turn of the century, as wild west shows and dime novels mythologized a largely vanished western past, the three-corners region was a place where outlaws, rustlers, and range war were still part of everyday life. The exploits of it's citizens provided new material for an urban population craving tales of Old West adventure.

The Daggett area settled down quickly in the 1900s, but the public demand for tales of western adventure did not abate. Local residents with literary aspirations found a ready market for their reminiscences and even found that the more sensational the stories, the better they were received. Authorship also brought a certain celebrity status. In such a climate, it is no wonder that writers sometimes exaggerated, colored the facts to put themselves or those that were close to them in a better light, or out-and-out fabricated information (telling tall stories was, after all, a western tradition). The curious result of this is that, though much has been written about the county's past, it is sometimes impossible to sort out what is fact, what is folklore, and what is simply untrue.

Much of what is known of the wild days in Browns Park comes from a handful of sources. "The J.S. Hoy Manuscript," the unpublished writings of rancher J.S. Hoy, is one of the few primary documents dealing with this subject. Edited by James G. Hodgson, who at the time was Director of Libraries at Colorado A & M College (now Colorado State University), Hoy's manuscript is a rambling attempt to chronicle the history of Browns Park. The original remains at Colorado State University, and there are copies at a few other research libraries in the Mountain West. It is based partly on research and partly on Hoy's own experiences. As a historical document, it is self-serving and often unreliable. Hoy generally did not get along with his neighbors, and he characterized most of them as thugs and criminals. His writings on Indians and Hispanics are bigoted, and not all his accounts are consistent. The manuscript contains three accounts of the killing of Charley Powers, for example, each varying significantly in details. Researchers should use this source with caution.

Another primary account of old Browns Park is William "Billy" Tittsworth's *Outskirt Episodes,* published in 1927. Tittsworth cowboyed in Browns Park and was a close associate of Charlie Crouse. Though there are kernels of truth scattered throughout the text, some of the stories in *Outskirt Episodes* are highly implausible. In a letter to Esther Campbell, Ann Bassett called the book "fiction" and asserted that it was the work of a ghost writer.

More plausible in many respects, but not without problems, is Matt Warner's *Last of the Bandit Riders,* written with the help of Murray E. King. The book recalls Warner's errant adolescence as a rustler and cowboy in Browns Park and his graduation to full-fledged outlawry in adulthood. Warner's stories are sensational, and he paints a picture of himself as a fast-gun outlaw and close associate of Butch Cassidy. Published in 1940, the book obviously was written for an audience smitten with Hollywood stereotypes. It portrays Warner as a larger-than-life character, yet Browns Park old-timers remembered him as a minor player among his outlaw contemporaries. Still, there is much in the book about outlaw life that rings true in light of modern scholarship, and its tale of Warner's evolution from young tough to armed robber is fascinating.

Though not a primary source itself, John Rolfe Burroughs's 1962 volume *Where the Old West Stayed Young* was based on a great deal of primary research. Burroughs was fortunate in being able to interview a number of people who had personal knowledge of events in Browns Park and northwestern Colorado. However, the most reliable account of doings in old Browns Park may be *The Bassett Women* by Grace McClure. Based on extensive research, this is perhaps as close a rendition of the truth as can be constructed from the confusing and sometimes contradictory accounts that are available.

What is known for sure about Browns Park is that it was a violent community that grew increasingly out of step with the "civilized" ways of a developing western America. The business interests that dominated government in the region worked hard to increase the penalties for property crimes and to enforce the rule of law. This brought people like those in Browns Park for whom rustling was accepted and justice was a matter of personal honor into conflict with an ever more powerful legal system. The writings of historian Richard Maxwell Brown show that such conflict was relatively widespread in the West. Brown's *No Duty to Retreat: Violence and Values in American History and Society* discusses similar situations in the western frontier communities of Tombstone, Abilene, and Bodie. A more concise presentation of these ideas appears in his article "Violence" in the *Oxford History of the American West.* Whereas most books on frontier violence are a retelling of stories, Brown attempts to make sense of the basic social conflicts that precipitated violent situations. It has become popular to dismiss frontier violence as a Hollywood fabrication, but Brown shows that the myth has a basis in fact and that the Old West was at times a very violent place.

While tales of rustling and outlaws dominate much of what has been written about Daggett County, there is a great deal more of historical interest. Three general histories of the area are worthy of mention. *Flaming Gorge Country* by Richard "Dick" Dunham and Vivian Dunham, a greatly expanded rewriting of the earlier booklet *Our Strip of Land,* covers the Daggett County area from the geologic past through the 1970s. The Dunhams' research was comprehensive, and it almost seems that every fact or story that they uncovered was included in the volume. The book was written in a folksy style that now seems somewhat dated or affected, and the authors admit that some of their tales may be more lore than history; however, the book is very engaging and a pleasure to read. Most of the book seems to be based on sound scholarship; however, the Dunhams were not overly critical of sources, and, as the notes are scanty, it is sometimes difficult to discern historical facts from entertaining stories. The book's anecdotes and outlaw yarns are not always believable.

Dianna Allen Kouris's book *The Romantic and Notorious History of Brown's Park* is a general history of Browns Park with an emphasis on the families that lived there. Like the Dunhams' work, it is based on an intimate association with the place and its people. This book is a very personal collection of family stories as they relate to, and come to constitute, the history of a place. Its discussion of the outlaw years in the park, however, shows neither the detailed research nor the depth of understanding presented by Grace McClure.

A third general history dealing largely with the three-corners region is *If We Had a Boat: Green River Explorers, Adventurers, and Runners* by Roy Webb. A Vernal native, river enthusiast, and professional historian, Webb has crafted a fine book on the history of the river and those who have closely interacted with it. *If We Had a Boat* looks at the story of the Green River corridor from the time of the exploration of William Ashley through the construction of Flaming Gorge Dam. It chronicles the voyages of explorers like John Wesley Powell, the exploits of river adventurers like Nathaniel Galloway and the Kolb brothers, and the development of commercial river running. Much of Daggett County's history is tied to the Green River, and Webb's book fills an important niche on the local historian's bookshelf.

For those interested in particular aspects of county history, a number of other works come to mind. Fur-trade enthusiasts will enjoy Harrison Clifford Dale's *The Ashley-Smith Explorations and the Discovery of a Central Route to the Pacific.* This book contains Ashley's own account of his exploration of the Green River and the rendezvous on Henrys Fork. Fred Gowans's *Rocky Mountain Rendezvous* also presents detailed information of the Henrys Fork gathering. *The Life and Times of James P. Beckwourth as told to Thomas D. Bonner* is another account of these events; but Beckwourth was a notorious storyteller. His thrilling story of rescuing General Ashley from the dreaded "Green River Suck" is known to be a tall tale, for example, and much of the information included in this book should be viewed with some skepticism.

The fur traders and trappers who visited the Daggett region considered the entire upper basin of the Green River their home. When the beaver trade ended, some of them entered into a brisk business with overland emigrants as traders, guides, or ferrymen. Their conflict with the Mormons for control of these businesses is well chronicled in *Fort Bridger: Island in the Wilderness* by Fred Gowans and Eugene Campbell. This book is especially noteworthy for its extensive use of quotations. Hope Hilton's *"Wild Bill" Hickman and the Mormon Frontier* also sheds light on the Mormon incursions into the Green River country. Hickman's autobiography, *Brigham's Destroying Angel*, written with the help of Mormon antagonist John H. Beadle, contains Hickman's own highly colored version of events in Green River County and the Utah War.

Perhaps no other portion of the American West was more thoroughly explored than the Uinta Mountains country. *Exploration and Empire: The Explorer and Scientist in the Winning of the American West* by William H. Goetzmann is still the best single volume dealing with the great government surveys of the post-Civil War West. It discusses the Clarence King survey of the Uintas and the diamond hoax, and it recounts both John Wesley Powell expeditions. Wallace Stegner's *Beyond the Hundredth Meridian: John Wesley Powell and the Second Opening of the American West* is a fine biography of the one-armed Major. Powell's own book, however, *Exploration of the Colorado River and its Canyons*, took liberties with the facts and combined into one account events from both his river journeys. The assembled journals and diaries of the crewmen on both Powell expeditions can be read in the 1948 and 1949 bound volumes of the *Utah Historical Quarterly*.

For insights into the day-to-day life of a survey party in the Uinta country, no book is more readable and entertaining than *The Passing of the Great West: Selected Papers of George Bird Grinnell,* edited by Robert Rieger. As a young man, Grinnell accompanied the O.C. Marsh paleontological expedition along the route of the newly completed Pacific railroad, and this was one of the signal events in his life. Grinnell's writings vividly recall life in camp and field. His account of a visit with the mountaineers on Henrys Fork provides a remarkably detailed description of Daggett County's earliest settlers.

The best single source dealing with the settlement and development of Daggett County is the Dunhams' *Flaming Gorge Country.* The authors lived in the county during the 1940s, and they talked with many of the area's pioneers. There are, however, other sources worth noting. *Links to the Past,* a collection of biographical sketches and family histories edited and published by Norma Gamble and Francie Anderson, tells of the settlement and development of Burnt Fork, Wyoming, and the Henrys Fork Valley. "The J.S. Hoy Manuscript" and Kouris's *History of Brown's Park* provide information of the growth of the ranching community in Browns Park.

Those interested in the development of the Sheep Creek irrigation system and the founding of Manila should look at the turn-of-the-century promotional pamphlet "Operations: Lucerne Land and Water Company." An original copy can be viewed in the Special Collections department of the Harold B. Lee Library at Brigham Young University. The pamphlet not only discusses the area and the available lands in Manila and Lucerne Valley, it also describes in detail the beginnings of the project and the construction of the Sheep Creek Canal. The text is illustrated with excellent photographs.

Another vivid description of Manila in the early days can be found in John M. Baxter's autobiography, *The Life of John M. Baxter,* published by the Deseret News Press in 1932. Baxter traveled to Manila along with other church officials to establish a branch of the LDS church there. His recollections provide insights into the harsh living conditions and grinding poverty experienced by Manila's early settlers.

Life in Linwood is the focus of the "Recollections of Keith Smith of Linwood, Utah as told to his Daughter Susan." The original copy of this manuscript history is housed at the library of the Utah State Historical Society. Linwood's most prominent resident, this Yale

University graduate turned rancher helped found the community and resided there until the town was inundated by the rising waters of Flaming Gorge Reservoir. Smith was a key player in Linwood and Daggett County affairs for seven decades. His reminiscences not only chronicle much of the county's history but are a fascinating account of his truly remarkable life.

Three theses also shed a great deal of light on county development. William Tennent's "The John Jarvie Ranch: A Case Study in Historic Site Development and Interpretation" looks at the life of John Jarvie and the Browns Park area, and Eric Swedin's "The Swett Homestead: An Oral History, 1909–1970" discusses ranch life in Greendale. Both are available at the Merrill Library at Utah State University. The best source dealing with schools is "The History of Public Education in Daggett County, Utah and Adjacent Areas," written by Donald Weir Baxter in 1959 at Brigham Young University.

For a woman's perspective on ranch life in the early decades of this century, the writings of Elinore Pruitt Stewart are both entertaining and instructive. Although Stewart was a resident of Burnt Fork, Wyoming, she wrote frequently about happenings in Daggett County, and her way of life mirrored that of her Utah neighbors. Almost all of her work consists of letters written to friends, some of which appeared in the *Atlantic Monthly* magazine; other letters were compiled into books. Her most famous works are her books *Letters of a Woman Homesteader,* published in 1914, and *Letters from an Elk Hunt,* published the following year.

Though she was not well known in her own time, Stewart's work was rediscovered in the 1960s and 1970s as interest developed in the study of women's literature. Her books were reprinted, and a movie based on her letters and journals, *Heartland,* was released in 1980. More of Stewart's letters were brought together by Susan K. George in the 1992 book *The Adventures of the Woman Homesteader.* Historical researchers, however, will find Stewart's letters of limited value. They are more literary exercises than historical documents. Stewart used them to indulge an interest in creative writing, and her correspondents were her audience. Most of the letters are short stories, inspired by the world around her but not necessarily renditions of fact. This is the opinion not only of some Daggett County residents but also of Stewart scholar and editor Susan K. George, who, in the preface of her book, acknowledged that, "Stewart's writings blur the boundaries of history and fiction." Elinore Pruitt Stewart's works are good reading, and they provide a woman's perspective on early twentieth-century ranch life. They offer insights into the daily life of the three-corners area, but they should not be taken as absolute fact.

Much has been written about Daggett County's outlaw heritage and the county's development through the 1930s, but those interested in studying its subsequent history will find the offerings limited. The story is scattered in random newspaper clippings, government documents, public records, and a handful of manuscript histories. Roy Webb's *If We Had a Boat* has some information on Flaming Gorge Dam and its consequences, as does the Dunhams' *Flaming Gorge Country.* A file of newspaper clippings pertaining to Daggett County, housed at the Uintah County Library in Vernal, provides bits of information on how Manila and the county grew in the mid-twentieth century. That is about it. One can only hope that, as a new century approaches, those who built Flaming Gorge Dam, the recreational economy, and the county's modern institutions will do more to record their experiences.

Fortunately for researchers in Daggett County, most of the sources mentioned can be found in nearby repositories. The local history collection at Manila High School's library has copies of much of the material, as do also the files of the old Daggett County Historical Society (presently kept by the Flaming Gorge Natural History Association in Dutch John). The Uintah County Library in Vernal also has a fine local history room that has many materials dealing with the three-corners country. The best source for historic photographs of Daggett County is the Sweetwater County Museum in Green River, Wyoming. This museum has several albums of pertinent photographs, including the images used by Richard Dunham in *Flaming Gorge Country.* Researchers are also encouraged to consult the holdings of the state of Utah's major libraries, particularly the special collections departments of the Harold B. Lee Library at Brigham Young University in Provo, the Merrill Library at Utah State University in Logan, the Marriott Library at the University of Utah in Salt Lake City, and the Utah State Historical Society Library in Salt Lake City.

Selected Bibliography

Adams, Henry. *Henry Adams: Novels, Mont Saint Michel, The Education of Henry Adams.* New York: Library of America, 1984.

Atlas of Utah. Provo: Brigham Young University Press/Weber State University, 1981.

Baxter, Donald Weir. "The History of Public Education in Daggett County Utah and Adjacent Areas." Master's thesis, Brigham Young University, 1959.

Baxter, John M. *Life of John M. Baxter.* Salt Lake City: Deseret News Press, 1932.

Beckwourth, James P. *The Life and Times of James P. Beckwourth as told to Thomas D. Bonner.* Lincoln: University of Nebraska Press, 1972.

Brown, Richard Maxwell. *No Duty to Retreat: Violence and Values in American History and Society.* New York: Oxford University Press, 1991.

Campbell, Esther, and Carole L. Jackson. *Visit "Miss Esther" Campbell.* Vernal, UT: Carole Jackson, 1995.

Carson, Kit. *Kit Carson's Own Story of His Life.* Edited by Blanche Grant. Santa Fe: Kit Carson Memorial Foundation, 1956.

Chronic, Halka. *Roadside Geology of Utah.* Missoula, MT: Mountain Press Publishing, 1980.

Coutant, C.G. *History of Wyoming and the Far West,* Vol. 2. New York: Argonaut Press, 1966.

Dale, Harrison Clifford, ed. *The Ashley-Smith Explorations and the Discovery of a Central Route to the Pacific.* Glendale, CA: Arthur H. Clarke, 1941.

Daughters of Utah Pioneers. *Builders of Uintah: A Centennial History of Uintah County, 1872 to 1947.* Springville, UT: Daughters of Utah Pioneers, 1947.

Day, Kent C., and David S. Dibble. *Archaeological Survey of the Flaming Gorge Reservoir Area Wyoming-Utah.* University of Utah Anthropological Papers no. 65, Upper Colorado Series no. 9. Salt Lake City: University of Utah, 1963.

Dellenbaugh, Frederick S. *A Canyon Voyage: The Narrative of the Second Powell Expedition.* Reprint. Tucson: University of Arizona Press, 1991.

DeVoto, Bernard. *The Year of Decision: 1846.* Boston: Little, Brown and Company, 1943.

Dunham, Dick, and Vivian Dunham. *Flaming Gorge Country.* Denver: Eastwood Printing, 1978.

Ferris, Warren Angus. *Life in the Rocky Mountains.* Reprint. Denver: Old West Publishing Co., 1940.

Flaming Gorge National Recreation Area Ashley National Forest, Forest Service, U.S. Dept. of Agriculture: Multiple Use Management Guide and Recreation Management Plan. Washington, D.C.: U.S. Forest Service, 1970.

Gamble, Norma, and Francie Anderson, eds. *Links to the Past.* Burnt Fork, WY: Gamble and Anderson, 1990.

Gates, Paul W. *History of Public Land Law Development.* Washington, D.C.: Government Printing Office, 1968.

George, Susanne K. *The Adventures of a Woman Homesteader: The Life and Letters of Elinore Pruitt Stewart.* Lincoln: University of Nebraska Press, 1992.

Goetzmann, William H. *Exploration and Empire: The Explorer and Scientist in the Winning of the American West.* New York: Alfred A. Knopf, 1966.

Gowans, Fred R. *Fort Bridger: Island in the Wilderness.* Provo, UT: Brigham Young University Press, 1975.

———. *Rocky Mountain Rendezvous: A History of the Fur Trade Rendezvous 1825–1840.* Layton, UT: Peregrine Smith Books, 1985.

Hamilton, William T. *My Sixty Years on the Plains: Trapping, Trading, and Indian Fighting.* Norman: University of Oklahoma Press, 1960.

Hilton, Hope. *"Wild Bill" Hickman and the Mormon Frontier.* Salt Lake City, UT: Signature Books, 1988.

Hoy, J.S. "The J.S. Hoy Manuscript." Edited by James G. Hodgson, 1952. Unpublished manuscript at Special Collections, Merrill Library, Utah State University.

Inventory of the County Archives of Utah, No. 5: Daggett County. Ogden, UT: Works Project Administration, 1939.

Jackson, Donald, and Mary Lee Spence. *The Expeditions of John C. Fremont.* Urbana: University of Illinois Press, 1970.

Jones, Holway R. *John Muir and the Sierra Club: The Battle for Yosemite.* San Francisco: Sierra Club, 1965.

Kouris, Diana Allen. *The Romantic and Notorious History of Brown's Park.* Greybull, WY: Wolverine Gallery, 1980.

Larsen, M.N. "History of Daggett County." Manuscript at Utah State Historical Society Library, Salt Lake City.

LeCompte, Janet. "Jean-Baptiste Chalifoux." In *The Mountain Men and the Fur Trade of the Far West,* vol. 7, ed. Leroy R. Hafen. Glendale, CA: Arthur H. Clark, 1955.

Limerick, Patricia Nelson, Clyde A. Milner, and Charles E. Rankin, eds., *Trails: Towards A New Western History.* Lawrence: University of Kansas Press, 1991.

McClure, Grace. *The Bassett Women.* Athens, OH: Swallow Press/Ohio University Press, 1985.

Olson, J. Kent. *Never Marry a Rancher.* Salt Lake City: Hiller Industries: 1979.

"Operations: Lucerne Land and Water Company." Salt Lake City: Lucerne Land and Water Co., n.d., Harold B. Lee Library, Brigham Young University.

Opie, John. "Environmental History in the West." In *The Twentieth Century West: Historical Interpretations,* ed. Gerald D. Nash and Richard Etulain. Albuquerque: University of New Mexico Press, 1989.

"Pinon O Pinon." Bulletins of CCC Company 1965, copies at Utah State Historical Society Library.

Pomeroy, Earl. *In Search of the Golden West: The Tourist in Western America.* New York: Alfred A. Knopf, 1957.

Powell, John Wesley. *Exploration of the Colorado River and its Canyons.* Reprint. New York: Dover Publications, 1961.

Reiger, John F., ed. *The Passing of the Great West: Selected Papers of George Bird Grinnell.* New York: Winchester Press, 1972.

Ritzma, Howard R. *Geological Atlas of Utah: Daggett County.* Salt Lake City: Utah Geological and Mineral Survey, 1959.

Smith, Keith, "Recollections of Keith Smith of Linwood, Utah as Told to his Daughter Susan." 1968. Unpublished manuscript at Utah State Historical Society Library,

Stansbury, Howard. *Exploring the Great Salt Lake.* Reprint. Washington, D.C.: Smithsonian Institution Press, 1988.

Statistical Review of Utah's Economy. Salt Lake City: Bureau of Economic and Business Research, 1960.

Steen, Harold K. *The U.S. Forest Service: A History.* Seattle: University of Washington Press, n.d.

Stegner, Wallace. *Beyond the Hundredth Meridian: John Wesley Powell and the Second Opening of the West.* New York: Houghton Mifflin, 1954.

Stokes, William Lee, *Geology of Utah.* Salt Lake City: Utah Museum of Natural History/Utah Geological and Mineral Survey, 1980.

Swedin, Eric G. "The Swett Homestead: An Oral History, 1909–1970." Master's thesis, Utah State University, 1991.

Tennent, William Lawrence. "The John Jarvie Ranch: A Case Study in Historic Site Development and Interpretation." Master's thesis, Utah State University, 1980.

Trenholm, Virginia, and Maurine Carley. *The Shoshonis: Sentinels of the Rockies.* Norman: University of Oklahoma Press, 1969.

United States Census, 1920. Washington, D.C.: Government Printing Office, 1924.

United States Census, 1930. Washington, D.C.: Government Printing Office, 1932.

United States Census, 1950. Washington, D.C.: Department of Commerce, 1952.

Unruh, John D. *The Plains Across.* Urbana: University of Illinois Press, 1979.

Untermann, G.E., and B.R. Untermann. *Field Guide to the Geology of the Uinta Mountains.* Salt Lake City: Utah Geological and Mineral Survey, 1961.

Utah Agricultural Statistics, 1971. Salt Lake City: Utah Department of Agriculture, 1971.

Utah Agricultural Statistics and Utah Department of Agriculture Annual Report, 1995. Salt Lake City: Utah Department of Agriculture, 1996.

Utah Statistical Abstract, 1983. Salt Lake City: Bureau of Economic and Business Research, 1984.

Utah Statistical Abstract, 1996. Salt Lake City: Bureau of Economic and Business Research, 1997.

Utley, Robert M. *Billy the Kid: A Short and Violent Life*. Lincoln: University of Nebraska Press, 1989.

Victor, Frances Fuller. *The River of the West*. Oakland, CA: Brooks-Sterling, 1974.

Warner, Matt, and Murray E. King. *The Last of the Bandit Riders*. New York: Bonanza Books, 1940.

Webb, Roy. *If We Had a Boat: Green River Explorers, Adventurers, and Runners*. Salt Lake City: University of Utah Press, 1986.

Wislizenus, Frederick A. *A Journey to the Rocky Mountains*. St. Louis: Missouri Historical Society, 1912.

Woolley, Ralf R. *The Green River and Its Utilization*. USGS Water Supply Paper no. 618. Washington, D.C.: Government Printing Office, 1930.

Index